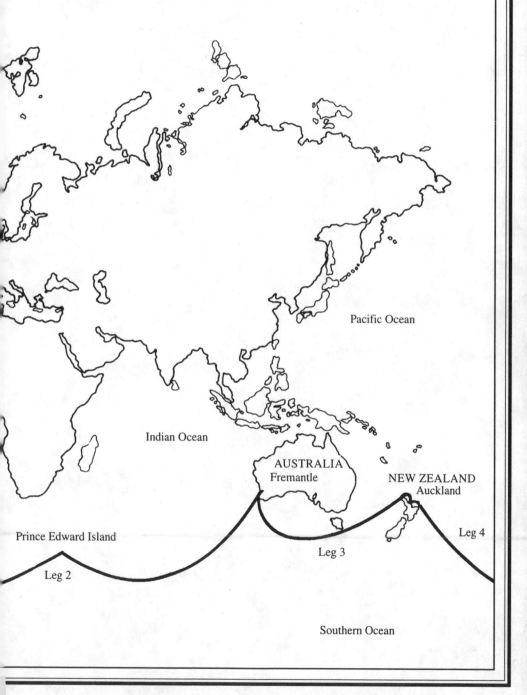

Leg 4
Auckland to Punta del Este
Depart February 20
Arrive mid-March
5,914 nautical miles

Leg 5
Punta del Este to Fort Lauderdale
Depart April 2
Arrive late April
5,475 nautical miles

Leg 6
Fort Lauderdale to Southampton
Depart May 21
Arrive early June
3,818 nautical miles

Pacific Ocean

Indian Ocean

AUSTRALIA
Fremantle

NEW ZEALAND
Auckland

Prince Edward Island

Leg 4

Leg 3

Leg 2

Southern Ocean

TAKING
THE HELM

TAKING
THE HELM

Dawn Riley
with Cynthia Flanagan

Little, Brown and Company
Boston   New York   Toronto   London

First Edition

Library of Congress Cataloging-in-Publication Data
Riley, Dawn.
    Taking the helm / Dawn Riley with Cynthia Flanagan. — 1st ed.
        p.   cm.
    ISBN 0-316-74550-2
    1. Whitbread Round-the-World Race. 2. Riley, Dawn. 3. Women
sailors — United States — Biography. I. Flanagan, Cynthia.
II. Title.
GV832.R54   1995
797.1'4 — dc20   94-47989

10   9   8   7   6   5   4   3   2   1

RRD-VA
*Published simultaneously in Canada
by Little, Brown & Company (Canada) Limited*

Printed in the United States of America

For my parents,
who gave me the imagination to seek new horizons,
and
for Barry,
the best discovery I made along the way

TAKING
THE HELM

1

Was it just an ego thing that made me think I could save this project? I am having second thoughts about this boat. Adrienne says that I shouldn't make any rash decisions because this will be great for my career. My answer is, Not if someone dies.

> — fax from Dawn Riley
> to Barry McKay

November 13, 1993

I couldn't sleep last night. The metal shutters on the apartment windows never stopped rattling: a constant fluttering of metal, sometimes slow and sometimes fast and frantic. It was the wind, the lulls and the high gusts that here, in this part of the world, they call the *pampero*. It blasts onto the coast of Uruguay and funnels onto the streets of Punta del Este, shaking the restaurant canopies and the window shutters, snaking around the high-rise apartment buildings along the beach, making the boats at the pier dance on the water, turning this resort town into one giant wind tunnel.

Even if the wind had been calm, I still would not have slept. I haven't slept well since I arrived in Uruguay a few days ago to get ready for this race. I've hardly eaten, except for a few *chivitos* (Uruguay's answer to the steak sandwich) at the Yateste café and the spaghetti I cooked last night here in the apartment. It was leftover from the last tenant, abandoned in the cupboard for a long time, and all I had for sauce was salt. But thank you, whoever you are who left it here. At least it was something in my stomach before I sail off into the land of freeze-dried food and icebergs.

As soon as I got out of bed this morning, I rushed over to the window, pushed open the shutters, and looked out at the sky and the sea. I had hoped for blue sky, sun, and a gentle breeze — just the way it was yesterday. The sky was gray. Rain was falling. And the wind whipped the wave crests on the sea into a froth of white.

A sunny day would have been better, for today, eleven women and I head out to sail across the Southern Ocean (the name used to refer to the waters surrounding Antarctica) in a sixy-four-foot boat that the crew calls the Old Red Bucket. I would feel better going on a boat called the Red Missile or the Red Warrior. Some powerful weapon to be reckoned with. But we have only this boat to take us across the Southern Ocean: a place with gale-force winds, icebergs, waves the size of city buildings, snowstorms, and the kind of cold that freezes your skin and creeps into your dreams.

Our twelve-woman crew, with the help of some of our competitors, finished working on the boat last night at eight o'clock. We have spent the last four days on our knees and contorted in small spaces, crawling over the boat, checking the engine, the systems, the keel bolts, the through-hull fittings. My back is stiff from hours of stooping over the boat engine, generator, and deck gear. My hands are sore from muscling boat parts into place. I have cuts that will someday join all the other scars I've collected on boats. I am exhausted from four days on the boat: disassembling, assembling, rigging, rerigging, wiring, splicing, bolting, fiberglassing. It has been a never-ending reconnaissance mission down into the boat's inner workings, then back to the work list that seemed to grow every time we came back to check off one more task: The List That Never Shrank. It is the subplot of our horror story.

The owners of this boat telephoned me just over one week ago. They asked me to come to South America and keep this boat and its all-female crew in the Whitbread Round-the-World Race, an ocean marathon sailed in six legs, as the new skipper. Key members of the crew mutinied after the boat completed the first six-thousand-mile leg of the race, from England to Uruguay, and the skipper announced the withdrawal of her boat from the race. Now the original skipper, who started the boat in the race when the fleet sailed from England two months ago, has already left for the States — not by boat, but by airplane, amidst circumstances that I am still unraveling. And here I am, a last-minute leader made out to be the lady mercenary of the high seas, hired to pull this boat and this crew together in what is an insane amount of time. Since the six-thousand-mile leg from England to Uruguay, our competitors have had nearly a month in port to get ready for the restart to Australia; we have had four days.

Soon it will be time to walk out of this apartment and down to the dock where the fourteen boats in this round-the-world race are berthed. The boats will be flying huge battle flags from their rigging: the nautical version of war paint. The spectators will come down to the waterfront, to stand at the edge of Uruguay before it drops into the Atlantic Ocean and wave good-bye to the brave sailors. It is time to go, I keep telling myself, but somehow I don't feel like myself this morning. I am not eager to compete, to fight, to find out who the best sailor is.

I take the last shower I will take for nearly a month. I pack what little clothing I have. My duffel bag, with all my cold-weather gear, was lost on the airplane trip from the States. By now my luggage is probably in Hong Kong or Tahiti. Someplace where a bag of thermal underwear, gloves, face masks, goggles, and hats are of no use to anyone but me. How I will survive the ice in sweatshirts and jeans, I don't know. But there's no time to worry about that now.

I pack my other tools of survival. My rigging knife goes into my pocket; I will keep this tool within easy reach from now on, in case one night I have to cut away lines or sails that endanger me or my crew. I strap my watch onto my wrist; it will stay on my body until I reach Australia. I put Gizmo — my stuffed gremlin who always travels with me, for luck and for company — in my duffel. I go through the logical, methodical, rote procedure of packing, but I don't feel ready to leave yet, and I keep remembering all the "what ifs" that kept me awake last night.

What if my crew and I had months to prepare for this race around the world? We could stack the odds in our favor. There would be time to build new sails, to overhaul the systems onboard the boat, to make the rig and the deck gear like new again, to do brain surgery on the electronics, to learn to sail this fast racing machine better. Mostly we need time to learn to trust one another's abilities as a crew, for few of us have sailed together before and this is a nine-month marathon: a 32,000-mile course through extreme ocean conditions from England, to Uruguay, to Australia, to New Zealand, back to Uruguay, to Florida, and back to England. In the first Whitbread race in 1973/74, two people had died by the time the fleet reached Australia.

What will this four-day, patch-it-so-it's-good-enough

marathon cost us once we hit the extreme ice conditions of the Southern Ocean? What if, what if: a hundred of them go through my mind up here, in this apartment hanging high over the sea with the wind whipping by.

Over the last four days, the faxes have rolled in, from friends and fellow sailors. Tracy Edwards — skipper of *Maiden,* the first all-female entry ever sailed in the Whitbread, of which I was a part in 1989/90 — faxed a huge "Well Done!" across the Atlantic, with a reminder to send many postcards home to her in England recounting our adventures. Eric Goetz, back in Rhode Island building America's Cup boats, sent his wishes for speedy sailing. Friends from New Zealand sent words of wisdom from Eastern philosophers about great purposes and transcending limitations. Claire Warren, who had raced as the doctor onboard with Tracy and me in the 1989/90 Whitbread on *Maiden,* was "jealous as hell" we were going without her, but she reported that support was strong in the United Kingdom and the British press was treating us fine.

Putting me onboard at the zero hour as the new skipper to strengthen the campaign makes a nice, neat storyline after the crew of the only all-female entry in this race nearly dissolved into mutiny. The truth is, after four days of nonstop work, sleepless nights, stress, tears, homesick moments, and little food, I know from the inside that this is no fairy tale.

On the outside, I have worked like a machine to follow a logical plan of action in a very short time. Inside, everything is coming too fast. The deadline to leave is here. The journalists have questions about the all-female crew with the new skipper; there have been calls to return to New York and Miami and London from this place that feels like the edge of the world.

I still have questions of my own about this boat and this crew. But as of this morning, I cannot think of one good-enough reason why we should not set sail for Australia today.

It's time to go. I zip my duffel shut, survey the apartment for any last remnants of four days that I hope will soon be a distant memory, and head out toward the stairwell, to the street, and down to the docks. The wind is still blowing and the sea is still white. The breeze whooshes the door shut with a thud — pushing me out of this high-rise apartment before I feel ready to leave.

Everything began with one phone call.

I left New Zealand, where I share a house with my partner in life, Barry McKay, a few months ago to race in several sailing regattas in the United States. On the night I received the phone call, I was back with my mom in Detroit, where I grew up sailing on the Great Lakes. The next day, I was scheduled to fly home to Auckland to see Barry and compete in a match race called the Steinlager Logan Cup. It was a gamble: the Steinlager Cup is a professional race for prize money. My last dime went toward a $950 plane ticket back to New Zealand and the $750 entry fee for the regatta.

On the eve of my departure, the whole family was over: sister, brother, grandparents. We were heading off to my cousin's performance in a 1950s musical revue at the local high school. Then the phone rang.

It was a faraway voice for me: David Glen from Uruguay. He told me news about the Whitbread I was not surprised to hear. And then he asked me a question that floored me.

Crew members of the *U.S. Women's Challenge* had mutinied, and the skipper announced she was withdrawing the boat from the Whitbread Round-the-World Race, explained Glen, who represented the boat's owners, Ocean Ventures Management, of New Zealand. The only all-female crew in the race could stop here at the edge of the Third World. But there was a slim chance the campaign could continue: it all depended on me.

Will you fly to Uruguay as soon as possible and consider being the new skipper? Glen asked. This is an American vessel, and you are the only American woman skilled enough to take command. If you take over, the boat sails on. If you don't, the project stops here. We need an answer by 8:00 tomorrow morning and the race starts in nine days. Good-bye.

"I don't want to do another Whitbread," I said as I hung up the phone.

"Another Whitbread?" said my mom. "Well, Dawn, that's what you wanted — to do a second Whitbread. We'll support you from here like the last time: have fund-raisers at home, follow you on ESPN, collect all your mail and messages . . ." Before I got a word in, Mom was off with full-speed enthusiasm for my next adventure, and once she told Grandma and Grandpa — who are both slightly hard-of-hearing — it was gospel, because it was too hard to undo a thought in their heads once it was planted in a loud and simplified way. "She's what? Where? What? . . . Oh, how nice," said Grandma.

I had not taken one step away from the phone and this offer from faraway Uruguay was considered a done deal by my mother. This is the woman who, along with my father, took me, my younger sister Dana, and little brother Todd out of grade school, moved us onboard a thirty-six-foot wooden cutter, and sailed away to the Caribbean islands.

We were a family band of crew pirated away from civilization by dreams of adventure and new challenges. I was
twelve; Dana ten; Todd seven. Soon after leaving, we three
kids were standing watches alone at night in the Atlantic
Ocean as we headed south toward the sun.

"Mom, hold on. You don't understand the circumstances."

"What's there to understand? This race is the ultimate
race for offshore sailors. Why wouldn't you go?"

"The circumstances are not at all perfect," I explained.
"It's not as if this were my program from the outset, and I
was involved in the design and building of the boat, selection
of the crew and shore-management team, selection of all the
gear and sails, negotiations with the sponsor. It's as if I were
adopting a thirteen-year-old and I had nothing to do with
her development up to this point, but now, I am totally
responsible for her life. Do you understand?"

"I guess I do. But if this boat has to stay in the race and
they need a female skipper, I don't know anyone better to
take the job on," she answered.

Mom was not one to provide me a trapdoor out of a challenge. But I still had my reasons for not wanting to take on
this job. I went to the concert with the rest of the family. But
a musical revue in a high-school auditorium became a
bizarre evening of speculation as my mind traveled to the
edge of South America.

The withdrawal of the *U.S. Women's Challenge* from the
race did not surprise me. I knew there were problems. I had
been piecing the story together from reading the newspapers, following the computer information networks that
reported on the race, reading the daily press releases and
position reports that could be obtained via fax, and keeping

my ear tuned to the worldwide underground of sailors who circulate stories of fact and fiction that transform the sailing world into one big soap opera of the high seas.

The original skipper of the *U.S. Women's Challenge* was Nance Frank, an American woman in her forties. She had been trying to pull an all-female Whitbread boat together for nearly ten years. When she began, her effort was a crusade in the truest sense. Ten years ago, a crew of all women competing in this grueling ocean race was unheard of.

Frank started sailing as part of Tracy Edwards's *Maiden* team in the late 1980s. Edwards was running a British-based effort to enter a female crew in the Whitbread, a race that started in 1973 and takes place every four years. I joined Edwards's campaign in 1989. Before I did, Nance Frank and Tracy Edwards parted ways, and Frank came home to the United States to field her own team.

Frank sailed a boat across the Atlantic to the start of the 1989/90 Whitbread. She and her all-female crew sailed in the starting area in England, but they did not officially start the race since insufficient funding prevented them from competing. Frank came to the starting line as a symbolic gesture; then she returned home to the United States to continue her crusade for the 1993/94 Whitbread.

I had never sailed with Nance Frank, but I knew she had thrown herself into a herculean task: she needed to be Joan of Arc with sea legs, to lead the charge, raise the money, skipper the boat across the violent oceans. Frank had never before completed a Whitbread as crew. Most skippers in this race start as crews first: they cross oceans and work on boats and spend their lives around the docks before they promote themselves to management. Even then, raising sponsorship and organizing a sailing campaign of this stature is a difficult job, especially for a woman, and especially for a woman in the United States. Corporate America has not yet embraced the sponsorship of sailing the way it has tennis or golf. All of us trying to make a career out of racing sailboats know the odds of funding offshore campaigns — and they are not good.

Still, I had questions about Nance Frank's abilities as a sailor. Yet the media grasped on to the simple story of a woman sailor trying to compete in a man's race. Frank was on television shows, in magazines, in newspapers. The news media never stopped to ask if she was competent.

Despite difficulties in raising enough funds to compete, Frank was tenacious. She secured a boat for the 1993/94 Whitbread. Up until the last moments before the start, Frank was still looking for a major sponsor, and reports of creditors who were hounding her broke in the press days before the start. The fact that the campaign was underfunded was no secret. Frank held on and sailed away from England with the Whitbread fleet in September 1993.

The money issue plagued the boat as it crossed the Atlantic. The sails on the *U.S. Women's Challenge* were constantly tearing. Sails are the engine of a sailboat: they harness the power of the wind to move a boat across the ocean. Funds must have been too thin to build the right inventory of sails. The crew was spending endless hours piecing a sail back together, only to rehoist it and have it shred again. The boat was effectively crippled. I wondered what crew morale was like and how high tempers flared racing a tired boat without enough cash to make it competitive or, maybe, to make it safe.

Days after the boat landed in Punta, key crew members

informed Frank that they would not continue into the Southern Ocean on this boat. It was mutiny, 1990s style. I did not know all the reasons behind the act. I only knew that if I took this job, I would be smack in the middle of a crew that had already fallen apart.

Taking over this doomed effort with only a few days to prepare was not my idea of a smart decision. After completing my first Whitbread on *Maiden,* I was asked to consider two different Whitbread campaigns for the 1993/94 race. I said yes, conditionally, if the sponsorship was right and if the crew could be coed. I had done the Whitbread once. What I wanted to do the second time was organize a winning campaign: secure the financial backing to build a fast boat, then pick the strongest sailors I could find — whether they were male or female — and mount a formidable effort. But the pieces never fell into place and I gave up hope of doing a second Whitbread.

But now, this proposal was being dropped in my path in less-than-ideal circumstances. Why was I considering it? All my logic said, No. Stop. Think about what you are getting into. The Whitbread is one of the toughest ocean races and it can be hell. I know: I did it once and I didn't want to do it again. Not on this boat. Not with a crew whose abilities I didn't yet know or trust. But this would be a great challenge. And if I did not take the job, the campaign would die, the women would fly away, and the boat would rot in Punta. I only had a few hours to decide. I had to talk to Barry.

Barry was still in New Zealand, and it wasn't easy to find him. He was getting ready to set sail around the world as crew on a ninety-two-foot catamaran that was challenging the record for a nonstop circumnavigation. When I got the call from Uruguay, Barry and the crew were out on a promotional tour of the country.

I finally reached him onboard *ENZA,* their round-the-world speed machine, and I filled him in on the phone call that was turning my life upside down. "I thought you might be getting a call," he said. "Guess you got to do it."

Barry's inside track did not surprise me, but his response was not what I wanted to hear — because, deep inside, my gut matched Barry's words: I did not really have a choice.

Yes, it was a steady job, but I would not risk my life for a paycheck. My schedule for the next months was set. After Auckland and the Steinlager Cup, plans for the first all-female America's Cup team in history were brewing. As the lone woman on the winning *America³* team in 1992, I wanted to be part of this new effort. It was the match-racing of the America's Cup I was working toward — the intense, head-to-head game of two boats in a battle of wits on the water that I thrived on.

But the offer from David Glen in that faraway phone call from Uruguay was not a simple question of, Will you take this job? It was an ultimatum for women's sailing. I had been part of the crew of the first-ever women's Whitbread boat in the 1989/90 race. We on *Maiden* were a team, and together we proved women could do this race. If the *U.S. Women's Challenge* stopped here and rotted away in Punta, all our work on *Maiden* would be lost. People would believe that the *Maiden* voyage was an isolated fluke, that women cannot compete in this grueling race.

When I went to bed that night, I already knew: I was going to Uruguay. If the details with the boat and the crew were in place, I would keep this boat in the race. The house went silent and the world went to sleep while I thought about how much work I needed to do once I answered David Glen's phone call.

As soon as I decided to consider the job, logic kicked in. I was unprepared. I needed the proper cold-weather gear. I needed crew around me whose abilities I could trust. And I needed to prepare myself to return to the personal hell of the Southern Ocean.

I had lived in many different places since the last Whitbread: California, Auckland, Michigan. Bits and pieces of my life were strewn around the world. I located my seaboots and had them shipped to Detroit. Ditto, my foul-weather gear. My mom drove me around Detroit to find long underwear. It was not yet ski season, and the hunting season was in full swing. Everything was wool. Everything was camouflage-colored and made for swamps and duck blinds. I needed clothes built from the synthetic fabrics developed for cold, wet conditions: polypropylene, polyester-pile Synchilla. "We can order you some, if you like," said one shopkeeper — and every one thereafter, like a broken record. But Mom and I continued on our scavenger hunt to find the off-season gear that would let me survive the Southern Ocean.

I spent the next days on the phone with David Glen; with the *America³* staff working on the all-female Cup syndicate; with Barry. They reminded me that this was not a simple task of flying to South America and hopping on a boat bound for Australia. I took a closer look at contracts and clauses, at safety matters, at all the things that could go wrong.

I was not sleeping well, and — with the time differences between the United States and New Zealand — the middle of the night was a good time to call Barry. I talked to him three, sometimes four times a night, dialing and redialing our long string of digits at odd hours to reach the other side of the world.

Barry is a boat builder by trade, and he was involved with the *Tokio* campaign — a New Zealand/Japan Whitbread effort skippered by the America's Cup sailor Chris Dickson — when the boat was being built and launched for this Whitbread. He knew the Whitbread 60 — a new type of ocean greyhound built specifically for this race — inside and out. I had sailed on *Tokio* in its early days, serving as part of the crew for a race to Fiji, but the winds were light. I needed a crash course in handling the Whitbread 60 in the extreme conditions we would face sailing from Uruguay to Australia through the Southern Ocean, so I fired my questions to Barry often, and as quickly as I could.

"When it's blowing fifty knots and you have to turn, is it best to tack or jibe? In what wind strengths do you switch from a Number Two to Number Three headsail? How do the boats surf in forty-plus knots and fifteen-foot seas? In what order do you fill your water-ballast tanks?"

Barry answered every question thoroughly, and my data bank on the boat started to build. But when he went over information I knew, I was short: "I know, I know." Barry was only trying to help, but I was impatient. I couldn't waste a second; I needed as much information as I could get in the few days I had before the start.

On top of educating myself about this boat, I had to consider the condition it was in after being maintained by Nance Frank and her crew. And I needed to know more about the skill level of the crew members who wanted to continue in the race.

Frank and three other crew members would not continue on. Some of the original crew were committed to staying on the boat, and I agreed to that. Barry and other experienced Whitbread sailors advised me otherwise: go down to Uruguay, fire all the crew, and then rehire. It was a question of understood loyalty, and they all warned me to do the tough thing early on. But I did not think there was enough time to fire the crew, then build up a new team.

The only crew member I knew was Mikaela von Koskull of Finland. Mikki, as we called her, sailed onboard *Maiden* in the 1989/90 Whitbread. She would be my only in, my link to understanding what had happpened onboard. Beyond Mikki, everyone else was a perfect stranger.

I would bring in three experienced crew. I tried to find Jeni Mundy in the Hamble, the area of England where the race begins and ends — and the region where many Whitbread veterans retire to. She was not home when I called, and I tracked her down having dinner with Claire Warren, our doctor from *Maiden.* Jeni was also part of the *Maiden* crew. I could trust her abilities as a good sailor, and I trusted her as a friend for life. "Hello, Jeni. Are you ready to get cold and wet again?" My invitation burned across the phone wire to England. Jeni, whose boyfriend Spike was already racing in the Whitbread on a New Zealand boat, knew exactly what was happening. She had just finished her masters in engineering, specializing in electronic communications systems, and she was job-hunting. Going back into the Southern Ocean was not the offer she had in mind. But the minute she heard my voice, she knew what I was about to ask. Her answer was yes.

It was a lucky coincidence that Marie-Claude Kieffer was at Claire's too. She is a Frenchwoman known for her talents as a solo offshore sailor, and I wanted Marie-Claude on the boat too. Jeni was going. MC, as we called her, would go too.

The third was Renee Mehl. She had been captaining racing boats in the States for several seasons. The guys call her Stick Chick, and she is just that: 100 pounds of pure determination. She was my light-air crew in college sailing, when we sailed two-person dinghies together in the mid-1980s at Michigan State University. Renee quickly became my all-weather crew: when it started to blow, she hung in and gave everything she could, even though she was as thin as a reed.

There was no time to lose. I was asking these women to pack up their lives, get to South America, and be ready to sail into the Southern Ocean — all within the space of a week. It was a lot to ask.

Finally, Monday came. I had been on the phone nonstop to New Zealand, Uruguay, and the United Kingdom, and I had done as much as I could from Detroit. I needed to get to South America, to meet the crew and inspect the boat. My flight plan was a long one: Detroit to New York. A night flight from New York to Buenos Aires. A short flight to Montevideo.

I got on the plane in Detroit, and I thought back to the day when I flew away from home to join the *Maiden* crew for my first Whitbread. That was five years ago. I had flown out months before the start to train in England and get the boat ready. I was scared, but it was a good kind of scared. I was going off to find adventure and see the world. This second Whitbread would be completely different: this was all about responsibility and weighing the odds for survival.

I have boarded a hundred planes before. But this time

was eerie: this plane was flying me into the vortex of what could turn out to be a disaster.

I buckled my seat belt, and soon we were off.

The timing of my arrival in Uruguay was carefully planned. I was one of the pieces on the chessboard, and the game was escalating toward check-checkmate. I hoped the people moving the pieces knew exactly what they were doing.

I arrived in Uruguay on Tuesday, November 9, with Renee. We landed on the hot, black tarmac, the airport building gleaming in the sun in the distance. We were both groggy from all-night flying, although both of us had the luxury of a nap on airport benches in Buenos Aires. Nance Frank was scheduled to take the same plane out of Uruguay, heading back to the United States.

Ocean Ventures Management had already repossessed the *U.S. Women's Challenge* by the time I arrived. After Frank announced her withdrawal from the race, Ocean Ventures stepped in and planned to keep the boat sailing around the world with my new leadership. But the boat and crew had been in a holding pattern in Uruguay since sailing the last leg from England. There was no way of knowing exactly what I would find in Punta.

As soon as we landed in Montevideo, we traveled along the long ocean road in a car sent to collect us, past small houses and large, green fields and giant billboards marketing Coca-Cola, cars, and other essentials of modern life that seemed so out of place in the rugged South American country-side. The long ribbon of road eventually fell down to the sea and into the oceanside resort of Punta del Este. As we came over the hill, Punta's waterfront high rises gleamed in the distance — and the pit of my stomach knotted up.

Life moved into full speed as soon as we drove past Punta's waterfront and into the parking lot where the fleets' containers were parked. Every boat in the race has an ocean-freight shipping container at each stopover, which they use as a land-based storage closet and work area. The containers lined the perimeter of the lot: yellow, blue, white, green industrial-strength, trailer-home-sized boxes chock-full of miles of line, wire, tools, workbenches, spare sails, leftover boat clothers, unclaimed sunglasses. The gear spilled out of each container onto a sun-baked tarmac. Groups of racers surrounded each container pow-wow style, inspecting sails, splicing lines, lubricating deck gear; wearing T-shirts stained by epoxy, grease, engine oil, and the road dirt kicked up by the cars whizzing past the lot. I spied a few women across the lot, which I assumed were my new crew. They looked lost amid the rubble of the containers.

We had a meeting to get acquainted, make crew assignments, and figure out who would do what to get the boat ready to race. Rather than a long planning session, it was a quick huddle on the field before the next play. The clock was already running down: the start was four days away.

The crew who sailed the leg from England knew the gear best. They needed to decide what sails we would take, what rigging we would need. The engineer, Gloria Borrego, would not be in Punta until the end of the week; someone had to put together spare parts and tools for Gloria and hunt through Uruguay to find any missing bits. The boat needed constant work, so we set up an eight-to-five workday. "We can leave at five if the work is done. If not, we stay," I informed them. Some of the crew balked at the overtime. That was too bad; the boat had to be ready.

The boat was berthed on the cement pier, and I was

anxious to see its condition. As I made my way down past the yacht club, past the local fishing fleet, one of the male Whitbread crews passed me on the pier with a smirk and a dubious greeting: "Jumping into the deep end, eh?" he said. His voice trailed away in the wind. Was it a joke? Was it a warning? I did not have time to stop and think about what he meant.

The crew dubbed the boat the Old Red Bucket, but this sailboat is a racing machine designed by Bruce Farr, one of the top naval architects of racing yachts in the world. The moniker only reflected the condition the boat was kept in. Launched in April 1992, it was the first of its kind to hit the water and has the first hull designed according to the Whitbread 60 rule, a parameter of design guidelines created specifically for the conditions of this around-the-world race. The 60s are beasts of their own kind: fast, purely functional, high-performance ocean flyers.

The red-hulled boat was at the end of the pier and I climbed onboard for my first survey. The boat is a stripped-out monocoque hull built to be light yet strong. Down below, the inside of the boat looks like an empty eggshell with few creature comforts. There are metal frames for bunks that swing down from the sides of the hull. There is a four-burner propane stove, a sink, and some counter space for cooking in the center of the cabin. There is no refrigeration, so the crew must eat freeze-dried food. There is one toilet in a space the diameter of a phone booth (an area called the head). There is no shower in the head, just a second sink the size of a salad bowl.

The aft section of the boat houses a Star Trek panel of electronics: computer, satellite communications gear, VHF radio, single-sideband radio, weather fax, electronic instruments that spit out a wealth of necessary data — speed of the boat, angle of the wind, depth of the water, and more. These instruments make up what is referred to as the navigation station. This area is the brain of the boat, the electronic link to the outside world, and the nerve center of the vessel — all packed into one small console, complete with a bench for the person tweaking all the dials.

Above deck, the boat is shaped like a sixty-four-foot torpedo. There are two large wheels, each with a diameter the size of a human armspan, in the aft section of the cockpit where the crew will helm the boat. The mast stands firm like a tree trunk, and it grows out of the deck and towers toward the sky. The deck is littered with ropes, lines, blocks, and winches that make the boat look like an oceangoing gymnasium or a floating torture chamber.

The work list was too long for the little time we had left before the restart to Australia. We needed a new mainsail, but without enough time to build a new one we took a secondhand main from *Yamaha,* another Whitbread 60 owned by Ocean Ventures Management. The winches, the mechanical drums used to trim the massive power in the sails, needed to be broken down and checked and put back together again. The grinding pedestal for the large primary winches needed to be rebedded in the boat: it was torn off the deck on the last leg. The systems onboard — the engine, generator, desalinator, steering system — needed to be serviced. The keel attachment and rudder bearings had to be checked; we could not survive without those underwater appendages. The mast and rigging needed to be surveyed: Were there any weak points? Would the mast stand up in the Southern Ocean? The electronics needed the expertise of a surgeon. They would feed us the kind of information we needed to sail swiftly and safely. Safety gear needed to be 100 percent perfect.

We had a lot of help from racers whose boats were ready to race, especially the *Yamaha* crew. Still, the days getting the boat ready became endless and exhausting and I was overwhelmed, not by the work but by the responsibility thrown at my feet. I told few people. Barry was my rock-steady confidant.

"So how was the day?" he would ask, with me holding back the tears because I wished I was there with him, at the end of a long day, sipping gin-and-tonics on the porch, inspecting the garden, and recapping a day's work while Miss Kitty purred on the windowsill and dinner cooked on the stove. During those days in Punta, I craved a normal, everyday life more than anything in the world.

"Do you have a day to talk about it?" I answered. "The boat's tired — and it needs a refit badly. But for now it's a matter of making the essentials good enough to get through the Southern Ocean. Our primary winches need rebuilding —"

"Dawn, wait," Barry interrupted. "What are you doing on the boat looking at the insides of a primary winch? You need to be taking care of the overall picture, looking at strategy, being the leader of the campaign. The crew is there to handle the details."

"In a perfect world, yes. But the thing is, if I don't do it, it won't get done. Barry, I need to be there taking care of details. At this point, the only crew I know I can rely on to get the job done right are the crew I brought in with me. As for the others, I am not sure what kind of job they will do, and I don't want to find out once we hit the ice region. I need to be involved in the details. It's a matter of survival now — not race strategy."

"OK, point taken. Anything else?" he said.

Having Barry to talk to made me sane, but in another way, it made me sad. Every time I talked to him I thought about home and how much I wanted to be there. Sometimes I cried, and I hate crying. There is no point to it. I just wanted someone to take me away — but there was no way anyone could or should: the responsibility of this boat was mine now.

Controversy surrounded our campaign, and it was clear that it was not going to go away. Ocean Venture's plan seemed logical: the crew mutinied, Nance Frank announced the withdrawal of her boat from the race, and Ocean Ventures — the ultimate owner of the boat — decided to keep the boat going by bringing in new leadership and a handful of new crew. It was not all that unusual for a boat to switch skippers during the race. *Intrum Justitia,* a Whitbread 60 sailing as a European entry, sent Swedish skipper Roger Nilson home with a knee injury and brought in Lawrie Smith, a talented British skipper. But Nance Frank was not ready to give in.

Once back in the States, Frank talked to the media about taking legal action. Newspapers reported that Frank's withdrawal from the race was only a tactical move, a last-minute call for help and sponsorship support, and that she did not mean to end the campaign. Susan Chiu, who was part of the original crew and a major financial backer of the campaign, told the *New York Times* that the takeover was "an act of piracy," and the paper posed the headline question "Piracy or Just Insolvency?" The media raised a lot of questions about what really happened onboard the boat. They pointed to Mikaela and navigator Adrienne Cahalan, both of whom were continuing on with me, as the ones who divided the crew into pro-Frank and anti-Frank forces. The boat looked like a banana republic of women fumbling through a coup d'etat.

Though I was thrown into the center of the controversy, I was determined to show the world that these problems did not exist because the crew was female. I was determined to set the record straight by sailing on.

The crew members who chose to keep racing had been living in limbo in Punta. Punta — a resort town where the locals party until the sun comes up — is not a good place to be in limbo. The women had nothing to do and little money, and after their six-thousand-mile leg from England to Uruguay, idle time became a perfect excuse for catching up on parties and sleeping late.

Together, our crew became a feminine United Nations, with sailors from the United States, Australia, England, Finland, France, Japan, and New Zealand. The youngest crew was Merritt Carey, a twenty-four-year-old from Maine. We all spoke English, but I sensed a gap. And I soon realized the differences were deeper than cultural.

They resented me. I was not part of the crew who had worked endless hours to get the boat ready for the start in England, working on a small budget and borrowing and begging for cheap labor and free goods. I was not part of the crew who got this boat from England to Uruguay. I was not part of the group who waited in Punta with a little money and a lot of uncertainty after the crew dissolved into mutiny. In their eyes, I had not paid my dues.

There was a state of chaos in Punta. But there was no time to unravel the stories and the sentiments. To survive, we needed to put behind us everything that had happened before and focus on rebuilding this campaign. Soon, we would be playing by the rules of the Southern Ocean, where there is no mercy for the weak and the unprepared. And so we spent the days in Punta on the boat, making every preparation that time would allow before we sailed toward Australia.

Jeni had flown in from London two days earlier with Marie-Claude. But Jeni — the tall and perpetually cool blond — was visibly nervous on the flight down. Marie-Claude asked her why, what's the problem? "I know what it's like where we're going," said Jeni. Enough said. She knew the Southern Ocean and Marie-Claude did not. Not yet.

Because I, too, had sailed those fearsome waters, on the eve of the start, as the wind flew under the moon and swept over Punta, I kept asking myself, Are we ready for the Southern Ocean? Are we ready for the Southern Ocean? The words kept running through my brain like a mantra.

I made a continual checklist in my head. Renee, do you have all the spares? Belts, impeller, oil, batteries, light bulbs, rolls and rolls and rolls of duct tape — that indispensable all-purpose marine Band-Aid. Mikaela, have you checked all the deck gear? Are any winches going to freeze or freewheel out of control? Are any blocks going to explode in our faces? Jeni, will the electronics keep talking to us all the way to Australia? Adrienne, can you show us the way there, navigate us through the icebergs and into the fastest weather systems? Merritt, have you checked the rig, forward and backward and forward again? Without a stick we'll never get there.

I had a lot of questions that would be answered with time. But I was anxious to learn how everyone would handle the Southern Ocean. I had sailed with four of the crew before — Jeni, Mikki, Marie-Claude, and Renee. I only prayed that the promises the rest of the crew had made on their résumés would prove true once we were in the middle of the ocean.

I wanted to tell them all that soon you will be living in the womb of a boat that will buck like a wild beast on the ocean. The hour of four o'clock in the morning will come. It will be as black as ink outside and ice will be all over the deck. You will be partially petrified and partially numb, and it will be your turn to go on deck and tame the wild beast. What will you be like then? But I could not ask the question because they could never give me an answer. Most of them had never seen the Southern Ocean.

The night before the start — when all the boats were silent and closed up for the night — I walked the pier alone. The multinational fleet of ten Whitbread 60s and four Maxis — the Maxis being an older class of boat measuring about eighty feet overall — were ready for the start. There were entries from England, France, Italy, Japan, New Zealand, Spain, Switzerland, the Ukraine, the United States, Uruguay, and one boat entered as a combined European entry.

Intrum Justitia, the European entry, gleamed in gray and yellow in the dock light; Lawrie Smith and several experienced Whitbread veterans would step onboard for the start. *Tokio,* the white-hulled boat with the splash of red graphics, would have Chris Dickson at the helm, a competitor known for his intensity and his focus on winning. *Winston,* an American boat with a red-and-white paint job like the pack of cigarettes, was entered by four-time America's Cup winner Dennis Conner; Conner would not be onboard on this leg, but coskipper Brad Butterworth, who was part of the winning crew of the last Whitbread, would be in command. *Yamaha,* also owned by Ocean Ventures, was the closest thing to our brother ship; the *Yamaha* boys finished third in the first leg, and they were in contention for a front-of-the-fleet spot. The Maxi *New Zealand Endeavour* presented a strong front with many Kiwi sailors who knew this course like their own backyard. This fleet had some of the best sailors in the world. But the level of the competitors did not awe me; I had raced against many of the skippers before. My concerns were the condition of our boat and the skill level of our crew. Four days of preparation is not enough.

When I arrived in Uruguay, the journalists were waiting to have their questions answered. The *New York Times,* the *Washington Post,* the *London Daily Telegraph, USA Today.* Why are you here? Where is Nance Frank? When did you become involved with this all-female project? Are you ready for the Southern Ocean?

Most boats in the race take months and months to train, sail-test, boat-test, and grow into a team before they are ready for this race. We had four days together as a crew. We never had our dress rehearsal.

Are we ready for the Southern Ocean? It was a good question that the journalists were asking. But the question stops being rhetorical this morning. I spent a sleepless night learning to accept the fact that whatever shape we are in as a crew, whatever shape our boat is in, we are setting sail for Australia today.

There is no more time left to prepare.

2

It's happening! After a frantic four days of scrambling to prep the boat, we are on our way and sailing to Australia. . . . Saw the Southern Cross last night. Incredible starry night. *Les etoiles sont brillant!*

> — from the journal of
> Renee Mehl

November 13, 1993

We started the race.

The fact stares at me from our logbook, where we recorded the time in black and white: Saturday, November 13, 1500 Greenwich Mean Time. I can barely believe we pulled it off. The Old Red Bucket is no longer a heap of fiberglass and stainless steel undergoing massive surgery at the dock. It is our express bus to Australia: next stop Fremantle, seventy-five hundred miles down the road.

Our start was anything but brilliant; I should have done better.

The first miles of the race turned into what we are starting to call a "shit fight." I'm sure this will be a popular term used many times before we reach the finish next summer in England.

The start of a race is all about adrenaline and split-second timing. An imaginary starting line is set up between a committee boat and a marker. The boats jockey around the small confines of the starting area. The objective is to time your route so when the starting gun goes off, you are positioned perfectly on the line with good boat speed and a clear path to fresh wind. The start can be just like a game of musical chairs when more than one boat rushes toward the same space on the line. Only the consequences are more expensive.

Sometimes, I hit it just right. Sometimes, a million things go wrong.

The day we left Punta, it was pissing down rain and the wind was up to about twenty knots. This is a lot of breeze for a crew who has flown a spinnaker — a big and powerful balloonlike sail only kept in control by the crew pulling all the strings at the right times — for only fifteen minutes. That was during our only practice session, and that fifteen minutes under spinnaker took thirty minutes to set up. That's an eternity, considering that the pros can hook up a chute (sailors' slang for spinnaker) in a minute and hoist it in about forty seconds. The mastman stands at the mast and hauls the halyard, the line that raises the sail up the mast, with lightning speed. As soon as the chute is up the trimmers pull the right strings, the big balloon sail fills with a crack, and the boat lurches forward with the wind. That's the text-book version. The crew of the Red Bucket had our own way of doing things.

On the morning of the start, I went down to the boat early and alone, to have a pep talk with myself. Punta had been chaos for me. People kept asking if I was scared, nervous, confident, crazy, or egotistical to take over this boat. (I knew I was all of the above, but I never let on.) On the morning of the start, the chaos would stop and I would pour all my energy into this boat, hoping to make it work like a machine.

I outlined a tentative watch system. Not one of us would sleep a full night from now on, and our lives would be ruled by the clock. One watch would be on deck for four hours, until a replacement team rotated in. The next four hours, the off-watch would be free to sleep, eat, read, write letters, listen to a Walkman, do whatever it is that lets them rest and recuperate from fear, stress, physical labor, and cold — until the clock tells them to go back out again.

I did not know all the crew's abilities, so I guessed. I made up watches that mixed those whom I figured to be strong players with the weaker ones. Each watch would have to operate as a team, and the personality and talent mix had to be right.

I carefully wrote down crew positions for the start. It would be a take-no-prisoners moment on the boat. Do your job right. No, do it perfectly. Mistakes mean, at best, a bad start and a disadvantage from the very beginning. At worst, mistakes mean a collision, a breakdown, or someone getting hurt. Everyone's job would be crucial.

I put Merritt Carey on the bow. An American from Maine, she works hard, she learns fast, and she does not seem to be afraid of many things. I sense that, for her, this race is not about ego — not about telling the world how good a sailor you are. She wants to learn to be a better sailor, so when Merritt doesn't know something, she asks. I could trust her on the bow. She would be my eyes in the front of the boat.

Gloria Borrego would be at the mast for the start, hauling the halyards that pull the sails up the mast. Gloria is our

engineer — an experienced mechanic who is used to working under pressure after her days of working in the NASCAR
pits. Once we head offshore, she will be in charge of maintaining the boat's systems: the engine, the generator, the
water-ballast system, the desalinator that turns salt water to
fresh, the charge levels of our bank of batteries and the supply
level of our stores of diesel fuel, our steering system. Gloria
flew in only a day before the start, and I had never met her
before. But she is strong, and I sense she wants to be part of a
well-oiled machine. I figured if I told Gloria to pump the halyard — harder, faster, harder — she would keep up the pace.

Leah Newbold is from New Zealand, a country of sailors
where Whitbread racers are national heros as big as American football stars. I imagined Leah as a kid with miles of
wiry, brown hair, staring out of her window from a house on
the hill, watching the Whitbread heros sail back from the sea,
dreaming of someday sailing home — just like them. This
race meant a lot to Leah. She was in the pit, a central part of
the boat where many halyard controls are located. Leah
would be overhauling halyards for Gloria and backing up
Merritt on the foredeck.

Kaori Matsunaga would be in the pit with Leah. Kaori is
from Japan. I heard of her when she tried to join the *Maiden*
crew. But at that time, her sailing skills were weak and her
English was not good, and she left the crew before I arrived
in England. I assumed she had gone back to Japan — to the
land of Madame Butterfly, where women are not known to
venture to foreign lands to compete in dangerous sailboat
races. Instead, she moved to New Zealand to improve her
English and she sailed Pacific Ocean passages. Now she is
back, a stronger sailor with better English. Kaori is determined.

Sue Crafer, our physiotherapist onboard from England, was working her way around the world — crewing on boats in the Caribbean, working as a physio with a film crew on Easter Island — when the Whitbread called. Sue's skills as a physio will be well used during our long ocean legs accompanied by muscle strain and body fatigue. Sue and Jeni would be the headsail trimmers.

Lisa Beecham, a doctor from Australia who joined the boat in Punta, would grind winches at the start for Sue and Jeni, to give them the mechanical advantage to trim the massive headsails. Once we head offshore, Lisa will be cooking meals, acting as general crew, and contributing her medical skills when needed.

Marie-Claude would trim the mainsail. She had a good eye for sail trim and she understood that the mainsail is a controlling power during a start. The main has to be let out or pulled in at the right time. Sometimes we would need to trim on and sail fast. Sometimes we would need to let the main flog and slow down. Marie-Claude is an experienced sailor, and I knew I would count on her once we headed offshore.

Renee was on a runner, a stay that helps to shape the mast bend and hold the giant tree-trunk stick upright in the boat. I needed her in a position that required finesse rather than brute strength.

Adrienne Cahalan, our navigator, is a lawyer from Sydney, Australia. She is a strong personality, she has strong opinions, and I am beginning to learn that she is never one not to voice what she feels is right. I learned that when I asked Adrienne to share the job of navigating with Jeni. I wanted a fail-safe watch system with as many checks and balances as possible. I planned for everyone to have a backup — in case something happened to that person and they could not do their job. But Adrienne refused, and she insisted on remaining indispensable as the sole navigator on the boat. At the start, I put her behind me, in charge of keeping time at the start.

Mikaela would be crew boss. Mikki is Finnish, and she can be bossy if she has to be. She understands how this boat works, she can catch a mistake before it happens, and she would oversee the crew work while I concentrated on driving. Unless she lapsed into Finnish at a crucial moment, we would be fine.

I would drive the boat. I would take full responsibility for a brilliant start or a disastrous beginning or something in between.

I penned the list neatly; it was the textbook map of our start. I put the paper in my notebook and crossed my fingers for my best-laid plan.

On the morning of the start, we dropped our dock lines in the pouring rain and drifted away from the pier with the engine in reverse. I kicked the engine into neutral, then forward, and we powered away. Good riddance Punta. Life there was a monster amusement-park ride — a mass confusion of the senses, all in one short burst of time. Finally I am traveling in a straight line.

By next spring, the race will stop again in Punta, and everything on this boat will be different then — that is, if we make it. If disaster or an iceberg or Nance Frank's dreams of redemption don't catch us first.

My mom gave me a handful of good fortune when I left Detroit: one New Age crystal for each crew. I portioned out the lucky charms down below as the rain pelted on the deck. One drop of rain makes a big sound on a boat like

ours, a rain-on-a-tin-can shower of noise. Sue Crafer
thought her crystal was rock candy and took a huge, enthusiastic bite. Sue, Lesson One: don't consume all your good
luck now. Save it until we reach Australia.

We motored out toward the start and ran the spaghetti of
lines that would control our headsails. I caught a look
between Merritt and Adrienne as they ran the lines on the
foredeck. There was nothing said, but I know what they
were thinking. We are really going: there's no turning back
now. It was a glance between two people diving off a cliff
into water that could be deep enough or too shallow. Only
way to find out is to jump in, headfirst.

Before we raised a headsail, an inflatable tender came
running to us at full speed. What was it, I wondered, that
had them rushing at top speed to us? Had someone said,
"No, stop this boatload of women from sailing into disaster"? As they drew closer, I saw my bag. My big duffel with
warm clothes. It had been found in the nick of time. We
stowed the bag below, raised a headsail, and got quickly
back to the business of sailing.

With the headsail up, and everyone in position, the boat
and the crew settled in for what I hoped would be their first
star performance. I studied the wind, watching how it
moved the boat. Was it shifting back and forth? Was it
steady? Was it clocking in one direction? Was it puffing and
changing intensity quickly so we would have to depower,
power up, and switch gears with the vagaries of the breeze?

For the first time in days, I could focus intensely on one
job. My head kicked into racing mode, killer instinct. We
could win this start.

The gun signaling ten minutes to the start blasted off.
Our start was already mapped out inside my head. Start at

the pin end, not the boat end. In relation to the wind direction, this was the favored end to start on. The next five minutes flew by as we jockeyed around the starting area.

The five-minute gun sounded. We timed the gun to the smoke coming off the committee boat: the noise of the cannon would take a few extra seconds to reach us, and we had to be exact on time. Five minutes: now it's countdown time.

"Four minutes. Three-and-a-half. Three minutes." Adrienne reeled off the time left as the seconds peeled away. Our boat handling was decent as we whizzed through the rush-hour traffic on the line. The time was getting down to the wire.

"One minute," yelled Adrienne. OK, I thought, this is where we make it or we don't. As we approached the pin end, the crowd of boats started to build. Everyone in the fleet wanted to be in that favored position.

"I can't get the boat into that crowd. MC, luff the main. Slow us down a bit," I told her. If we could delay, a slot might open up. But the boats were bunched tightly together, making a wall of sail. The watch was running down. We had to get to the line.

"No room here. We have to run the line. Trim for speed, keep those sails working," I instructed them. I sailed the boat along the start line, away from the pin. Time was crucial now and as the clock ran down to zero my adrenaline ran high.

"Thirty seconds, twenty, ten," Adrienne called. OK, we were powered up, sails were trimmed.

"Merritt, how many boat lengths to the line?" I called. Merritt stood at the bow, eyeing the starting line. She held out one finger, signaling one boat length, or about sixty feet, to the line. It was crucial to time our placement so our bow would hit the line exactly at the starting gun. The cannon onboard the committee boat blasted with a shotgun explosion. We crossed the line and hoisted our spinnaker. All fourteen boats surged through the choppy water over the line, most with spinnakers flying. We all sprinted toward the turning mark at Punta Ballena, three miles away.

We were on the line at the start, but not in the position I had wanted to be in. So we concentrated hard on squeezing every tenth-of-a-knot of speed out of our boat. Jeni and Sue were working together to keep the chute full, to keep it flying and pulling for speed. Lisa was ready to crank the big coffee-grinder winch, poised to move any second. MC worked the mainsail, constantly adjusting to keep it working efficiently. I drove while I eyed our sail trim, the position of the other boats, and our boat speed as it read on the electronic knotmeter mounted on the mast. The pedal was down and everyone was focused on her job. It would be like this for weeks now.

We had to jibe to make the mark. I knew this could be a violent turn in this breeze if we did not handle the sails right. The crew started grinding in the mainsail, but it wasn't coming in fast enough. I should have held it longer, but we had to turn. I spun the boat on its keel. The new runner, which helps keep the mast upright in the boat, was not pulled in fast enough and the old runner was still too tight. Now our boat speed was way down, and we were losing steerage. With the main strapped in by the old runner, we spun too far and tacked — forcing our sails over to the other side of the boat, like a drunk person overnavigating a turn. We had to use the jib to get us back on course.

No one was hurt and nothing broke — except our pride.

The TV crews and journalists were out there in press boats. Barry would see our start on New Zealand TV tonight. It was very embarrassing. But we got the boat back under control, reached off for speed, and picked up again in the fleet. *Intrum Justitia* was first to reach the turning mark, and they turned the corner and headed out for Prince Edward Island, the next turning mark of the leg. It would be about twelve days before any of us reached that point.

A fleet of a hundred boats filled with well-wishers, press, and families of the crews came out to wave the Whitbread boats on to Australia. On land, spectators drove out to the hills at Punta Ballena — where a modern artist's version of a fairy-tale castle sits, like a funky, white wedding cake in the sky. Some of the families would be crying to see their loved ones sail away into the Southern Ocean. Some of the spectators would be happy to have seen the spectacle of the fleet charging off to Australia. By nightfall, they would all be back on land, safe at home in cozy, dry houses. We would be wet, with spray washing on deck, eating a dinner of freeze-dried food.

A pack of 60s — *Tokio, Yamaha, Galicia 93 Pescanova, Brooksfield* — rounded the mark together, turning in formation like a flock of geese navigating the airstreams. To the world, we were that small: a few birds making a long trip. The pack was followed by British entry *Dolphin & Youth,* and *Hetman Sahaidachny,* a Whitbread 60 from the Ukraine, rounded next. *Hetman* caught the mark and started dragging it downwind. It looked like a fiasco, but it actually made our angle to the mark easier. Thank you, *Hetman,* for small favors.

At the fairy-tale castle at Punta Ballena, we turned the corner for Prince Edward Island, dropped our spinnaker, hauled in our sails, and settled in for what I knew could be a long night.

The weather forecast called for a gale — a Force 8 wind of forty knots — and we were headed upwind, which is the most uncomfortable point of sail. Most inshore boat races would be canceled with a wind of such intensity. But in off-shore racing, conditions are constantly changing and as ocean racers we have to handle whatever conditions we encounter — and still keep pushing the boat as fast as pos-sible without falling over the edge to damage. Or disaster.

So I waited for darkness to fall — the blanket of black that makes every job onboard that much harder. If some-thing breaks on deck, we have limited visibility to make the repair. If someone falls overboard, she is that much harder to find. Obstacles are obscured by the dark. Massive ships become skeletons of running lights floating through the night on an invisible horizon. Everything disappears in the dark — except the kind of uncertainty that haunts until day-break.

Sailing in the dark requires sharp eyes and a strong mind. But the crews' minds and bodies are still geared for land life, and fatigue will set in during this first night at sea. It will take days for us to get used to living by the watch system of four hours on duty, four hours off. It will take days before catnaps will fuel us to peak performance. We will have to sail carefully in tonight's Force 8 wind.

We sailed into the night with our sails close-hauled. The crew had already stowed the minimal gear they brought onboard. A list of waterproof wear to stay warm and dry was allowed: foul-weather gear; a drysuit with rubber seals at neck, feet, and cuffs to keep water out; a fleece jacket, long underwear, boots, mask, balaclava, hat, oil-rig gloves and glove liners. Four changes of underwear were allowed. Most everything else was shared between watch partners: Walkmans, tapes, books, goggles to wear onboard in the heavy spray. We only had what we needed to function, for weight onboard had to be kept to a minimum. The boat's only opening ports would remain closed to keep the water out, and down below we would live in an enclosed capsule of air that would have a distinct stench by the time we reached Australia. For now, everything was clean and dry. Each crew had one cubbyhole for stowing gear, and on either side of the hull was a set of hooks for hanging wet clothes and foul-weather gear. We labeled each crew's hook with a black marker. It made for an orderly display, like the Christmas-stocking station of a large family.

As the clock neared 1900 hours — our nightly dinnertime — Lisa fired up the propane stove, transforming feather-light, space-age bits of freeze-dried food into a curry. I had no appetite. Whether it was nerves or an allergic reaction or little enthusiasm for the cuisine, I could not get any food down. So I stayed on deck.

The boat settled into a steady upwind motion, and we moved out in a moderate breeze, powering forward at about ten knots. A boat has a language of its own — the groans of winches easing, the pounding of the water on the hull, the purr of the generator: it has its own way of telling you what is going on. With time, I would learn to translate all the noises and know which ones were normal grunts and which ones were trouble signs. But I was not yet fluent in the Red Bucket's tongue, so I listened for every noise as we headed into our first night.

For hours, I was busy watching the boat — feeling how it moved and listening for any telltale signs of trouble. The on-watch crew was on deck with me, trimming the sails and keeping their weight on the high, windward side of the boat to balance out the heel of the hull. My head and my eyes stayed focused on this sailing machine that was taking us farther and farther away from life as we knew it.

The Force 8 wind was showing no signs of rearing its ugly head, and the latest weather fax showed us pointed toward a high-pressure system of fair weather. Maybe tonight the breeze will stay calm. Maybe tonight will be a long-awaited chance to build our fragile confidence with smooth sailing.

The boat settled down under the cover of darkness. Our white sails flew like a ghost over the water. The red compass light turned the compass into an eerie crystal ball of fire, smoldering at the wheel and pointing us toward the future. The sky was magic: a billion stars. The horrors of the Southern Ocean seemed a million miles away tonight, as we flew toward Australia through a sky of diamonds.

As we soared upwind, I took a break to look back, one last time. Uruguay had vanished. We were all alone now.

3

This crew has already mutinied once. Be careful.

— Advice from Barry
McKay to Dawn Riley

November 15, 1993

"Dawn, wake up, wake up," said Jeni, who had been on deck before coming down below to wake me. She was dressed in a foul-weather jacket, and her hair was half-wet from the spray outside.

"Yeah, OK. OK. I'm awake. Is it time for my watch already?" I answered from my bunk.

"No. . . . We're tacking," Jeni informed me.

It was a loaded response — because that was not supposed to happen. I had been trying to get three hours of sleep during the midday sun, to rest up for sailing that night. Maybe, during that time, the crew received new weather information, giving us clues to the location of a low-pressure system with better breeze. Maybe it was tactically right to tack and change our course. But it was wrong for the crew to make this decision without consulting me.

Jeni knew. She had raced on Whitbread boats before and she understood that, however military it may seem, there is one ultimate authority on the boat: the skipper.

Jeni looked at me and understood what was going

through my head. I wanted to go up on deck, chew out the crew who made the call, tell them tactical moves are not to be made behind my back.

Give them the benefit of the doubt, I told myself: the crew is green and unprofessional, and they don't understand the chain of command. Or, are they purposely overriding my authority? It was like the sitcoms on TV I used to watch as a kid. On one shoulder was the angel, wearing white. She was saying, "Don't be too hard on them. This is an understandable mistake." On the other shoulder was the devil, with horns: "Come on, come on. Go kick some butt. They are intentionally overriding you. Are you going to let them get away with that?" Those were the two extremes. The crew was new to me — too new for me to understand their motivation for making decisions without me. How was I supposed to react?

I started to get out of my bunk, but I was halfway out when I pulled myself back. I could tear up there and chew everyone out for tacking, but that could be war, alienation, and an explosion of the delicate balance onboard among virtual strangers who were now living together in a small capsule and careening toward dangerous waters. It was only our second day out, and we had too many hard miles to go together to risk a war onboard.

The angle of the boat's heel began to change, sails flogged overhead like muffled thunder, and the monster coffee-grinder winches growled through the boat. I hadn't been dreaming that the crew had turned the boat into the eye of the wind to sail ninety degrees away from our original course, to change our strategy while I was asleep. It wasn't a bad dream. We were really tacking.

Everything resettled down below in the cabin as the boat

rocked over onto its other side. The water ballast that we pumped through the hull was shifted to the opposite side of the boat, to counterbalance our new angle of heel. Hanging clothes and foul-weather gear followed the pull of gravity and swung over to hang at a new angle. Canisters of tea, coffee, and sugar secured in the galley budged over an inch or two. Jeni went back on deck — silently — to get back to the business of trimming sails, and as my body shifted in its prone position in my bunk with the motion of the hull, I remembered something Barry had said to me. It was something I had wanted to forget.

It was during one of those middle-of-the-night phone calls between Detroit and New Zealand, during the days I considered and reconsidered this project from the security of my childhood home.

"This crew has already mutinied once," Barry told me. "Be careful."

"Barry, don't be so dramatic. It's not like that anymore," I told him. The word "mutiny" carried too much weight. To me, it was a word that belonged to the days of Columbus and pirates, to offshore passages on brigantines when men were men and women were absent. No. A modern-day race was not the same as the sea tales of old.

"Dawn, be careful," he said again, after I rebuffed his warning. And only now did I wonder to myself, should I have taken his warning more seriously?

I needed to find a strategy for these kinds of situations, and I decided that I could only lead gently, by example — not by brute force. I had never had a hard time taking command of a boat. But this was different. This was integrating an existing crew with new members, and it could be a walk through a minefield of personalities. Take one step back, I told myself, and let the mechanics of the crew develop naturally until we are a solid team. This seemed to be the logical route, although I will admit that part of me wanted to be an absolute dictator.

By now I was already awake. I got up, put on my layers of clothing, and went on deck to get ready for my four-hour watch. Once I was on deck, all I focused on was the sails, the trim, the boat speed — the things I could fix. I said nothing — absolutely nothing — about the tack.

The wind had been light, and now it was growing lighter. By 0200 hours we switched to a bigger jib for more sail area and more power aloft. We hoisted the Number 1 genoa. It looked worse than the smaller Number 3 jib — and I thought that sail was bad. According to the last position report we received via fax from race headquarters, we were in ninth place in the ten-boat Whitbread 60 class. Our speed-made-good (SMG), the speed we averaged between our last two known positions, was about three-tenths of a knot below the average of the class. We had to make better speed if we were going to stay with the fleet all the way to Australia.

By November 16, our fourth day at sea, we had sailed into a region called the Roaring Forties. This forty-degree-latitude belt is usually true to its name: roaring and raging, with full-blown warnings of the Southern Ocean miles ahead. But we had not yet seen any signs of the region's bad temper. For four days, high-pressure systems bringing fair weather, lighter winds, and sun rolled over us. I was sunburned. Jeni was gleeful on our fourth day out: ". . . here we are, barefoot in the Roaring Forties," she exclaimed, as she helmed the boat as shoeless and sockless as a Caribbean sailor, enjoying her "holiday" from job-hunting in this exotic ocean. I could not complain about the lack of harsh weather. I was warm and dry, wearing only one pair of heavy socks, midweight long underwear, T-shirt, polar-fleece-lined pants, jacket, and foul-weather gear to keep the damp out.

The Red Bucket still needed work. The rudderpost — the post that runs through the aft section of the hull and attaches to the rudder, and a notorious source of leaking water in many boats — was letting water seep in. But we could sponge the water out of the aft section of the boat faster than it was coming in. We had limited tankage for fresh water — thirty gallons — so we had a desalinator to transform salt water to fresh. Marooned sailors who drink salt water get dehydrated and ultimately go mad. The water maker was a vital piece of gear, but it was sucking too much air. We had a system of water ballast that pumped movable liquid ballast throughout the hull. We could empty the tanks, or fill them completely with a total of about five thousand liters of salt water — the weight of approximately forty women — to balance out the heel of the boat and keep us sailing at the most efficient angle. There were eight tanks, four on each side, and a system of pumps that shifted the water from side to side. But the system was slow and sluggish. The work list was still long, and it inspired a roll-the-eyeballs reaction: Long Live the Red Bucket.

In reality, it was no joke.

The boat was not 100 percent ready for the Southern Ocean — and neither was I. After several days out sailing, I thought my eating problem would sort itself out — but I was still having a hard time getting the freeze-dried food down. Every time I tried, my throat swelled up and I was not sure there was enough room to get anything down. I don't know if it was nerves, or an allergy. But the lack of food made me light-headed. My mind was not clued in to the boat yet. I was going through the motions: living on a four-hours-on, four-hours-off watch schedule, looking at Adrienne's weather maps, studying position reports, helming the boat, and trimming sails. But my head and my heart were suffering from some strange kind of jet lag. In my mind, I was not really here yet.

When I was not working on deck, I went below and fired up the laptop computer and wrote: messages, letters, questions, news; to Barry, to the office of the all-female America's Cup effort *America³*, to our shore manager David Glen back in Auckland, to my mom. I needed outlets, someplace to vent steam and rant and rave and say what I honestly thought. The crew's level of experience was not as high as I hoped it would be. We were not falling into a solid team quickly enough.

I faxed the office of *America³* with a cheery voice: *All is well here. Much warmer than the last time around. . . . If we average 11 knots, we can be in Australia around December 9.* I wanted to know what was happening, when announcements might be made about the historic, first-ever female Cup crew. For my own sanity, I had to keep thinking ahead to career projects beyond this boat.

I faxed Barry as much as possible. If I had not taken this job, I would have been at home in Auckland with him. I missed our 120-year-old house on Vine Street that we restored together. For a short time, before I came back to the United States last summer, Barry and I had a nice life in New Zealand. I was scraping paint, sanding, rebuilding, refinishing; doing odd jobs to make some money; working in the garden; going to barbecues and having friends over. After college, I never had a nine-to-five job. I moved onto boats, raced them and maintained them, and traveled to the racing circuits along the East Coast and in the Caribbean. After years of living out of duffel bags, vans, boats, and crew houses, and working on the boats that follow the seasons like migrating birds, our rehabbed house was the first real home of my own I ever had.

Barry was privy to my stream-of-consciousness spewing off this boat, and my faxes filed in the computer held all my innermost thoughts. *I miss you. Yes, I still start to cry when I think of what I am giving up to do this. . . . I hate it here. Maybe it will be better in a few days. . . . I still don't know if I am going to continue after Australia.*

At this point, it would not have been constructive to tell the crew everything that was going through my mind. Everyone in the crew needed an equivalent: a journal, a friend to write faxes to, letters about frustration and fright that were written and — maybe — never sent. It didn't matter: writing it all down was only a way to find an outlet while living in a 24-hour-a-day work environment with no privacy.

I reported to Barry on wind conditions, boat speed, sail handling, and how the crew situation was progressing. Our lack of boat speed and our less-than-expert sail handling could be corrected with better sails and more time in this scary-fast boat. It was the crew situation that I did not have a handle on.

I knew the crew I brought in with me at Punta, except for Lisa Beecham, our doctor, who was in Punta and willing to join the crew at the last minute as medic and cook. I knew Mikaela from our *Maiden* days in my first Whitbread, and that she was a solid watch leader and an expert helmsman who knew what the Southern Ocean was all about. Kaori, from Japan, impressed me as neat and orderly; she cataloged all her belongings in Ziploc bags and followed orders to the letter. Merritt, on the other hand, was the one who was always foraging through the cabin in search of her hat when it was time for a watch change, or walking around the cabin wearing one waterproof seaboot in desperate need of its mate; once on deck, Merritt was a solid and dependable sailor. Leah was a no-bullshit kind of crew: always on time for watches, always willing to pitch in. Gloria was talented as an engineer, but she had less sailing experience than most of the crew and seemed more content to stay below deck and tinker with tools. Adrienne struck me as a natural-born leader, and she had built up a lot of loyalty among the original crew.

My insights into the crew, at this point, were only superficial, but there was one thing I was certain of: in Punta, two distinct camps of old crew and new crew took shape. The new crew that I brought into the program — including me, Renee, Marie-Claude, and Jeni — flew into Punta with a killer instinct. Let's put this boat back together, we all thought. Let's erase the past and start all over again. The old crew of Adrienne, Mikki, Leah, Merritt, Kaori, Sue, and Gloria had a right to be cynical. They were a big part of the reason why this boat had even made it to Uruguay. So what if Dawn had done the America's Cup and the Whitbread before? So what if Marie-Claude had done a million single-handed races all over Europe? So what if Renee had sailed with America's Cup sailor Paul Cayard in the 50-Foot Worlds? What are they doing on our boat? I knew the thought went through their brains. Constantly.

If the old-crew-versus-new-crew situation escalated into an explosive situation, I knew I would have to make crew changes. I confided this to Barry in the faxes I wrote to him. But no one on the crew could know my thoughts. Each of them had enough pressure without the added stress of worrying that her job might be in jeopardy.

At this point in the race, we had not yet hit the hellish conditions of the Southern Ocean. In this fair, high-pressure weather, the old crew may have figured that they didn't need me and my new crew. *We can survive without you, thank you very much,* they might have been thinking. But if the crew wanted my job, I wanted them first to walk through my dreams.

Ever since we left Punta I had been having a lot of visions in my short bursts of sleep between watches. Some were strange, and some were simple to make sense of. The ones about the boat were not full-blown nightmares; they were all my concerns painted in black humor. Nance Frank appeared in midocean. Boats appeared thousands of miles from nowhere to watch us race. There were people who came onboard and clawed our sails to bits. The dreams that were not set on the boat were fantasies of everything that was missing out here: a hot shower and fluffy, white towels, a deluxe hotel room, a meal of fresh fruit, Barry.

One day, we were racing in the middle of the ocean. The sea was filled with icebergs, but we were all wearing bathing suits. I did not think it strange at the time, but in that patch of ocean thousands of miles from the mainland were all these boats who had come out to watch us race: tugboats, inflatable dinghies, cabin cruisers, big catamarans. The people on the boats were all waving and cheering. I don't remember who they all were or where they came from. There was one other boat in the race. We were having a close race with it, and we were both approaching a small island. But we could not get past the spectator boats to sail around the island. We were trapped. We had to go over the land. I said we could make it to the finish. I jumped into the water and picked the boat up by the keel and balanced it on my shoulder. The boat was way too heavy. My feet were sinking into the mud, and I was getting crushed. But I made it to the other side of the island and slid the boat off my back and into the water.

All the people cheered, and we won the race.

November 19 marks our seventh day at sea. We have covered approximately thirteen hundred miles. The weather is still relatively warm and dry. Some of the nights are magic, and our boat flies over flat-water seas that are mirrors to a thousand points of starlight. They are skies of "Star light, star bright . . ." for my nightly wish-upon-a-star. The fair weather has given us time to settle into the routine of living at sea. But I am anxious to see how we hold together once we hit the worst of the Southern Ocean.

We have taken a dive south. *Tokio,* the Japanese/New Zealand entry that is winning the Whitbread 60 class, and the Italian 60 *Brooksfield* — named for its clothing-company sponsor — have also chosen a southerly route.

When we reach Australia, two winners will be named: the first Whitbread 60 into Fremantle and the first Maxi. But those are just two of over a dozen first-place trophies that will be awarded during this race. At the end of each of the six legs, trophies are awarded at a prize-giving ceremony held during each stopover to the first Maxi and the first Whitbread 60 to finish that particular leg. Then, the times for each individual leg are factored into an overall standing, and at the race's end two overall trophies will be awarded at a prize-giving ceremony in England for the best time around the world in each class. But for now, trophies are not foremost in my mind: we are all sailing south to search for low-pressure regions, hoping to be the first boat to catch their swift ride.

Not everything is fine onboard. The head (our marine toilet) blew up today. That's a major problem with twelve women onboard, and Renee, Mikki, and Gloria spent a sunny day down below fixing it. The head is not industrial-strength: only a system of hoses, valves, and a hand pump that can't take much abuse. The head has to be rebuilt once we reach Australia, but for now, it's the only one we have onboard. If it breaks again once we hit snowstorms, it is going to be a cold trip to the outhouse.

We need to maintain a regimented routine onboard. Everyone is on a schedule of four hours on watch, four hours off watch — except Adrienne, who is free to float and navigate when she needs to, and Lisa, our cook. If anyone gets hurt, I will put Lisa on deck and let the injured crew member stay in her bunk.

With Adrienne and Lisa floating, we have ten crew left, so there are five people on watch at all times. There is a watch leader for each watch; I lead one watch, Mikki leads the other. If we flip five people every four hours, the performance of the boat will suffer: when five new people come on deck, they have no sense of how the wind has been behaving, how the seas have been running, and how the boat has been handling in the conditions. So I have set up teams of two and three people who will rotate every two hours. Kaori and I are paired together; Mikki and Gloria are a team; Jeni, Renee, and Merritt make one three-woman group; and MC, Leah, and Susie make up the other. This way, when one two-woman team goes below and the second two-woman team comes up on deck, there will be three people who have already been sailing the boat for two hours. They will know the patterns of the wind and the weather for the last two hours, and they can educate the new watch to keep the boat running at optimum performance. There is no downtime: we have to keep pushing until we reach Australia.

Meals are served at the time of a watch change. Lisa prepares the food twenty minutes before the change of watch. The new watch eats before getting dressed to go outside; when they finish eating and are dressed, they tag a partner on deck who can now come below and eat and go to bed. The remaining crew not due for a watch change get fed in bed. Breakfast in bed sounds nice. But on this boat, it is not silk pajamas under a fluffy duvet with a tray of orange juice, coffee, croissants, and a rose in a silver vase. Meals are plastic bowls of freeze-dried curry, or chile, or pasta with a mystery sauce, served to you in your damp sleeping bag in a metal-framed bunk.

The hour of the day is a relative term. As we sail across the ocean we keep entering new time zones. This will be the case on every leg, so for each leg we have to design a system of adjusting the hour onboard to slowly phase ourselves into the time of our land destination.

On this leg, we change the hour of the day onboard as we need to. When dinnertime becomes the hour of sunrise and lunch is the middle of the night, we adjust the hour onboard to keep pace with the cycles of the sun. Altering our clock as we head toward Australia is not a hardship. The most confusing thing is figuring out a schedule for taking birth-control pills: Was that yesterday that I took one? But yesterday is now today in this time zone, so maybe I have missed a day? This is one problem the men do not have.

We cannot see the other boats, but we know exactly where they are. With our satellite-communications systems onboard, the race organizers can poll the fleet positions from a remote site. Our SatCom C bleeps twice when they take our latitude/longitude position: a high sign from land, even if it is only a computer who has found us here, in the middle of the ocean. The electronic tracking system used by the race committee enables race headquarters to issue a report back to us every six hours, which Adrienne collects and deciphers. It tells us the latitude/longitude positions of the other boats; their speed-made-good; their velocity-made-good (VMG), which is the average velocity made over the leg and used to predict velocity to the leg finish; their average compass course sailed; and their distance to the finish. The fleet is spread out all over the ocean, but the program factors the order of the yachts, using VMG and the distance remaining to the finish of the leg. It enables us to have a visual plot of the entire fleet — just like a board game: Parcheesi on the high seas for survival stakes.

Adrienne receives weather maps via our satellite-communications fax capabilities, and the maps plot out the position of the high- and low-pressure systems, the barometric-pressure readings in the centers of the systems, the movements of the fronts. We have to superimpose this information on our charts of the ocean, and plot our hunt for the rewards of low-pressure systems with stronger winds and rougher weather. It is not enough simply to sail into a low-pressure region. In the Southern Hemisphere, the lows circulate in a clockwise direction, so we have to sail along the backs of the system — to hit the right place in the cycle and get the strongest push from the wind. It is like walking across a river on floating logs: if you don't hit the right part of the log, you fall, lose your balance, and have to search for the next ride.

Our instincts on navigating this part of the ocean are right, but our boat speed is not what it needs to be to keep pace with the leaders. Our sails are tired. Our boat handling is less than expert. I am constantly coaching the crew (or is it nagging?) to race with the big picture in mind, to push for those extra tenths-of-a-knot in speed and keep to our compass course.

Part of me feels like a failure because we are not winning. But part of me knows we don't have the tools we need to triumph on this leg. The goal is to get to Australia in one piece with a decent finishing time. If all works according to plan, a new sponsor will be actively supporting the campaign once we reach Australia, and our wish list to David Glen for new gear and repairs grows longer every day.

David Glen of Ocean Ventures Management (OVM), who is now back in Auckland, is acting as our sole shore manager. With sponsor negotiations in the works, OVM is backing us until a sponsor is onboard, and David Glen is our link to land until a sponsor brings in a full shore crew. His name has been quickly abbreviated by all of us to DG. The nickname has an identity of its own when pronounced in all our different accents. Marie-Claude's French-accented "Deeegheee" makes his name sound like a French movie star's. Leah's New Zealand twang makes him sound like a Maori warrior. My unadulterated American makes "DG" sound like a Texas country boy. Merritt applies her unique American/Australian lingo — picked up working her way from home in Maine, and through the Caribbean, on boats with Aussie crews. However the name sounds, DG is our key contact on earth: he is our link to possibility, to getting the tools we need to make this campaign succeed.

We fax DG nearly every day on our SatCom C — our satellite-communications gear that allows us to transmit text. Soon we will become the remote harem that he can banish at will with the flick of a computer switch. But for now, the mail will roll off the SatCom C at a rapid pace: *Dear DG, we need new snatch blocks. Dear DG, we need new genoa track stoppers; the last one flew off like a speeding bullet from the end of the track. Dear DG, we need a new mainsail; this one is holding up like a well-worn rag. Dear DG, how about some new shives, an assortment of ball bearings, some new main-sheet blocks? Dear DG, our rudder is groaning and leaking; we need a new rudder seal, or a new bearing, or maybe both.*

P.S. DG, Christmas is only a month away.

It is time for me to climb into my bunk for my off-watch sleep. I write a quick fax to Barry to fill him in on the crew situation, on our ETA in Australia, on my mood swings from frustration, to disappointment, to depression, to anger.

I need to get some sleep: count sheep and think of Barry. It is not easy to sleep when the boat feels so alive. There are voices and footsteps on deck. The ocean passes by, inches away from where I lie, and the waves turn my bunk into a water bed with an earthquake motion. The ease of tension off the winches makes a strange sound: like the song of a whale, a long and eerie cry that lingers too long in the air.

Gizmo and I drop off to sleep, amid the sounds of life at sea.

Each day we see more signs of Southern Ocean life. There are seals sleeping on their sides. They keep one fin up and stick it out of the water like a small flag. As soon as our hull approaches them, the seals look up indignantly and swim away. *In this vast ocean,* they must be thinking, *can't you find your own place to go? How dare you disturb our sleep!*

Dolphin & Youth — the only British entry in the race, skippered by twenty-two-year-old Matt Humphries, the youngest skipper in the fleet — reported being followed by a pod of killer whales. Kaori saw some penguins, and in her excited Japanese accent, she called them chickens; we are all having a laugh, thinking about the farm birds on a glamorous world tour. I saw pilot whales; and petrels and albatross dance in the air along our wake. I wish I could hitchhike with them, soar away and be free. But that would be quitting.

We have ventured farther south into the fifty-degree-latitude belt. The conditions are getting more extreme, with bigger seas and stronger winds. The carnage onboard has escalated — the blown-up sails, the wear and tear on our bodies, the close encounters with potential disasters. I am having a harder time getting to sleep.

We have passed *Hetman Sahaidachny,* the Whitbread 60 from the Ukraine. We have now set our sights on grinding down the lead of *Dolphin & Youth.* We are catching fast sleigh rides in the "Screaming Fifties" — the nickname for this latitude belt where the winds really do scream. The shape of our hull is not a heavy-displacement triangle wedge that bulldozes through the water. Our hull has a flatter bottom and thin fin keel, and it skips, dances, and flies on the water and sometimes bows down like a torpedo into the surf, producing a motion that is wet and wild — sometimes a graceful-bird flight and sometimes a hold-on-for-dear-life ride. Screaming along is fine — as long as nothing shatters or explodes. When it does, the carnage destroys our equilibrium and mayhem prevails. It is quite clear that we are not yet expert at recovering from disasters.

Two days ago, we were soaring: moving at 24.8 knots with our Code 7 spinnaker flying, cruising through the ice-cold sky and finally making good headway. We were pushing with the Code 7 for about six hours, and everyone was wearing ski goggles so she could see through the spray washing on deck. Then wind went forward and increased to 35 knots.

"We have to drop the chute," I told the crew, "quickly."

Everyone on deck has a job during a spinnaker takedown. One end of the sail has to be released, and the halyard that holds the sail up has to be eased down. The rest of the crew pulls in the yards and yards of spinnaker cloth that drop into a shapeless mass as soon as the wind spills out of the sail. Merritt knew we had to act fast, because the wind was getting stronger and changing direction. It was getting harder and harder to hold this sail, and the boat was protesting like a wild animal that does not want to be harnessed.

Merritt wears a harness like that of a rock climber when she is working on the bow, and she hooked a halyard onto her harness so she could go aloft in the rigging without falling into the water.

"Merritt, go when you're hooked in and ready," I called.

"Yeah, OK," she said, and as she answered, Merritt shinnied out along the twenty-seven-foot-long spinnaker pole that hung horizontally over the icy ocean to release one corner of the spinnaker for the takedown. She blew the end of the sail free. As the halyard was let down, the pressure on the sail was supposed to unload, allowing the crew to pull the miles of cloth into the boat. But just as Merritt spiked one end of the sail away, allowing it to fly free, the Code 7 blew up: like a piece of cloth with a built-in detonator.

As the wind snapped the sail to pieces I could think of only one thing: just a week out and already our best heavy-air spinnaker is toast. We have an entire wardrobe of spinnakers, each coded with a number. But each spinnaker is built to handle the strength of a certain wind range, and each one is cut to handle different wind angles best. The odd-numbered spinnakers are for reaching, when the wind is coming across the beam of the boat or over the aft quarter. The even-numbered spinnakers are for running, when the wind is blowing directly over the stern, the back of the boat. The low-numbered spinnakers are for light air; the high-numbered spinnakers are for heavy air. Without the right sails, we are crippled.

We salvaged what bits we could of the exploded sail: the rest was gone forever. We bid farewell to our heaviest reaching spinnaker: good-bye Code 7, you will be missed.

The down-to-the-bone Southern Ocean freeze is slowly descending upon us. November 21, our ninth day out, is our first ice-cold day, and I am now wearing five layers of clothes. We all sleep in our clothes and wear them for days. At the beginning of each leg, I will issue a list of what clothes the crew can bring onboard. We usually have enough underclothes to be able to change once a week. I might add, no one smells very good.

The cold makes me remember the days on *Maiden* in this region: the ice-cubes-in-your-face spray, the frozen hands, the frostbite on patches of exposed skin, the middle-of-the-night watches in snowstorms, the hold-on-and-hope-we-don't-die moments of speeding wildly on the edge of control, the times when you are soooooo frozen you feel you cannot carry on any longer.

On day nine, I noticed two chilblains on my face — patches of skin inflamed by exposure to cold. Snow showers have been falling through the fog, and on day nine we saw our first iceberg: a mountain of jagged ice that was beautiful — and very dangerous. Icebergs are floating rocks. They move and shift position and they have teeth. Our only defense is to find them before they find us by spotting them on the radar or with our own eyes.

The worst times in the ice regions are at night. Ask Renee about the midnight-to-0400-hours watch one morning. The sky was black velvet and a forty-knot squall moved through. The boat found her own groove in the waves, picked up her tail, and was launched. If we were on a fast collision course with the ice, we would never have known it.

Racing through the ice on a black night is never a comforting feeling. It is a ninety-miles-per-hour drag race down a dirt road. Without headlights.

With every watch and every incident out here, we gain more experience on this boat. But things are not yet right, and I question myself and my game plan of laissez-faire leadership. It was a decision made in a fit of hope, when optimism colored my logic more than anything else. The strategy depends on time: time for the past to unravel itself and time for us to reknit ourselves into a solid team. It is not happening fast enough. I fax Barry nearly every day and I write in my journal, always with some encouraging note to try to convince myself that we are progressing as a crew: *I think the crew is coming together now. . . . Things with the crew are slowly working themselves out. . . . I am feeling better about the crew situation and I think we have made progress.* Am I kidding myself? Can all of us, each with our own complicated past history with this campaign, our own fears about racing into the Southern Ocean, and our own gaps of missing experience on this kind of boat, come together in a short time like a TV movie with a two-hour timetable? I have an answer, but I am not willing to accept it.

People are getting hurt on deck. Renee was thrown across the cockpit by a wave the other day, and her stick-figure body crashed into a winch. The only major damage is a sore torso and a purple-black-and-blue tan. Still, we put her in her bunk, kept her below for two watches, and fed her painkillers. Other people have been surfing on deck: Merritt took a long ride down the leeward side of the boat when a wave crashed on deck and carried her away. Although we all wear a safety harness, a leash that you wear to attach yourself to the boat, it is no fun riding a powerful wave toward cold oblivion. Leah's hand was crushed by the spinnaker pole — the pole we use like a boom to hold out one side of the spinnaker. MC almost lost two fingers when a rope clutch, which holds a loaded line, slipped as she started to unwrap the line off a winch. The loads on the winch drums are amazing. A snapped halyard or sheet running off a winch could sever a limb. MC is an experienced sailor and she has seen the damage that a loaded line can do; the rope clutch should have held the pressure. But the lack of experience of some of the other crew is all too clear out here. This boat is a beast. If we do not handle her properly, she will turn around and snap our heads off without a second thought.

There are times when the crew forgets that, and we need to keep thinking ahead to new disasters. What would happen if that shackle blew up in my face? What if that halyard snapped? How would we react if the rig fell down? Who would go for the hacksaw, the halyard, the life raft? Who would grab the rations of food and water and the life jackets? This is the way I program my mind on every boat I sail on: a computer spreadsheet with a million scenarios of carnage.

If we had been thinking this way, we could have saved ourselves three days of drifting with too little sail up. Three whole days. It's a lot of time in a race like this.

It happened at the funeral for our Code 8 symmetrical chute, which is built for downwind sailing in "30 to 40 knots." That's the instruction-manual version. It was only blowing twenty-five to thirty knots, and Kaori was at the helm until we heard a snapping noise from aloft and our spinnaker suddenly turned into a loose, out-of-control, elephant-sized piece of cloth that was falling toward the water. The top of the sail attached to the halyard had blown out. The chute fell to the water, became buried by the weight of the sea, and acted as a huge sea anchor. It took most of us to pull it on deck, and in the process we wiped out part of our lifelines, which form a "fence" around the deck to keep things and people from falling overboard. While we wrestled with the wet elephant, MC grabbed the wheel from Kaori.

"MC, don't slow the boat down. Keep up some speed. . . . Keep up some speed!" I yelled several times, because these boats lose steerage when there is not enough forward momentum. But before she heard my instruction, it was too late. The boat slowed down and drifted into a dangerous angle, the wind caught the boom and sent it flying fast over the cockpit: a runaway tree trunk traveling at breakneck speed. Leah and Kaori became the victims of the mayhem, getting nailed with the mainsheet — the line attached to the boom that controls the trim of the main. Kaori may have a broken arm, and Leah has a bruised kidney. The mainsail tore in three places.

We pulled the torn mainsail off the boom and replaced the sail with a small trysail. It took six hours to get the trysail on, including time to file the cars on the trysail down because they would not fit into the mainsail track.

My hopes for a decent finishing time for this leg vanished when our mainsail crashed over and tore apart as easily as if it were a paper napkin. It would take days to hand-sew the mainsail back together. With that sail damage, we lost a big source of our power. Forget the race; it's just survival now.

Icebergs, snow squalls, and crash-and-burn scenes are becoming common occurrences onboard. We are all bruised and beaten. Sue broke her tibia when she was thrown by a wave into the metal-bar traveler that runs across the cockpit. She limped for four days before she told Lisa, our doctor, that her leg was sore. Lisa felt the bone, and, sure enough, it was broken. But Sue has taped up her leg, and she is trying to stand her watches. Beyond the normal wear and tear and frozen skin, my carpal tunnel syndrome is coming back after hours and hours of standing at the wheel and flicking it with a fast wrist motion to keep the boat moving in the waves. I still cannot keep much food down. We keep getting beaten up — in part because our sails are not holding up in this weather, and in part because we do not know this boat well enough to prevent disasters from happening.

After our mainsail shattered, my frustration and moments of depression transformed into full-blown anger. The torn-apart mainsail lay in the cockpit for three days. Anyone on watch who was not trimming sails or helming the boat was obligated to sit in the cockpit filled with snow and sew. I was so angry: the powerful sail that we desperately needed to keep our speed up lay in the cockpit — a dead mass of white.

"This didn't have to happen," I said, as Jeni and I sat one day on a freezing gray day, sewing together.

"I know, Dawn, you're right — but all we can do now is fix it," she said. Jeni is a stability factor on the boat: intelligent, competent, always willing to be part of a solution rather than causing a problem. "But God do my hands hurt."

The mainsail is made of bulletproof Kevlar, and pushing each stitch through this material was hard work. Plus, my hands were stiff from the cold, and we had to wear rubberized gloves — the kind they wear on oil rigs — to keep our hands from freezing in the cold spray. I kept stabbing the needle through my gloves and into my hand. By the end of a sewing session, I could turn my gloves upside down and water poured through the holes like a sprinkling can. So much for waterproof gloves.

Jeni and I kept sewing, uttering a chorus of obscenities when the puncture wounds really hurt. There was nothing else to say, sewing stitch after stitch and suffering through the self-inflicted stabs.

"Jeni, when we get to Australia, I'm off this boat," I said.

"Me too," Jeni answered quietly, as we continued to sew in the ice-cube-temperature air.

Maybe it is only a case of temporary sanity, but I want to get off this boat more than anything in the world. Unfortunately, it will not happen soon.

We are only one-third of the way to Australia. We have five thousand miles to go.

4

There is no word yet from *Brooksfield* after the maritime rescue center in Canberra picked up her distress signal this morning. The event has shocked us into taking it easy and working as a team. . . . We will make it to Australia safely.

— fax from Dawn Riley to
Barry McKay

December 3, 1993

On the morning of December 3, a shock wave ran through the fleet.

At 0718 hours, the Maritime Rescue Coordination Center in Canberra, Australia, picked up a distress signal from the Italian Whitbread 60 *Brooksfield.* There was one signal. Then, there was silence.

No one knows what happened. The single distress signal could be a mistake — but *Brooksfield* could also be in serious danger. *Brooksfield* did not respond to the 0755 fleet position poll, and the race committee has not been able to raise the vessel by radio or by satellite, leading us to conclude that their electronics are not operating.

I trust that Ian Bailey-Willmot, the race director, is in his office in England on a raw December day trying, and trying, and trying to raise the boat, fearing the worst has happened but hoping this is a mistake, wishing he could reach a large hand through the sky and pull the boat to safety. I think of the families of the crew, who have no way of knowing if their loved ones are safe, and of Jenny Fitzhardinge, the race's press officer, who is engaged to one of the crew onboard. Soon, the story will be in the press in Italy, New Zealand, England. There will be a small world of people looking for news from this boat — the needle-in-a-haystack speck lost somewhere on the ocean.

The rescue center in Canberra and race headquarters have only one clue to the puzzle: they can track the latitude/longitude position where *Brooksfield*'s EPIRB, the emergency position-indicating radio beacon, sounded the distress signal. When that waypoint is obtained, race organizers will at least know exactly where *Brooksfield* was when she signaled for help.

The race organizers send periodic updates when new information is found. They want to assure us all that everything possible is being done to find answers. They remind us that the sounding of *Brooksfield*'s EPIRB could be a mistake: in the last Whitbread, in 1989/90, there were seven similar occurrences of distress signals, and in every case, the boats and crews were safe. But, in my gut, I do not believe it is a mistake. I have my own theories.

If their electronics are out, it could mean they lost their entire mast and rigging and, therefore, all their antennas. If that were the case, it could be only a matter of a few hours before they jury-rig a new antenna and send a signal out to the world. They could also have lost their keel — the underwater appendage that keeps these boats upright. If that were the case, they could be dead: no one can last very long swimming in water the temperature of ice cubes.

Gloria, our engineer, is an ace mechanic. She performs miracles with the minimum tools and supplies we have onboard. But she does not have as much ocean-sailing experience as some of the other crew, and I know it is hard for her to make any kind of sense out of this morning's news.

"Dawn, what do you think has happened? . . . Could this happen to us?" she asks. I can only answer honestly. But despite my theories, I have a strong glimmer of hope that, whatever has happened, everyone onboard is going to be all right.

A search is organized. At 1036 hours, the race director asks the two boats closest to *Brooksfield*'s last-known position — the American Whitbread 60 *Winston* and the French Maxi boat *La Poste* — to turn back and conduct a search-and-rescue effort. They will head for the waypoint of 50°08' S, 81°03.1' E. From there, the nearest landfall is 427 miles away at the Kerguelen Islands, a dependency of France, where the French maintain a naval meteorological station. Australia is 2,000 miles to the northeast.

From what we know, *Brooksfield* was in an intense low-pressure system when the distress call sounded: on her last schedule, she posted a speed-made-good of 16.3 knots, one of the fastest in the fleet. To average that pace, she must have been flying. But we knew *Brooksfield* was pushing. A few days ago, the boat posted the longest run in a twenty-four-hour period, sailing 380.0 miles in a day. Was she pushing too hard?

December 3 is one of the most frigid days yet: a bleak dawn with icebox-temperature winds of twenty knots. It is snowing and sleeting and we are all wearing somewhat wet clothing. Goggles help us see through the spray on deck. We all take turns at the helm for thirty minutes at a stretch, then go below to make a hot drink. The teapot and the cocoa tin are the most sought-after pieces of gear onboard.

Later that day, I fax Barry many times. There are many things I need to tell him.

> We are sailing in 20 knots and the sun has finally come out and we are making 12.8 knots toward Freo; it is cold, but we are not in the same weather as *Brooksfield*.
>
> There is no word yet from *Brooksfield*.
>
> We are still waiting for news from *Winston* and *La Poste*.
>
> I pray I never put you through the worry that the families of the *Brooksfield* crew are going through, and that you never do the same to me.
>
> I love you.

Love letters. Assurances that we are still here and we are fine. Notes about a package I mailed or a new contact number for DG in Fremantle. Progress reports. Today the missives bounce like crazy off the satellites, all aimed home for Barry.

Winston and *La Poste* should be able to reach the area of the distress call around 2100 hours GMT, which will be the hour of first light locally. But I hope for news before then; I hope that it will only be a few more hours before *Brooksfield* can jury-rig a system to make a transmission. But for now, we can only wait for news and pray that everyone is safe.

During these long hours of waiting for news, our crew is silently grounded by one thought: something could be very wrong on *Brooksfield*. The incident is shock therapy for all of us, and it reminds me that we are responsible for one another's lives, more so here, in this race, than with any other class of boat.

How many times have crews and I made a decision to take a chance, put up the bigger sail, push the boat to its limit. In some races, five seconds means the difference between winning and losing, so you drive the boat harder, stress the rigging, test the sails to their maximum wind-range, sail too close to a rocky region trying to catch a favorable tide. Push, push, push. And for what? A piece of silver, a boat owner's ego, proof that you are the better sailor? Today, during the hours that we wait for news of *Brooksfield*, I know too well that — out here, in these conditions — sailboat racing is no longer just a game.

Hours have gone by, and still no word. We all have to put speculation about *Brooksfield* in the backs of our minds so we can focus on our boat: as of this afternoon's schedule, we still have 2,580 miles left to go — and we could soon be facing the same kind of weather *Brooksfield* found. We have been driving through the sleet with our largest, heaviest jib — our heavy Number 1 genoa. The wind shifts so we can put up our Code 5 reaching spinnaker to get more speed out of the boat. Everyone is cautious and methodical during the spinnaker set. No mistakes, no dramas, please.

Once the Code 5 is up and pulling, Merritt and Jeni wrestle the big Number 1 genoa down to the deck, fold it, and move it below deck. The sail is a huge, wet mass that adds even more moisture down below. The condensation below deck is a problem; clothes are damp, sleeping bags are soggy. When I crawl into my bunk after a watch — the bunk we all call the coffin, because there is so little room between it and the cabin ceiling — I take a chamois and wipe down the area above my sleeping quarters, which is dripping with condensation. I always collect a cup of water. The heater would help dry out the cabin, but Gloria has warned us that we have only one-quarter of our diesel supply left. We need to conserve the fuel — to run the generator and keep our power supply up to operate our electronics, communications gear, desalinator, lights, and other equipment — so we have to do without the luxury of a heater.

At 2300 hours, a fax comes over the SatCom C. It is not news of *Brooksfield*, but very, very welcome word from Barry: *It does not sound too good for* Brooksfield. *Let's hope they are alright. You be bloody careful out there, OK? . . . I really miss you.*

At 0032 hours GMT on Saturday, December 4, as dawn was breaking over the Southern Ocean, *Brooksfield* was found by *La Poste*. The boat was damaged, but the crew was safe. For now, that is all we know. For now, that is enough.

The Southern Ocean is teaching us its lessons: respect the sea, because I can snap you in half like a little twig if I want to; never think you are special or too important, because I can be arbitrary and unfair and I don't care who gets in my path of destruction.

I learned to respect the power of this place when I sailed the Southern Ocean for the first time, onboard *Maiden* in the 1989/90 Whitbread. This ocean — the water of the Southern Hemisphere that circles around Antarctica — has its moods. Some days the sun gleamed off the ice; the seals waved hello with their fins and the penguins swam by, and they welcomed us to a magical mystery tour of this place that is free from human beings, unbound by land, and endless. Some days, the Southern Ocean was a gray planet with no life at all: everything was still and frozen and desolate. Some days, the Southern Ocean came alive to inspire terror: every time the boat pounded off a wave, it seemed as if the hull would explode; every time a gust of wind hit, you waited for the sails or the rigging to blow up in your face. With every mood, the feeling of anticipation — of what the next day or the next nightfall would bring — was almost the worst part.

I sailed out of the Southern Ocean understanding how the astronauts must have felt when they landed on the moon and saw a place that was so strange and beautiful and alien to human eyes. On *Maiden,* we all paid a price to venture deep into untouched terrain; when the wind raged and the waves turned into mountains of water, and we were all fatigued from days of too little sleep and too much cold, I knew we had only ourselves to rely on if something went really wrong. Not even the shipping lanes come through this part of the ocean, so we needed self-reliance and a survival instinct. The Southern Ocean is temperamental — and help is very, very far away.

It was a challenge to make sense out of a place that was so big and powerful. It was easiest to think of this ocean as a force that could not be controlled or understood: like a supernatural spirit or a god. I could deal with that category — a class of being that does what it does with absolute power and no apologies. People died in the Southern Ocean. Maybe some deaths could not be avoided. But the misjudgments in seamanship and the failure of man-made equipment that resulted in death, those were the tragedies.

Today, we are miles from the patch of ocean where Tony Phillips received his burial at sea in the 1989/90 race; but the memory of what happened colors this place for me. It was November 12, 1989, when *Maiden* received a call from *Creightons Naturally,* the British Maxi boat. They were calling for Claire, our doctor. They had lost two men overboard during a crash jibe in a westerly gale; both men were in the water a long time before being brought back onboard. Claire coached them on resuscitating the victims over the radio; she stayed up all night to counsel them on complications that arose. By morning, Bart van den Dwey was stable. Tony Phillips never made it back to life. On November 14, at 1000 hours GMT, he was buried at sea. The fleet observed the tragedy with a moment of silence. I felt sorry, but — even more — I felt angry. Could his death have been avoided?

For me, the 1989 race already had a specter over it and had since our first stopover in Punta del Este. Punta held a lot of memories, both good and very bad. The first time I sailed there in the 1989/90 race, *Maiden* was on an upswing: we had had a good first leg from England; we were coming into a racing form as a crew; our confidence in the boat and in ourselves was growing. Punta was a new place, filled with beaches and bronzed Brazilians. The titles on the newsstand were all strange and foreign, the café menus were exotic to me. The place had its own kind of allure.

Punta was the first stopover for the entire fleet, and it was our crew's first chance to become better friends with our Whitbread colleagues. I was quickly nicknamed "Detroit" by some of the Kiwi crew members. I liked being named for my hometown. I was not from a blue-blood, blue-blazered yachting family, and Detroit fit: my all-American home-town, the land of hamburgers and Buicks. The crew on *Maiden* continued our friendship with some of the crew members of the USSR entry, *Fazisi*. Before the start in England, they had come over to our crew house for a party. They stayed to help clean up and fell in love with our vacuum cleaner and our dishwasher, modern contraptions that they had never used before. None of us could say their names right, so two crew members were granted with English-language animal titles: Crocodile and Elephant. For all our purposes, the nicknames worked just fine.

When our Whitbread crew was not working on *Maiden*, to ready her for the next leg of the race, we explored Uruguay. We went to cafés and pubs with Whitbread friends. We climbed to the highest point of land in Uruguay, which was only a one-hour climb up a hill piled with rocks. We ate at the base of the hill of rocks in a funny green restaurant, where the decorations were faded and old, where reruns of the *Beverly Hillbillies* were always playing in Spanish, where the clock was always a few hours off. The place was in a time zone all its own, but that suited us all fine; it was an escape from the pressures of the race.

One night, I went to the Café Fragata on the main boulevard for pasta and wine with Crocodile and Elephant. They were both preoccupied with worry about the coskipper of *Fazisi*. He had been missing for several days, and the crew knew the coskipper had been depressed. He resurfaced there, in the Café Fragata, on the television news one night. There, in full color, was Alexei Grischenko: he had hanged himself from a tree.

This race pushes people and boats to the edge — and the Southern Ocean was the most extreme example of that. In that part of the ocean, my mind was clear from pollution, and alcohol, and the pressure of land life. I had a vocabulary of emotions there that I did not have in everyday life: terror and exhilaration, an appreciation for the natural beauty of a place that was alien to humans, my coldest misery, and — ultimately — a strong feeling of confidence that we had survived.

It was then that I began to understand that this race — crazy as it may have seemed — made sense. I had always wanted to find the outer limits of my abilities on a boat. This was my chance.

Some sailors have a strange attraction for the Whitbread. They say it is a misery. And when they reach the finish line in England, they truly believe they will never do this race again. But a lot of us return.

Maybe all of us are just junkies for living in the extremes.

On December 4, we passed thirty miles south of the Kerguelen Islands. Renee — a woman who is not expert at waking up and who would benefit greatly (as would everyone else onboard) from an intravenous coffee line run directly to her bunk — has interrupted her precious four-hour, off-watch sleep to see the large, snow-covered mountain that rises out of the Southern Ocean. The sight of land is uncommon to us as we travel this long oasis of ocean; passing the Kerguelens is an event.

The islands are beautiful and unreal looking: a mirage of still, snow-capped peace pushing out of the ocean. Renee stayed awake long enough to know she was not having a wild sea dream. She was back down below to her bunk as soon as she was convinced the snow-mountain island was real.

"Daaaaahhhhmn," Gloria remarked in her Texas drawl. "Looks pretty cold over there in all that snow. And this is supposed to be their summertime? . . . Damn."

MC waved to her French countrymen, the fifty or so people who live on Kerguelen and maintain the meteorological station. There is no airstrip and a supply vessel comes out to the islands only twice a year. I hope they are all good friends, those fifty people of Kerguelen.

Huge mood swings swept over the boat before we reached the Kerguelens. On Thanksgiving Day we did not eat turkey, but we gave thanks for getting our mainsail stitched together. We finally hoisted it back up, and we began to fly again. Then the luff (the section of the sail that runs along the mast) ripped. We shortened the sail, by taking a fourth reef in the main, and started sewing again to repair the torn luff. The injury count was rising, and we added two wrenched shoulders and one stab wound (self-inflicted) to the list. Snow squalls and forty-six-knot winds moved through four days after Thanksgiving, and on November 29, at the pitch-black hour of one o'clock in the morning, local time, we rounded Prince Edward Island, which is a mark of the course. Fifteen minutes later, another breakdown occurred: our main halyard, which holds the mainsail up, broke. Adrienne did an emergency rope-to-wire splice in the cold and the dark. The next day, Merritt went up the rig to rerun a new main halyard, and she found all sorts of problems: a halyard shive about to fall out, a missing nut, compression cracks in our spinnaker pole, a broken car for our mainsail battens. The only positive side of our continual falling-apart was that the crew was becoming better at recovering from disasters. God knows we were getting practice.

On December 2, I hit a confrontation. Head-on.

Some of the original crew confronted me about my criticizing their ability in print. The only place I did that was in my private correspondence to Barry, and so at that moment, I knew: any shred of privacy I had was gone; all my innermost thoughts put into that computer were now public knowledge among some of the crew. By now, some of them knew my thoughts about the possibility of crew changes, and I could see, on their faces, what was going through their minds: *Am I going to go? Will I be put off the boat in Australia — just like that — after working so hard to get here?* I had my reasons for keeping my concerns secret.

Their reading my correspondence pushed me over the edge. Those were private letters between Barry and me — and no one else. I called a meeting. I told the crew that no one was to read anyone's faxes. I told them that I was concerned that if the team could not pull together, there might be crew changes. But we were not at that point. I explained that there was no use confiding this prospect to the entire crew: everyone would only worry about keeping her job. I apologized for being negative about them, but explained that I had had a life that was happy and relatively stable, and that all that had changed in twenty-four hours when I decided to take this job. I told them that our troubles were to be expected when we put a crew together at the last minute and headed into the Southern Ocean on a fast, high-performance boat that is difficult to sail. Then I opened the meeting up to discussion.

Some of the crew said they felt things were all right, under the circumstances. Some of the original crew dredged up more private thoughts from my faxes and challenged them.

I wanted to lead this crew gently, by example, until this group of twelve women — women from all over the world who hardly knew each other before heading into this treacherous ocean — could come together and become a team. After the meeting, I realized we don't have the luxury of waiting for this to happen.

Then, on December 3, *Brooksfield* vanished, falling out of the electronic tracking system with no explanation. Were they dead? Were they alive? Not knowing made us all stop and think: that could have been us. It shocked us into a new attitude: we have to work together if we want to make it in one piece to Australia. On December 4, the attitude onboard was 100 percent improved.

The meeting and the shock therapy of *Brooksfield* helped us in a backhanded way. Yes, the crew had read my faxes. Were they looking for a weapon to use against me? Or were they clawing for their own survival, to stay in this campaign? I wanted to believe the latter. We would have more struggles, and now I sensed that some of the original crew believed that they — and not I — should have been the natural heirs to this campaign when Nance Frank announced her withdrawal. I know better who I am dealing with, I told myself. But I am too pragmatic to dwell on past history. Move forward: the past is the past. I'll take the new crew attitude, however we got it, and just hope it is not a temporary reaction to what could have been *Brooksfield*'s tragedy.

On December 4, I started to look fast-forward with blinders on: twenty-four hundred miles to Fremantle. I began to plan for Australia. A sponsor would be coming onboard, if all went according to plan. There would be press announcements, a full refit for the boat, new sails, new shore-based staff — and realistic hopes for our program with a new-and-improved boat and budget. I asked the crew to begin writing their bios: each crew member would have her own media following in her homeland, and this information needed to be organized before we sailed into port.

Renee began with her rags-to-riches tale. "I was born a poor white child on Harsens Island, Michigan — a remote rock in the delta of the St. Clair River. My parents owned a small airport. My first taste of sailing was on the sixteen-foot

Snark we won in the local church raffle," Renee carried on. She went to Michigan State University with me, where we became friends sailing together on the sailing team. She moved on to run racing boats on the Great Lakes, and then worked in the East Coast race circuits running from Maine to Florida as captain and crew. She raced 50-Footers — a class of inshore racers that were shipped around the world to race in places such as Saint-Tropez, Tortola, Sardinia, Palma de Mallorca. She and her boyfriend Mike kept a home base in the United States, at Mike's house in Annapolis dubbed the Sparkin' Blue Vinyl (named for its in-bad-taste vinyl siding and its proximity to a power plant), which is a place a lot of yachties call temporary home — whether they are paying rent or not. But Renee is mostly on the road, sailing along the East Coast and across to Europe, to find work as a captain or paid crew for races, and for offshore deliveries from port to port. An entire moving community of sailors support themselves this way.

Gloria was born in a hotel in El Paso. At age nine, she moved to southern California to become a beach bum. It was there that she was introduced to sailing, but she also had a dangerous curiosity for learning how things worked. "One weekend, during the Super Bowl, I snuck outside and took my father's car apart. . . . After that, they kept the tool chest under lock and key." When she was eighteen, Gloria got interested in building race cars; while she studied electro-mechanical engineering in college, she worked in the NASCAR pits. Later, to earn money for more school, she managed a sailboat rental outfit on Grapevine Lake in Texas. Her first real job was with an engineering company, working on the applications of high-vacuum technologies, "which makes fixing the head [our marine toilet, which kept breaking] a walk in the park." Gloria escaped the "pencil-pocket-protector" world of an engineering company and moved onboard a 110-foot yacht called *Alpha Centauri,* based in Fort Lauderdale, to work as the boat's engineer. When *Alpha Centauri* cruised down to Key West, Gloria thought she had found paradise. She got off the boat to make a life in Key West, and there — in the funky island home of Jimmy Buffet — she met Nance Frank and joined the *U.S. Women's Challenge.* "And the rest," concludes Gloria, "is history."

It was hard to top Gloria's colorful life story — so the enthusiasm for bios began to wane.

To document the life and times of the *Women's Challenge,* the name we will sail under until a sponsor is onboard, Gloria and Renee created a new morning talk show with a minimum amount of on-air talent and our video camera. Gloria was the anchor; the video work was shaky, as we pitched and crashed in the waves. Our anchorwoman was not the picture of on-screen glamour, for the waves pummeled her in her brief on-deck monologue. Gloria and Renee gave up on the outdoor scenics when the waves washed Gloria away from the set one too many times. They went below to wake the off-watch crew. That is when the talk show turned to a horror show: none of us are pleasant when it's time to wake up to a cold, wet boat and do the thirty-minute dressing routine of putting layers and layers of clothing on while the boat pitches like an amusement park ride. Gloria and Renee, On Location in the Southern Ocean: the footage would not be snatched up by the networks. For us, it was entertainment enough.

Our cast of crew characters was building, but — unfortunately — the press releases would only use the facts and leave the near-cartoon versions that we spun during our on-watch hours out of the official version.

Planning for Australia lifted all our spirits. I could not wait to fly to England and spend Christmas with Barry, while he waited for the right weather conditions to begin his sail around the world on the fast *ENZA* catamaran. The plane reservations were a problem: not knowing exactly what day I would arrive, our travel agent had to be creative in switching dates at the last minute. The bottom line was that the ticket "would cost moonbeams," as Barry put it. But it was worth it. Everyone had her own plans. MC's Richard was coming out from England. Renee faxed Mike to see if he could do the same. Kaori was going home to Japan for the holiday. It was hard to keep our minds in the present tense. But we had to: we were still not free from the dangers of the Southern Ocean.

On the night of December 5 — when the sky was pitch-black and the phosphorescence in the water turned the wave crests to glow-in-the-dark whitecaps — we could have lost our entire mast. A thirty-eight-knot gust of wind accelerated us into a wave that threw us, like a skidding car, into a turn, backed our large mainsail, and nearly brought our mast down.

It happened at 2230 hours local time. I was down below at the nav station when I started to feel the hull spin. I ran on deck in my thermal underwear, grabbing someone's jacket on the way up. Renee was already on the preventer, a line controlling the boom, and easing the boom back to a safe place. We eased the sail slowly back and carefully tensioned the runner to control the rig.

We were floating in a helpless, sideways angle to the waves — the same situation as a turtle on its back. We would stay like that until we could get the sails sorted out and pulling again. Waves crashed into the side of the boat. One washed me down, but I managed to get up. Then another one came. It washed me off my feet, and took me away. All I can remember is that I did not have a safety harness on: I was free-flying into the ocean, and I kept thinking to myself, *There is no way in hell I'm going into the Southern Ocean.* The only obstacle between me and the ocean was a stanchion, a metal "fence post" that holds up our lifelines. I smacked my head hard on the metal post. Then I vomited and shook uncontrollably.

The crew forced me to go below and get out of my wet clothes. I managed to mouth a few numb words to make sure everyone understood how to get out of this situation: "Get a headsail up. Start moving forward." I went below, slowly got my wet clothes off. I was so mad at myself for having to go below. I tried to think of things I could do while banished to the cabin, but I soon realized it was futile. I was cold, tired, not thinking straight. I crawled into my bunk and slept for a full seven hours.

I would not recommend swimming in your underwear in the Southern Ocean. My head hurt for several days. It did not help that my hat was too tight on my head, which was newly enlarged after hitting the stanchion. But I could easily forgive the metal post in my way: it may have saved my life. On the positive side, our recovery time was improving. The mainsail was damaged again, but it only took us twenty-three hours to sew the sail back together and rehoist it.

Friends and family were getting faxes through via DG with news of Christmas festivities at home; we had Christmas trees decorated in our honor and holiday greetings were sent via the satellites. We had almost forgotten that the world was getting ready for Christmas.

As we neared Australia, we sailed in a generally northeast direction up into the Indian Ocean. Our latitude numbers slowly clicked down, the air temperature started to warm, and we sailed away — at last — from the ice. Some days were so calm and sunny that we could actually stay dry on deck; on the first dry day, I combed my hair out for the second time in a month.

The warmer weather was welcome respite from the long, cold watches of the ice region, and all of us took advantage of it by thawing out and having a sunbath — although the air still had a lot of winter in it. But the sun and lighter winds were also an omen of the Southern Indian Ocean High — a high-pressure region of light wind we would have to cross before reaching Fremantle.

After all this time, I did not want to get stuck floating in a no-air parking lot and lose the precious time we needed to log a halfway decent finishing time. Plus, we were nearly out of food and low on fuel — and thus limited in our ability to make fresh water.

The weather contrasts at the end of this leg could be stark: one night you could be surfing in snow squalls; a few nights later you could be wallowing with no wind, floating up and down on the sea in big ocean swells. I knew from firsthand experience; in the 1989/90 race, *Maiden* sat in this area for nearly twenty-four hours, waiting for the breeze while we watched the boats behind us creep up on our three-hundred-mile lead. Fortunately, the boats behind only caught up by fifty miles. It could have been worse.

We watched the weather maps carefully for the location of the high. We were in seventh place, with *Hetman Sahaidachny*'s ETA set several hours ahead of ours. There was still time to make up some ground.

On December 9, the first Whitbread 60 pulled into Fremantle. The British skipper Lawrie Smith led his crew on the European entry *Intrum Justitia* to a record time from Punta to Australia: 25 days, 14 hours, 39 minutes. In his Whitbread 60 — this new breed of modern ocean racer — he cut an amazing one-and-a-half days off the 1989/90 record set by race winner *Steinlager 2*. Smith also made a record 24-hour run for a monohulled boat of 425 miles. These boats were scary, but they could fly.

Five more boats rolled into Fremantle on December 9, and we followed the position reports with envy. By midnight, the crews on the Whitbread 60s *Intrum* (Europe), *Tokio* (New Zealand/Japan), *Yamaha* (New Zealand/Japan), and *Galicia 93 Pescanova* (Spain), and the Maxis *Merit Cup* (Switzerland) and *New Zealand Endeavour* (New Zealand) would be swapping war stories and getting showers of champagne for as long as they could last before dropping off into their first solid sleep since leaving Punta twenty-five days ago.

We were still sailing, still wearing soggy clothes, and our sewing brigade was active with tears still occurring in the mainsail. But we were managing to skirt the no-air, high-pressure parking lots to make up some time.

The morning of December 13 would be our last dawn at sea. The day grew into a picture-postcard scene on the ocean: the sky was blue, the clouds were white and puffy, and the wind was firm. We flew toward Freo, logging speeds of around twenty knots. The crew's spirits were soaring: we were close to completing the toughest leg of this race.

None of the off-watch crew could sleep; there was too much to do and too much excitement about the prospect of reaching Australia. Showers were the first order for those not on watch. It was still cold — the crew wardrobe was two pairs of thermal underwear, waterproof drysuits, and foul-weather gear; individual styles were revealed in the odd assortments we assembled for our head, foot, and hand gear. (Sue had already set a fashion trend: Ziploc bags on your feet go with anything.) Most showers were taken — much to the cook's chagrin — at the galley sink. Some hardy souls (including Lisa, our cook) stood outside on the aft deck for open-air, freshwater bucket showers. However you could get it, a shower felt luxurious after being wet and salty for a month.

Our ETA was sometime around midnight. Racing to catch the afternoon sea breeze, we hoisted our Code 5 reaching spinnaker to fly into the night. Darkness fell and a sky filled with stars settled in over our heads. The stars reminded me of our first night out, as we flew away from Uruguay. That South American nightsky was far away now; the heavens of Australia are even better — and chock-full of good luck. Renee counted twenty-two shooting stars: one for each of us to wish on, and a bunch to spare.

At twenty-nine minutes past midnight, we crossed the finish line off Fremantle to take seventh in the Whitbread 60 class and log a leg time of 30 days, 1 hour, 29 minutes. It was easy to forget the bad times now: at the end of the long Southern Ocean road, we were — after all — triumphant. Some of our competitors suffered debilitating damages: *Dolphin & Youth* had to make an unscheduled stop at the Kerguelens to repair their rudder. The Maxi *Endeavour* lost nearly one-half of her mizzenmast. *Brooksfield*'s damage was a delaminated area around the rudderpost, leaving a hole in the aft section of the hull that caused her to take on three tons of water.

I promised myself that I would quit this program many times over the past month, and — in the private thoughts I keep to myself — I still reserve that right. Sponsor promises have been made, but before we set sail again on this boat, I need to see proof of many improvements: better sails, a complete refit for the boat, time to train as a crew, a belief that this crew is committed to working as a team, and the funding necessary to be truly competitive. Without those essentials, there is no point in carrying on.

Yes, we made it across this ocean unscathed. But those shooting stars of good luck came out to meet us tonight for a reason. I believe they have been with us for many, many days — all the way across the vast Southern Ocean.

5

Taking over a rebellious crew is risky enough business at the best of times. Doing so a few days before putting to sea, to cross some of the most treacherous waters in the world, is almost an act of faith. . . . Dawn Riley was the woman who took that decision, but she had the background to make it.

— *The Independent*
(United Kingdom)

December 17, 1993

"Dawn, what's your contact number in England?" asked Howard Gibbons, our new shore manager, as I ran through the boatyard in Fremantle one last time before leaving for the airport.

"I'm staying at Marie-Claude's house in the Hamble. MC has the number," I answered, as I was clicking through a checklist of my own inside my head: money, airplane ticket, credit cards, passport . . .

"You're going to sponsor headquarters in Amsterdam next week, right?" asked Howard. "And we will set up some interviews with the British press while you are near London. . . . And we'll keep you posted on how the work with the boat is progressing. . . ."

Howard — who was brought onboard with our new sponsor — filled me in on all the necessary details before I flew away. I was only half listening. One, because I knew Howard well, and I knew he would handle all the details properly. He had been our shore manager on *Maiden;* he knew the race, he knew where to park containers in Punta, he knew where to find crew houses in Auckland, he knew where to stage sponsor parties in Fort Lauderdale — and he knew the nature of the Whitbread beast. Two, because I had one small yet very important detail on my mind.

I am supposed to be flying out of the country and my passport is missing. This is one plane I cannot miss: the flight to see Barry in England, the flight I have been looking forward to all the way across the Southern Ocean. Damn these details. They are not easy to keep straight when you are living on a boat, housing your belongings in a few duffel bags, and constantly on the move across oceans and past continents. I have also been working on the boat all morning, which is now hauled out of the water for a refit. I am wearing a Heineken-green one-piece bathing suit with our new sponsor logo emblazoned in white, and shorts. I am flying to England in the middle of December and I am dressed for the beach.

Details.

"Oh, and Dawn, Happy Christmas," Howard called as I raced off to find Adrienne.

Adrienne is Australian, she knows Fremantle, and she is a take-charge kind of person. She was also the last one at the chart table — the place in the nav station where all documents are kept onboard the boat — when we sailed into Australia and cleared through the customs entry procedures. If she did not know the whereabouts of the crew passports, she at least could be my guide on a wild-goose-chase ride through Fremantle to find them. It is ironic: we had transported ourselves between continents, across the rugged Southern Ocean, intact except for some minor injuries and some repairable damage to the boat. But when it came to globe-trotting the easy, everyday way by hopping on an airplane, things got screwed up.

The first place I looked for Adrienne was at our container. She wasn't there, but while I was there I rummaged through the boat gear inside: snatch blocks, lines, charts, pencils, spare halyards, cassette tapes, broken sunglasses, paperback novels, a few spare tea bags. No passport. I rushed down to the boat and popped my head down the aft hatch. The nav station was swimming in wires, tools, and navigation equipment. Adrienne was not there — so I looked in the chart table. It was nearly empty.

I finally found Adrienne at the *Yamaha* crew house. She was as clueless as I was about the whereabouts of the passports, but she said she would help me look, and we jumped into the crew car. I racked my brain about passports as Adrienne sped through the streets of Freo like a local: Where the hell could they be?

The car wasn't Formula One, but it still traveled fast, and, um, by the way, Adrienne, did we do that last turn on two wheels or four? We raced: fast turn left, left, right, left, park, fly out of the car — back to the boat, to check again and double-check. No passports. No sign at all. I kept thinking, thinking: what happened that night, the night we cleared customs in Freo, and then it hit me. "DG! Maybe he has them. Why didn't I think of him before? Adrienne, let's go. Let's go. We have to find DG." Quick dive back into the car. Race to find DG.

Sure enough, DG had found some of the passports in the galley after we cleared through customs on the night we sailed into Freo, and he had stuck them into his briefcase. For safekeeping. With my passport in hand, Adrienne and I sped to the airport.

"Will we make it? Will we get there?" I asked. Again, and again. I was dying of the heat. Soon, I could be someplace cold: quaint English country villages and Christmas snow. Well, maybe freezing rain. That's if I make it: if I don't miss this flight.

"How much farther? How much longer?" I bugged Adrienne, again.

"We're going to get you there. We have time," she assured me.

We drove fast into the airport. I was halfway out of the car before we stopped, and I yelled a thanks and a Merry Christmas back to Ad as I dove through the front door, duffel flying behind me — fortunately not on a collision course with the exiting travelers — to the ticket check-in.

"Hey, you are one of those Heineken girls. The lady sailors going around the world," said the ticket agent, as he methodically went through my paperwork. "I remember checking Dennis Conner through here in nineteen —"

"Yup, yes, that's me, yup, oh really, and thank you very much but I am in a bit of a rush . . ." It was nice to see that the general public in Freo follows sailing: that would never happen in the United States. But I was too rushed to stop and talk. I grabbed my ticket and ran and ran and, finally, reached the calm, cool flight attendant collecting boarding passes. She allowed me — looking more like a crazed refugee from the surf scene than a bona fide passenger — onto the plane bound for Singapore, then London. I fell into my seat. At long last, I could relax, be a passenger, have a rest — and Barry was only hours away.

The past few days had been exhausting — maybe more so than sailing across the Southern Ocean. On the boat, life is focused in one small place. The goals are clear, everyone has a set watch schedule, everyone has a purpose, and the idea is to keep the boat running like a machine. Once we reached Fremantle, schedules became the outline of what was supposed to happen, for land was filled with outside influences and demands on all our time that came from every direction. Sailing on the boat had the potential to work as perfectly as the rotation of the planets; when we hit land, someone revved up the spin cycle to create a universe in a washing machine that had the potential to spiral beyond our control.

We had landed in Fremantle in the early-morning hours of December 14. By nine o'clock that morning, press interviews were scheduled. Preparations for repairs to the boat and our sails had to start immediately. But the most welcome task was getting ready for a press conference scheduled for December 16.

The company Heineken had agreed to become the title sponsor of our campaign. They made their sponsorship announcement on the sixteenth and were very good at pampering our crew on the eve of the event. In between working on the boat and settling into our plush rooms at the Perth International Hotel, the crew had facials and massages and hair styling, meals of fresh fruits and salads that were a welcome change after dining offshore on freeze-dried cuisine, and a new wardrobe of crew gear emblazoned with Heineken logos. We were in the Land of Oz (a sailor's nickname for the faraway land of Australia) and — like Dorothy and the Tin Man and the Scarecrow and the Lion — we received makeovers and renewed hope for the future.

The sponsorship announcement had a few camp moments:

I wore a big, white shirt over my *Heineken* crew shirt. As the sponsor was being announced, I peeled my white shirt off to unveil my Heineken colors. I wondered if a man would be asked to do this. I believe the mastermind behind the act was DG and, maybe, Ben Pincus, the man from London who would assist in managing the sponsorship. Ben was slick; he spoke the language of Hollywood and Fleet Street, and still had some kind of rapport with us — the weather-beaten women sailors who lived an odd kind of adventuring life, so different from the London business-women Ben probably knew. Now, there was an entire family of shore support crew. Jan Beijerinck of Heineken would oversee all matters of sponsorship. Victoria Stacey would be our public relations person and all-around organizer, and she seemed pleasant — able to juggle five jobs at once, speak many languages, and still manage to smile. DG would still be our project manager on matters relating to the boat and sails. Howard Gibbons rounded out the core of shore crew, all of whom would be at every stopover from now on to organize us and our campaign.

We were finally getting the support to be a viable, competitive campaign. While I was in England, new sails would be cut and recut, the boat would begin a complete refit, the hull would get a new paint job in Heineken colors, and the crew would receive stipends, plush hotel accommodations, and a Christmas holiday.

I settled back into my upper-deck airplane seat, feeling very satisfied about the new potential for this Whitbread campaign.

Seat-belt lights flashed off, headphones were circulated, and the pilot's welcome sounded through the cabin. Australia fell away fast below our wings, and we soared into the time zones ahead — to England, to Barry, to the place where the Whitbread race begins and ends.

Going back to England brought back memories. The south coast of England is where my Whitbread adventures started in 1989, with the all-women *Maiden* campaign.

A friend had told me the *Maiden* syndicate was looking for qualified women sailors. I faxed my résumé over to England, and within hours plans were being made to fly me to London.

I didn't mind leaving the States. I was working in the waters of Florida and the Caribbean, and living in the Fort Lauderdale area in a variety of accommodations: on boats, sometimes in boat vans, and in an odd assortment of crew houses — some of which were plush, and some which were total dumps. I was finding work day by day, and — if I was lucky — month by month. I did everything from delivering race boats hundreds of miles away to the Caribbean for a series of races, acting as part of a racing crew trimming sails and grinding winches, prepping a boat and all its gear for a regatta, and — when all else failed — making sandwiches for racing boats and scuba diving before sunrise to scrub the bottoms of the racing boats clean. I wanted most of all to be racing. But as a woman, it was always a case of proving I was strong enough, a good enough sailor, and able to fit into the mostly male society onboard — whether it was as raunchy as a locker room or as polite as a tea party. It was always an uphill battle, but I was willing to put up a fight.

Cash flow was, at best, erratic. But, when times got hard, there was always a friend with a couch, an extra berth on a boat, a loan of ten bucks until next week. There was a small community of people who worked on race boats and an unwritten code that we would help one another. *Maiden* could be a boon: steady work for a year and a home — even though it would be moving around the world.

I arrived in the Hamble in early summer, five months before the start of the 1989/90 Whitbread, ready for adventure, with my prize possessions in tow: offshore sailing gear, my favorite T-shirts and shorts branded with the names of boats I had raced on, my stuffed gremlin Gizmo, miniskirts to wear to the bars at night, and three hundred British pounds sterling in my pocket — nearly every cent I had.

Soon, I was settled into the "Pink House." That was where the *Maiden* crew lived. A number of the Whitbread syndicates had set up camp in the Hamble, to prepare for the start of the race. The boys of the Whitbread crews were jealous of our campsite, but it was perfect for our crew: painted pink, nestled on the shores of the Hamble River, complete with six bedrooms and five bathrooms. It was luxury compared to some crew houses I had known. Plus, it was close to the King & Queen, the pub that became command central for Whitbread sailors. It was where we picked up gossip, picked up tales of the Southern Ocean and the doldrums, picked up news of what our competitors were doing, picked up boys.

The Pink House was a sailing sorority, of sorts — a culture I was not used to. Growing up sailing, I was often the only girl on the boat. There were other women involved with the racing campaigns — the boat owner's wife, the girlfriends of the crew. They seemed nice, but I never truly fit into their group. When it came to the crew onboard, I was also not — and never would be — one of the guys. I had no female-sailor-racer role model to follow, so I had to figure out my own way of survival — both on the boat and in the social aspects that surrounded the competition — to keep doing what I loved most: racing sailboats. The Pink House was a new world.

Mornings in the Pink House started at 6:30. A trainer from the local school worked with us weekday mornings on circuit training, aerobics, jumping rope, sprinting, sit-ups, push-ups. Many routines were a cycle of short bursts of energy followed by a brief rest — energy burst–rest–energy burst–rest–energy burst–rest. Some reps ran eight to ten times, and we recorded our heart rates each time. It was valuable training, since most work on a racing boat requires a burst of high energy followed by moderate exertion. Two days a week we invaded the public pool in Southampton for forty-five minutes of lap swimming. It became a passing contest: swim harder, swim faster, pass the girl in the next lane, win the imaginary prize. We were a team — but we were also very competitive.

After workouts, we went home to the Pink House for a breakfast of cereals, toast, cheeses, espresso. There, the mood regressed. Breakfast-table discussion was The Night Before: who met whom last night, who wished she had met whom last night, who wished she had not met whom last night, who acted civilized and went home early or read or took a long walk, who learned what about which campaign in our after-dark reconnaissance missions to the pub. The discussion mingled with our morning ritual of reading our horoscopes in the *Sun*. This was my initiation into the world of British tabloids, and, to me, the man-gives-birth-to-baby-alien and starlet-spied-with-married-millionaire headlines of American grocery-store newsstands paled in comparison.

"Gemini should not compromise her principles . . . Scorpio should expect unexpected news . . . Virgo needs self-discipline . . . Libra should exercise her imagination . . . Sagittarius may find romance today . . ." I cheated. I picked the bits from all the star signs that I liked and applied them to me: I always visualized positive things happening.

Breakfast-table gatherings also had a serious purpose: this was where we covered the business of the day. Each crew member had an area of responsibility — rigging, navigating, mechanical systems, sails. We reported in, scheduled the workday, masterminded comings and goings for a crew of twelve women who relied on one boat van and one boat car.

Every Whitbread crew lived like a tribe: ate together, slept under the same roof, exercised together, depended on one another. I still needed to create one route of independence — one escape hatch to the freedom to go my own way — and so I gave up car privileges and adopted the crew bicycle. It was a rattletrap vehicle, but the brakes still worked. Well, sometimes they worked; it was all in the technique. I learned that after I sped one too many times down the long hill through Hamble — past the old village from another century — into the modern world of the boatyard; the laboratory of fiberglass-foam-Kevlar-carbon-aluminum-titanium boats with psychedelic paint jobs. This was where we worked every day, preparing our boats to sail away in September.

I also found hideaways for solitude. One was an old, abandoned airfield; it was a good place for long walks. I started going to church early Sunday mornings. People who saw me walking home on Sundays in a skirt just assumed I was returning from a late night of partying or sleeping around. But I was used to rumors about myself. I often felt like an outsider and never fit the expectations of what a girl from Detroit should be. Other people seemed to mind more than I did. But in this case, I refused to defend my going to church on Sunday; it was private.

Life in the Pink House settled into a schedule. The days were spent on the boat and in the boatyard: wiring, compounding, welding, installing new deck gear, sanding, testing sails. Nights were spent at the King & Queen. We needed time to sail, and some of this was done far away from England, at regattas that were opportunities both for training and for more press exposure. Months before the start of the Whitbread, there were already TV crews from England, free-lance photographers from Paris and Milan, columnists from London. We were portrayed — both in print and in the rumor mill — as many things: the tough offshore hussies who should be locked away from the sons of England; the silly girls with no idea of what they are getting into; the crusading, courageous women sailors; the female answer to Peter Pan and the Lost Boys; the soon-to-be damsels in distress. No one knew quite what to make of us.

British-born Tracy Edwards was our fearless leader. Her initiation into the world of big sailing boats came when she worked on charter yachts that commuted from the Caribbean to the Mediterranean, on boats that made wintertime stops in Antigua, Tortola, and Grenada and moved across the ocean to summer in Sardinia, Saint Tropez, and Palma de Mallorca. The charter yachts doubled as floating luxury hotels, taking guests for a week of sailing, diving, port visiting, swimming, dining afloat. But Tracy got hooked when she started racing sailboats and using a boat to perform like a racehorse — instead of a pack mule. Tracy was not always the perfect picture of rational behavior, and she had a temper. But she had a passion for what she was trying to do. Leading a boatload of women into this race, Tracy faced rank after rank of skeptics who threw hurdles up at every turn; she needed to be passionate about her cause.

The *Maiden* crew went to Geneva to compete in a lake regatta. It was a crazy race, with seven hundred boats crossing the starting line at once, and we were the star attraction. We stayed with a friend of Michele Paret's, a French member of our *Maiden* crew, in a storybook house nestled in the foothills of the French Alps, with pastures out back for horses and cows, and rows of fruit trees. The summer Alpine mornings were beautiful. I jogged in the valley, through the shadows of the mountains, past long, green pastures. Then I came home to the house in the foothills with the heated swimming pool, and had fresh french bread and sweet butter for breakfast. I was a Julie Andrews character incarnate, about to burst into song from *The Sound of Music.* Life seemed pretty good.

In late June, our Whitbread crew sailed *Maiden* up to Ireland with some of the other Whitbread boats, to Cork, to participate in a Festival of Sail. It was a long trip up through light winds. A lot of the crew got seasick. I finished one book, read the engine and generator manuals from cover to cover, wrote postcards, and ate too much. It was a boring sail, but Cork made up for it: good racing and interesting nights in the pubs. I thought I had started a romance in Cork with one of our Whitbread competitors; but when we all returned to the Hamble, it was clear to me that I was a nice convenience. I was convinced, again, as I was with cyclic regularity, that all men were jerks.

On one day off, I stole up to London with two friends. One had forgotten his shoes on the dock in Hamble, so we all traveled barefoot in sympathy — to Big Ben, Houses of Parliament, along the Thames, Buckingham Palace.

The region of England surrounding the *Maiden* camp — the people, the cities, the villages and pubs — were all a strange new world. I would never have seen any of it had I not been there on *Maiden*. Sailboats were always my ticket to see the world.

The year my parents took me, my sister, and my brother out of school to go sailing, we left from the Great Lakes and headed toward the Hudson River, out into Long Island Sound, up to Maine — and then south: to the Bahamas, the Virgin Islands, and as far south as Grenada. We saw things we never would have seen had we stayed at home: endless horizons, dolphins who escorted us through the ocean, island waterfalls, coral reefs swarming with Technicolor fish, and people who did not live like the people at home in Detroit. When we returned to land a year later, life changed. We stayed in the Detroit area but moved to a new house on a canal off Lake Saint Clair, and I became even more involved with sailboats.

Sailing was always part of our life. Mom told me that she baptized me first, then took me sailing. My dad taught me to sail on the Great Lakes, and we took summer cruises up to Canada. I also sailed in a program called the Sea Explorers. It was like a yacht club for boys and girls from ages thirteen to eighteen, and I was the commodore. As soon as the snow thawed and the water got warm enough for sailing, I was rushing from school to go out on the boats.

After our family cruise, I was seriously hooked — not only on the kind of cruising our family had done, but on learning more about racing. We did not belong to a yacht club, but when I sailed at different clubs, I bugged all the boat owners I met, telling them I wanted to go racing with them. They would say, "OK little girl, someday. . . . Now run along," and they would wish me away with a smile and a pat-on-the-head look. I made a surprise rebuttal: "Fine. How about tomorrow? *I'm* free." I sailed with all the good sailors I could, so my teachers were many. Eventually, the boat owners started to ask me to come onboard for races.

Mom and Dad divorced in my senior year of high school. In the confusion, money for my college tuition was nonexistent. Living with my mom and my sister and brother in the house on the canal, I would never have gotten financial aid. I moved into a $200-a-month basement apartment in Grosse Pointe. I worked my way through community college with the hope that later I would qualify for financial aid after being self-supporting for two years.

I had a lot of jobs during the school year: I unloaded trucks, flipped hamburgers at fast-food restaurants, cleaned houses. I ran large racing boats during the summers on the Great Lakes, and I worked off-season in a sail loft building sails. After two years, I got my financial aid, even though, when the aid officers saw a white blond with a Grosse Pointe address apply for assistance, they always asked: "Is that apartment where you live your aunt's house? In a parent's friend's house?" I was accepted to Michigan State University. By that time, the dust had settled with the divorce, and Dad offered to help me out with tuition. "No thanks," I told him. I had worked too hard to get my independence, and I was not going to give it up.

I raced small, two-person dinghies at Michigan State as captain of the school's sailing team, and I finished my BA with hopes of heading to Madison Avenue to get a job in advertising. After graduation, a Great Lakes boat owner offered me $150 a week to take his forty-five-foot sailboat down to Florida for the winter and take care of it so he and his crew could fly down every few weeks and go racing. After sending a round of résumés to New York with no firm offer, I accepted.

The big event of the season was an international series of races called the Southern Ocean Racing Circuit (SORC). The top race boats came — the hot new designs, the big, grand Maxis. The race started on the west coast of Florida, then we raced over to Fort Lauderdale, and then out to the Bahamas. It was a new world, and there were a lot of sailors (almost all male) who supported themselves by running big racing boats. I had every intention of heading north to New York to become an advertising executive before I saw the SORC. But once I saw others making their livelihood from racing boats, I decided that I would do the same. For now. I did not have an apartment or a steady job, but I managed. One job led to the next, then to the next: a one-week job racing in Antigua, a three-week delivery to the Leeward Islands, an overhaul in a yard in Fort Lauderdale. The jobs usually came with a place to crash — a berth on a boat, a couch, a crew van. Eventually, I was earning what was to me a decent living doing what I loved, traveling along the East Coast and down to the Caribbean on racing boats.

Then *Maiden* came along. Getting a long-term job racing around the world was pure serendipity. But it would keep me on boats and carry me to a new part of the world, and so I packed my seabags without a second thought and flew to England.

Although *Maiden* was — in part — a dream come true, it was not all fun and games. Racing boats is hard work if you are really out there to win; it is pushing the boat to the edge, pushing yourself to your limit, walking around the minefield of egos in a crew. When it came to the condition of *Maiden*, I made a big decision: it was worth fighting the "this will have to be good enough" attitude. We were already collecting excuses for our all-woman team. We had to push beyond that to do everything we could to build a no-excuses campaign.

When the boat was hauled for the first time, I was appalled by the condition of the underside of the hull. The paint had orange-peel texture and some flaking. I had just come from Florida, where I worked on 50-Footers and One-Tonners. They are racing machines that we wet-sanded down to our last piece of 600-grit sandpaper and buffed until the hull's undersides shone like a mirror.

At first, I made myself less than popular by striving to push *Maiden* into true racing form. But that came with the territory: I wanted to win.

A few weeks before the September start of the race, Tracy sent me to Peterborough to visit the Perkins Diesel training facility. I was focused on absorbing as much information on our diesel as I could; when we were in midocean, it would not be a case of calling a repairman for help. I had to learn how to fix any problems that developed.

Tracy called during my crash course. Marie-Claude Kieffer, who had been on our crew as a watch captain, was off the crew. The start was three weeks away: would I take Marie-Claude's place?

I was glad I was away from the crew to consider the offer. Our camp was already divided. Yes, Marie-Claude had her faults — but she was a strong sailor, she lived with the crew in the Pink House, and she had her followers. Tracy had been living in her own house, apart from the crew, and sweating out the game of trying to convince sponsors and donors that a crew of women could compete in this race. Allegiances took their natural course.

I was just starting to find my place in the crew, and being put in Marie-Claude's shoes, as a bookend to Tracy's command, would not be easy. I could already feel the isolation that being a leader would bring.

The next day I left Peterborough to meet the crew for a photo shoot in London, at Picadilly Circus. I told Tracy that I would take the job.

Come September, we sailed away from England in the silver-gray-hulled *Maiden*. We were the first all-female crew ever to compete in the Whitbread. Tracy was the navigator, and I led one watch while French sailor Michele Paret led the other.

We never did return to the carefree days we had had in the Pink House. Once we sailed from England, we had a task to complete. It would take some nine months to finish the race.

When we did return to England, we returned triumphant, finishing second in our class. We proved a crew of women could compete in this grueling race. And I had one major race campaign under my belt, which I hoped would be my passkey to more campaigns at the grand prix level.

There were Christmas winds blowing outside Heathrow Airport when I arrived from Fremantle. At least I had found long trousers and a jacket to cover my surfer-girl attire. I could not find Barry in the airport or waiting curbside, but I knew there was a chance he could not come and collect me. I was supposed to meet the *ENZA* crew and help them sail the boat down the coast. That is, if everything was still on schedule with the boat.

I dialed the number I had for Peter Blake, the legendary sailor from New Zealand who was one of the skippers of the *ENZA* campaign.

"Hello, this is Dawn Riley. Would Barry McKay be there?" I said when a woman answered the phone.

"Hello, Dawn, it's Pippa Blake. You've missed them. They are already sailing the boat down to the south coast. So you are lucky, I guess — no escort to collect you, but you miss out on what is probably a freezing sail!" said Pippa, Peter's wife.

"Well, after crossing the Southern Ocean, I can't say I am disappointed," I said. Peter Blake had sailed five Whitbreads, and Pippa knew all about the Southern Ocean.

"Take the train down, and I'll collect you at the station. The boys should reach the dock sometime this morning," said Pippa.

I navigated myself to the wrong bus, then to the right one, and on to the train to the south coast. When Pippa arrived at the station, she told me that *ENZA* was just about to pull into the dock. I had not seen Barry since August, and I hoped to at least have a shower. But vanity would have to wait: I was too eager to see him.

He was still on *ENZA* when I arrived, coiling lines and folding sails and straightening up after the sail. He was salt-sprayed and tanned and windblown, and more handsome than the photos I carried of him across the Southern Ocean. It had been five months.

We said little. We walked down the dock, away from everyone around the boat, and just held each other. For a long time.

Breakfast was a Swedish smorgasbord at a friend's house in the village. Their little daughter was buzzing around with a contagious case of Santa-Claus-is-coming excitement. Their Christmas tree had pink-flamingo lights. Friends came over to Barry and me to say, Hi, Good to see you, Won't talk long, I'll leave you two lovebirds alone, Merry Christmas, Good sailing — all short greetings to leave space for Barry and me to try to make up for five months.

But that was hard to do. Our life together hit a mountain-sized speed bump when I got the call to fly to Uruguay. Taking the Whitbread job forced me to cancel my trip back to New Zealand. Presto chango: it would be a few more months before we would see each other again. Our faxes, via the satellites, to and from the Southern Ocean, became the one thing we had between us: they became everything — from love letters, to shoptalk, to proclamations of disgust.

> Dear Barry, I miss you. I still cry when I think of what I am giving up to do this race.

> Dear Barry, It is cold and wet, and we are doing 12.6 knots over the ground.

> Dear Barry, When it gets bad out here, it means so much to know that you are there for me.

> Dear Barry, I hate it here.

They were only cryptic words that we tried to build our relationship on. It didn't work, and when I landed in Australia, the one thing I felt I needed to do more than anything was to be with Barry.

In a few short days, I would fly back to Australia to keep sailing around the world. Barry and the crew of *ENZA* were waiting for the right weather systems to attempt a nonstop, global run for the Trophée Jules Verne. As soon as the right weather arrived, *ENZA* would sprint out of the English Channel on a mission to better the Around-the-World-in-

Eighty-Days record. We were going in two different directions, and every time you go to sea there is a percentage of a chance that you may never return. But we had Christmas together.

We settled into the house that Marie-Claude and Richard shared. Richard had gone to Australia to spend Christmas with MC, and they offered us their home. It was a beautiful, white farmhouse, complete with a huge fireplace.

Barry had some work to do on *ENZA* — small, final preparations and stowing provisions. Mostly, the crew was waiting for the right winter winds to take off on.

We had a civilized schedule of long sleeps, long dinners, long talks, long walks. Sailing was the furthest thing from our minds. As far as I was concerned, the Whitbread fleet could have been on a different planet, although I did get phone calls from Howard nearly every day with news, updates, instructions regarding appointments that I needed to keep.

It was Christmas Eve, and neither Barry nor I had started our Christmas shopping for each other. The solution was a trip to London, to Harrod's, the Knightsbridge emporium where anything and everything could be bought, for a price.

We boarded the train in Eastleigh and sped through the raw December weather to London. I liked watching the scenery go by: row houses, fields, cottages, and pastures. I was the fly on the wall watching what I imagined to be the picture-perfect lives of the people of England.

"Hey, Dawn, how long have we been going out?" Barry asked. He caught me a little off guard; I was somewhere else, imagining the lives going on inside the cottages covered with roses, with copper pots in the kitchen and a few kittens underfoot.

"What? Oh, well, what, about four-and-a-half years or so?" I answered. Barry and I had met during the last Whitbread, when he raced on the winning Maxi, *Steinlager*. And we both raced in the America's Cup. I for the Americans; Barry for the Kiwis. We would be together, and then our sailing careers would take us away to different parts of the world, and we would think that maybe this can't work. But we always came back for each other. "Barry, why do you ask?"

"Oh, no reason, really," he said.

Well, by now the imaginary lives in the rose-covered cottages were fading away. It started to rain.

"Well, Dawn . . . do you want to have children?" asked Barry after a stop at a country train station.

"Barry, we've talked about that before. Why do you ask?" I said.

"Oh, no reason, really," he said.

And so it went: a few questions, and then some quiet miles of train travel. They were all things we had talked around before. For some reason, Barry was asking for answers today, and I didn't know why.

When we arrived in London, the grand avenues were full of the excitement of Christmas. Taxicabs and cars and holiday-red double-decker buses carried people to shops and parties. Londoners dressed in elegant city-clothes whisked out of shops with their arms full of presents. We window-shopped, but we saved our purchases for Harrod's.

As soon as we walked through the door, Barry took my hand and led me over to the jewelry department.

"OK, Dawn, what do you want for Christmas?" he asked.

"Only you, sweetheart," I joked.

"Well, then pick one out," he said. I was not sure what he

meant, and I hoped with all my heart that he meant what I thought he meant. But I did not want to say — and then feel like a total idiot.

"What do you mean?" I asked, to be safe.

"Go ahead and pick one out," he said.

"Pick one out? Barry . . ."

"Well, I'm not going to ask you twice," said Barry.

"But Barry. You. Haven't. Asked. Yet." And Barry then did the formal thing, the pop-the-question.

"Will you marry me?"

I answered without hesitation. This was my secret Christmas wish, and I knew what the answer would be a long time ago.

"OK, follow me," I said, and I pulled him away from the counters to find the diamond rings: we were in the costume jewelry department.

The counter of diamonds was gleaming. I am not a diamonds kind of person — but I would be, just this once. I needed a ring that was somewhat flat: if it got caught on a line or wire on the boat, I could lose a finger.

Barry and I both agreed on one, and pointed. "We'd like to see that one, please," I said to the young saleslady, who wore an expression more regal than the Queen of England.

"These, hrrrrrrmmmph, are diamond engagement rings," she said, as she looked at both of us over the rim of her glasses.

"Yes. We know. Could we see that one, please?" We did look a little scruffy, wearing somewhat weather-worn clothes and both of us looking as if we lived outdoors, which — essentially — we did.

"Oh. Yes. Of course," said the young and snooty saleslady.

It fit. Perfectly. So we decided to buy it. "We'll take it. . . . Oh, by the way, how much does it cost?"

Our credibility shrank even further in the eyes of the saleslady. But it didn't matter. That's the one we wanted, so we would buy it.

"Well that *is* a fast decision," she said, and she was quick to reel off the price, thinking maybe she would scare us off.

We sat down and quickly made the necessary arrangements to pay for the ring. I am guessing, but we may have been the fastest decision makers in the engagement-ring department our saleslady had seen. Ever.

"And how long have you two been engaged?" she asked in her most fake-polite saleslady voice with her most fake-polite saleslady smile.

"Oh, well, about five minutes or so. Is that right, dear?" I said, turning to Barry, when what I really wanted to tell her was that we had just met, waiting to use the bathroom — ". . . *Isn't it romantic?*" But I thought I would spare her.

"Oh . . . How, um, nice," she said, as she walked away to check our credit. Barry and I just looked at each other and laughed.

When she returned, Barry slipped the ring on my finger, and we walked away satisifed customers.

"Good luck to both of you," was her parting shot.

My lack of domestic skills had caused a slight accident as we were rushing to catch the train from the coast that morning, so I wanted to remedy it with some presents for Barry. I had washed Barry's jeans, but they were not dry in time, so I threw them into the oven and wound the temperature dial way up. I baked them instead.

"See, Barry, they're only charred," I said when I took them out of the oven and brushed them off. "These black bits will come right off." I went to brush off the jeans — and they fell apart. So I bought Barry some new jeans, and a new woolen coat. I wanted to find an antique globe to commemorate his voyage on *ENZA*, but I did not see the right one as we roamed through the London backstreets.

At the end of the day, we hopped the train to the south coast, then went to the market to find a turkey for Christmas dinner on our way home from the train station. That night, we went to mass in the small village church that I had attended during my *Maiden* days. We kept our engagement a secret, just between the two of us, until Christmas Day.

On Christmas morning, we woke up to snow on the ground. It had fallen throughout the night before Christmas, wrapping the frozen winter gardens and the cottages of the Hamble in a veil of white. It was a storybook Christmas, in Marie-Claude and Richard's white house with the red door and the black shutters and the red-berry holly bushes.

Barry and I spent Christmas Day alone and took a trip out to Stonehenge. The long plain of monoliths was cold, stark, and mysterious — but everything I wanted was right there, as Barry and I walked together around the primeval circle of stone.

That night, when we got back to the farmhouse, we called our folks. Barry's parents live in New Zealand, in an area called the Bay of Islands. When we called, they were off cruising on a friend's sailboat for the holidays.

I called my mom back in Detroit. She was happy for us. "You've given me the best Christmas present you could ever give me," she said, through happy tears.

"Barry, you have to ask my dad for permission," I told him.

"Why? You never ask him for permission to do anything,"

he answered, with a big smile. "No, really, it's OK. You call him," he said.

I dialed Dad's number in San Francisco. After my parents' divorce, Mom stayed in the house on the canal in Detroit and Dad eventually moved to the West Coast.

"Hello, Dad, it's Dawn! Merry Christmas!"

"Dawn! Merry Christmas. Where are you?" he answered. "I'm in England. With Barry. And Barry has something to ask you . . . " I really wanted to watch Barry do the traditional thing. But Barry was conveniently not in the room. "Dad, we got engaged!" There was a silence at first.

"Engaged? . . . Far out!" was the reply of my father.

Far out? My fifty-something Dad thinks our engagement is far out. For that matter, why not groovy? Or cool? Dad, after all, had become Californian through and through. But both Mom and Dad seemed happy with our news, and I know they wished us the best and crossed their hearts and fingers for us. They know both Barry and I are free spirits drawn to the ocean — and that those kinds of people are somehow different, somehow a little wild, somehow hard to pin down in life.

Our round of family phone calling finished and holiday dinner eaten, the night sky settled over the Hamble as Barry and I sat by the fire in the white Christmas farmhouse. The moon had risen over the rooftops, and the stars were scattered on the horizon. The roar of the ocean was very far away from the peace of this hearth and home.

Christmas Day passed by too quickly. After midnight, the cottages around us turned out their Christmas lights and disappeared in the dark, one by one. We stayed awake. Our fire glowed on with the moon, and the village around us was silent under the snow.

6

If this boat has nine lives, our sponsor Heineken just gave us a second chance: a refit for the boat, proper funding, a chance for a new crew attitude.

I took the helm of this boat in Punta. But in my mind, the race starts here, in Australia.

— from the journal of
Dawn Riley

January 17, 1994

In the last thirty-six hours, I have had five hours of sleep. Most of them were in wet foul-weather gear sleeping on top of wet sails, because the waves are throwing me out of my bunk. I am a walking zombie. So is everyone else onboard.

The waves are big as we sail from Australia, past Tasmania, and on to New Zealand: as big as buildings of several stories. There goes a six-bedroom house in Grosse Pointe, a lakeside cottage. We're just about to ride an entire office building.

We are a cartoon: twelve women on a white-and-green boat riding up monster waves. Then we drop, sometimes two, three stories down, smash, into the rock bottom of the trough. Everything on the boat shakes and rattles. Pot lids escape from the galley and people fly. Some of us fall down; some of us only lurch a few feet forward on deck. It has been like this for days.

The fourteen-boat Whitbread fleet sailed away from Fremantle on January 9, and we have been at sea for nine days. We had light winds as we sailed past the south coast of Australia, but the wind has gotten stronger in the last forty-eight hours as we have headed into the Tasman Sea.

The fronts keep rolling through, bringing thirty, forty knots of breeze and monster seas. We have only been flying small jibs and a double-reefed mainsail — a reef being a "tuck" in the sail that reduces the sail area and, in turn, reduces the power. The boat cannot take much more horsepower aloft in these conditions.

Renee has become our cloud forecaster, predicting the weather from the look of the sky. She has given the clouds over the Tasman Sea a special name: the Highways of Destruction. A bank of big ones is approaching.

"We'd better take another reef and get the Number Three down," says Adrienne, as we round Tasmania and the wind builds to near-hurricane force.

I know we cannot afford to do any maneuvers, because the force of the wind will explode our sails if we let them flog. I figure — in a split-second decision — we need to keep the pressure on and hope that everything will withstand the force. I am not hasty with my decision: a split-second is all the time we have.

"Hang on," I tell the crew, and I do the very same. Although I have goggles on to see in the spray, I cannot see through the white water rushing on deck. My helming technique goes out the window. I am merely holding on for dear life and trying to keep this boat upright.

The wind flattens the sea. The pressure on everything onboard — sails, winches, blocks, the rig — loads up, tightens, stresses to what I think is beyond the maximum load.

Any second I expect an explosion: a detonated sail, a sonic crash of the rig. But we ride the fifty-eight-knot gust and fly, hitting a speed of twenty-five knots without breaking a thing. "Interesting sailing" is what I might report to the press. Scary as hell is the truth.

Maybe the Tasmanian devils are laughing at us as we fly fast past Tasmania — the boatload of cartoon women in the *Heineken* mean-green machine. But we are not laughing. I, for one, am glad to be in one piece.

Merritt, our rigger, has a newfound pride in our rig, the sturdy mast she has dubbed Harriet the Hardy. "Hey, Harriet, you did all right, eh?" Merritt says in her American-Australian lingo.

I have a newfound pride in all the crew. These conditions are difficult, and everyone is handling them fine. Had we had this breeze on the last leg, it would have detonated a sail and shattered our composure. But things are different now.

Australia was our turning point.

I had not expected it to be, for that would be too perfect: we sail through the Southern Ocean, our sponsor officially comes onboard, we become a real team and sail happily away.

Happily-ever-after tales belong to women who wear glass slippers. But in Fremantle, I began to believe we could turn our fate around.

I flew back from England just before the New Year. Dave Powys, a Whitbread veteran who sailed the 1989 race on the Maxi *Rothman's,* agreed to take over the boat's refit while I went to England for Christmas.

Our boat went into the boatyard in Australia looking like a red-dyed pistachio nut, and she emerged a porcelain-smooth white hull with green racing stripes. Our new name, *Heineken*, was branded over the stern. The systems were overhauled. The rig was checked and restepped. New sails were built. We now have the right inventory of running rigging: ten-, twelve-, fourteen-, and sixteen-millimeter sheets and lines, spare shackles, shock cord, new halyards.

We were lucky to have Dave Powys, and the work was on schedule when I returned — although I do believe Dave was pulling his hair out. Our sponsor needed to build a photo bank of the team, so our shore crew kept the team busy going to opal mines, taking trips to Rottnest Island, having holidays in the outback, being in parades. The go-carts were reported to be a highlight: Susie went the wrong way on the track, Renee was a speed freak and is considering a career change, Jeni was the pace car, and Gloria gave everyone the racing tips she learned during her days of working in the NASCAR pits. Everyone got a T-shirt: "I Survived Howard and Ben's Day Off." I trust it was fun. But not for Dave, who needed worker bees.

During our first leg together, sailing from Punta to Freo, we sent daily reports from the boat to two U.S. journalists. They put our reports on the "Sailing Forum" of the CompuServe computer information network. By the time we were in Freo, we learned that people were logging on to the network to follow our story. Checks started to come in: for $20, $25, $100, $250. They all had a common message: I wish it could be more; I hope this helps; I enjoy reading about the race.

We made contact with an educational program in Boston called Ocean Challenge. The organizers had created an innovative school curriculum using computers so the kids could follow the race and learn about geography, weather, oceanography, reaching goals, and other topics. In Freo, we received curious letters from the students: *Do you anchor at night? What do you eat? Is it hard to sleep at night? Do you have a dog on the boat? Do you have video games onboard? Do you see dolphins and whales? What do you do if it is someone's birthday on the boat? Do you ever get scared? . . . We hope you win. We like your boat the best. We can't wait til Fridays because that is the day we find out about the race. Your friend, Sinserly, Love, Love and Kisses . . . P.S. Please write back!*

The boats in the fleet corresponded with children around the world, and we also had the capability to exchange faxes with the kids while we were sailing. In Freo, we began to feel a groundswell of interest and support.

A metamorphosis of our boat and our crew slowly began to take hold, and the wave of desperation from our Southern Ocean leg subsided. The sudden personnel changes in Punta, coupled with the stress of sailing into the ice on a boat that was prepped for the conditions during a frantic, four-day fix-it session, created anxiety in all our minds. The crew had private questions that remained unanswered all the way to Freo: Will we make it to Australia in one piece? Will there be more crew changes once we reach Fremantle? Who are these new crew who have been put in charge of our boat?

I knew we would have our personality clashes, but I made it clear in Freo what I expected of the crew: "I expect total loyalty and respect for this boat, this crew, and this campaign. . . . This project began eight days before we left Punta and will end approximately one week after we finish in England. Then, this campaign will become part of your personal preparation for your career in sailing or your character or whatever it is you go on to do in life." Period.

My lay-the-law-down statement of what I expected of this crew, the growing support of the computer-network followers, the curiosity of the Ocean Challenge students all sparked a new beginning for our crew. But we had a lot more hard work to do before setting sail again. Leah is a former aerobics instructor, so we worked together on training schemes for the team.

When I finished the last Whitbread on *Maiden* and set my sights on the America's Cup, I had very little money and no means to join a gym to get myself into condition. So I created exercise routines around running, walking, and stairclimbing using chairs, picnic benches, and a minimum investment in weights. Crunches, flys, reverse flys, and curls could be done in a backyard, at the beach, in a basement. I used rocks and unopened tin cans for weights when I was away from home. Leah and I worked out a plan; everyone needed more upper-body strength and better aerobic conditioning for the short bursts of exertion on the boat.

The 0600 hours wake-up for workouts was not a pretty sight. Pumping coffee into their bodies was far more popular than pumping iron. But the crew fell into step and began showing better form on the weights, better syle on their reps.

What we needed most was time on the water practicing maneuvers: spinnaker hoists, spinnaker jibes and takedowns, tacks, sail changes. The sailing was a good photo opportunity for Heineken, so we managed several days on the water.

On the first day out, the boat was packed with the crew and boyfriends who came out to visit for Christmas, cameramen, photographers, press. We were tripping over one another. The boyfriends kept stepping in and hauling lines and giving instructions, even though I tried to get the point across: *Gee, thanks, guys, but you won't be here when we go back into the Southern Ocean.*

That night I talked to Howard. "Tomorrow, everyone is off: the cameras, the TV, the press, the boyfriends. They can ride in a chase boat and watch. But tomorrow, the crew needs time alone." Howard understood.

The next day, we focused on spinnaker work. It was not perfect, but we worked it like a drill. "OK, Leah, good job in the pit. Try two wraps on that winch. Mark the topping lift with a marker so you know how far to ease it in the jibe. . . . Marleen, coordinate more with Adrienne on the runners in the jibe; you have to time yourselves. . . . OK, Merritt, make me feel better and don't stand in that deadly area between the spinnaker pole and the headstay. . . . Renee, switch places with Kaori. You do the cleanup on deck after the spinnaker takedown. . . . Gloria, why do you keep falling down?" We did spinnaker hoists, jibes, spinnaker peels, take-downs, headsail changes, tacks, jibe sets. After our final day of drills in Freo, I saw a glimmer of what our crew could be. We executed maneuvers with finesse, and we were ready to set sail from Australia on January 9 and race the next leg to New Zealand.

Rather, we thought we were ready to sail for New Zealand. At the restart on the ninth, we did not go for just one mistake in our spinnaker work; we went for the snow-ball effect. Our spinnaker trimmers tripped up on their timing in the jibe and our new, green spinnaker wrapped around our headfoil. Wrapping a spinnaker around a head-foil is like those Chinese finger-handcuffs: the more you pull, the tighter it gets. We got the green chute unwrapped, ripping it in the process. We put up our Code 6 chute; the spinnaker pole tripped itself loose and one of our sheets got caught under the boat. Our earlier practice sessions turned into a slapstick comedy of errors at the start, but the worst fallout was only embarrassment.

We cleaned up the mass of lines and sails that lay on deck after our avalanche of errors at the start, and we rode the sea breeze to Cape Naturaliste. By nightfall, we had twenty-five-knot headwinds and pounding seas. Anything not nailed down (including the crew) was prone to levitate. Our SatCom A dome — the dinosaur-sized egg we carry in the bow so we can make voice and video-footage transmissions — nearly rocked off its perch; after that pounding, we could not get a signal out on the SatCom A. This was not good for Heineken, who needed us to make regular calls and video feeds to fuel our story on land. Until Jeni could diagnose the problem, the reports would have to go out as postcards faxed from the sea: *Sailing is beautiful. Wish you were here.*

By first light of the next day, we were tacking along the south coast of Australia in light winds. We had five boats in sight: three Maxis, and *Brooksfield* and *Dolphin & Youth* — the two Whitbread 60s we had the best chance of wrestling with for a midfleet finish.

The wind was fluky, unpredictable, patchy. All the competitors were gambling with their tactics. We could head offshore and hope to find a breeze that no one else was finding. Instead, we opted for the inshore route and sailed closer to land than the rest of the fleet. Everyone on the boat had to tread quietly and with a light foot: sharp, heavy movements of the crew would create an adverse force to the hull as we ghosted quietly along the coast.

We exchanged blows with *Dolphin* and *Brooksfield,* always watching them from the corners of our eyes. We monitored everything they did; they did the same to us. By the

January 11 position report, *Dolphin, Brooksfield,* and we were only three miles apart. I was not able to sleep during those first days out from Australia; the sailing was too close. Then, to add to the tension, the wind melted away to nearly nothing and Australia began to disappear in the haze: Fremantle, Perth, Cape Naturaliste, Cape Leeuwin. One by one these places vanished away.

At only 3,272 miles, the leg from Fremantle to Auckland is the shortest leg in the race. But it has the potential to be the trickiest. There is a high-pressure ridge — a moving minefield of light air. And then there is the Tasman Sea, which could deliver any kind of condition. We were warned by the weather experts, who gave us little data to go on except to expect the unexpected of this unpredictable, spooky sea that flows around Tasmania.

The rest of the fleet is in a close battle. As of the January 11 position report, New Zealand America's Cup skipper Chris Dickson was helming *Tokio* within only five miles of *Intrum Justitia* and *Yamaha.* One British journalist described Dickson perfectly: "boundless talent and . . . demonic intensity." No doubt, the mood on *Tokio* was tense, you-can't-hear-a-pindrop quiet: no bad tacks, no bad sail changes, no mistakes allowed. The mood onboard *Winston* must have been very different, for *Winston* knew something that none of us knew.

After leaving Freo, most of the fleet rounded Australia's Cape Naturaliste, then headed for Cape Leeuwin to wrap around the south coast of Australia and on to the southern tip of Tasmania. Most of the fleet, that is, except *Winston.*

With America's Cup sailor Dennis Conner onboard, *Winston* did not follow the bend of Australia's south coast. Conner and his crew took a deep dive to the south. And no one else followed. Less than two days out, and *Winston* already had a thirty-four-mile lead in the Whitbread 60 class. Her average speed was double what we were all logging. Plus, she was outrunning the high-pressure, no-wind zone that was sitting right down on top of the rest of the fleet. *Winston* was flying away like a bird on an airstream; the rest of us were caged in high-pressure weather.

Winston is out to prove herself. The current standings in the Whitbread 60 class are based on what some feel to be an overly generous time allowance given to *Winston* for being part of the *Brooksfield* search-and-rescue effort. Yacht racing has a legal code just as land-based society at large has the law. In a hearing not unlike that in a civil court, the International Jury of this race awarded *Winston* 21 hours, 28 minutes, 30 seconds for turning back and sacrificing her standing in the race to search for *Brooksfield.* That block of time rocketed *Winston* into second place on that leg, approximately one minute behind leg winner *Intrum Justitia.* The leading Whitbread 60s are in a rage, and they will lobby for the hearings to be reopened in Auckland.

The outcome of the *Winston* hearing would not affect our position on the Southern Ocean leg, but I was haunted by what was developing on this leg. If I could sleep well, I would be having nightmares about not listening to what the old man had told me.

Two days before the start, the man had been hanging around our container. We were busy dragging sails down to the boat, packing up spare running rigging, going over checklists of supplies to be stowed onboard.

"Hello. Good morning, ladies. You getting ready to sail on Sunday?" he asked. A lot of people always wanted to stop and make small talk, ask for a T-shirt or a sticker. We just didn't have time to chat with everyone who passed by.

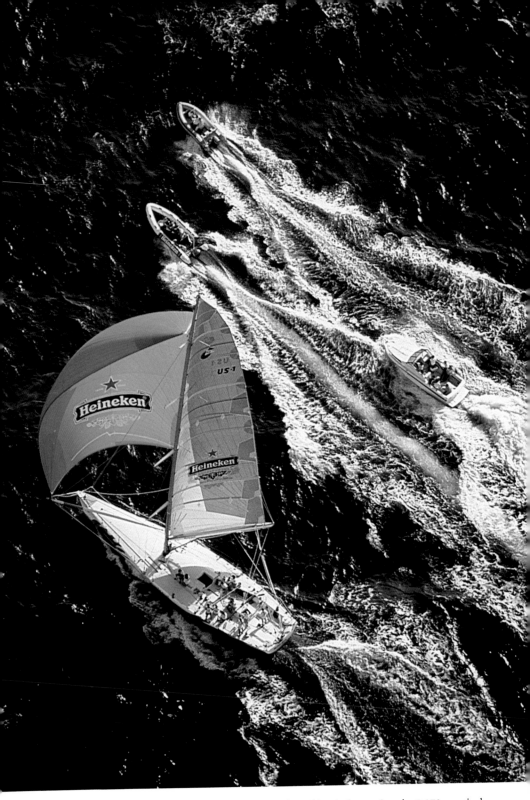

Heineken sails under spinnaker toward the port of Auckland after racing the 3,272-nautical-mile Leg 3 from Fremantle, Australia (*David Branigan/ALLSPORT*).

The *Heineken* crew in Southern Ocean attire, complete with goggles to aid visibility in the constant spray of seawater coming over the deck (*ALLSPORT*).

Mikaela von Koskull at the helm of *Heineken* while the on-watch crew sits on the windward rail to balance the heel of the boat. In addition to crew weight, the water ballast system was also used to balance the heel of the boat (*KOS/KOS Picture Source*).

Navigator Adrienne Cahalan studies weather patterns in the navigation station of *Heineken*. On some legs, Cahalan slept in the "nav station" to be ready at all times to study new weather information as it came in via fax (*David Branigan/ALLSPORT*).

The crew on the bow of their Whitbread 60. Front row, left to right: Leah Newbold, Kaori Matsunaga, Gloria Borrego, Adrienne Cahalan, Merritt Carey, Dawn Riley. Back row, left to right: Marleen Cleyndert, Jeni Mundy, Renee Mehl, Lisa Beecham, Marie-Claude Kieffer, Susan Crafer. Missing crew from photo: Mikaela von Koskull (*David Branigan/ALLSPORT*).

Heineken receives a warm welcome in the Fort Lauderdale heat. Pictured, from left to right, are crewmembers Mikaela von Koskull, Jeni Mundy, Marie-Claude Kieffer, Dawn Riley, Kaori Matsunaga, and Gloria Borrego (*KOS/KOS Picture Source*).

Heineken pulls into Fort Lauderdale—low on food, diesel fuel, and other essential provisions—after a rough 5,475-nautical-mile leg from Uruguay (*KOS/KOS Picture Source*).

Heineken arrives triumphant in Auckland after a strong finish in the Australia-to-New Zealand leg while a sea of cheering crowds awaits their arrival on the shores of Auckland (*David Branigan/KOS Picture Source*).

Heineken finally sights land at the end of an arduous transatlantic leg from Florida to the finish of the race in Southampton, England. The crew suffered the loss of their rudder on this final leg of the race. *Heineken* is racing here with a jury-rigged rudder system fitted to the stern of the boat (*Stephen Munday/ALLSPORT*).

"Yeah, yeah. We're busy getting all our supplies ready," I said, bent over a pile of spare line, barely looking up at him.

"Any of you girls from around these waters?" he asked.

"Well, Adrienne is Australian. From Sydney," I answered, my head still in a pile of line.

"Well then, I'll give you some advice about Sunday. You see, you'll start, you'll head to Cape Naturaliste. You'll want to hug the shore, stick to the south coast and sail along the beach. But I tell you, don't. Get offshore. Fast. Just keep going offshore," he said.

"Well, ummm, thanks. Thanks for the advice," I said as I picked up my lines and carted them down to the boat.

I remember thinking, thanks, whoever you are. Everyone always has an opinion about how to sail this race.

Now, I am kicking myself. Why didn't I at least think about what he said? *Winston* had — whether they talked to the same local-knowledge informant in the container park or had their own sources. We could have been out there with *Winston*, flying on that airstream.

I had to control my "if only" thinking. We were on a different route now, sailing on in light air and making only single-digit speeds.

Before we left Freo, I changed the watch system by appointing Jeni as a watch captain. This way, I would be free to float and to be on deck when I felt I most needed to. In the first part of this leg, that was most of the time. I was helming a lot, thinking about our next move, the next tack, watching the positions of *Dolphin* and *Brooksfield*.

Everyone was watchdogging her own area of the boat. Adrienne never left the navigation station; she stayed glued to the information coming in, not leaving even to sleep, catching catnaps at the chart table. MC kept her eyes on the sails — their trim, their shape. Between watches, Jeni was trying to diagnose the problem with the SatCom A, running through manuals and miles of wiring. Merritt may have been our resident Pig Pen in the boat's living area, but she was neat and tidy on duty, careful to have all the lines in the bow section in perfect order in case we had to change sails quickly. Leah had her lines in the pit coiled, and she was ready to handle the halyards, if we needed to make a sail change.

Heineken became a twenty-four-hour laboratory. We were the team of scientists wrestling around the clock with one problem: How do we improve our position in this fleet? With the light, fluky weather, the pressure showed no sign of letting up.

These first days out were exhausting, nonstop, intense. They reminded me how much I love racing sailboats.

Aotearoa, the Land of the Long, White Cloud. It crept onto our horizon today. We cannot see land, not yet. But the skinny finger of cloud that hovers over New Zealand marks the islands like a neon sign: the land of long, green pastures and silver seas is near.

The sun is getting ready to set as we sail upwind in light northwesterly breezes with only a few hours to go until we reach Cape Reinga at the north tip of New Zealand. The wind keeps clocking, forcing us away from the course we need to sail to reach the cape. If the breeze shifts any further, we are screwed. We will have to tack to reach the cape, and if we do, we will lose *Brooksfield* for sure. We both should round the tip of New Zealand tonight, when the cape is awash in starlight. Until then, we can only sail as fast as we can.

From the cape, we will slide down the coast of New Zealand, into the Hauraki Gulf, and toward the sea of spectators waiting on the Auckland waterfront. By sunrise, we should see New Zealand's Pacific coastline — Tutukaka, Takapuna, Whangarei. We hope to finish in approximately twenty-four hours' time.

Brooksfield is our nemesis now. We traded leads with the Italians several times as we crossed the Tasman Sea. The January 19 position reports logged *Brooksfield* twenty-one miles behind us. The Italian crew then took a hitch to the north, and *Brooksfield*'s pace wound down to the slowest speed in the fleet. But I could not help thinking that maybe her crew knew of a cold front moving in from Australia and bringing a fresh breeze. I wondered when I plotted *Brooksfield*'s position: latitude 38°45.99' S. Why is she up there? What does she see in the weather ahead?

By January 21 our positions had closed up again. Our prediction — based on our current speed and relative positions — had us into Auckland ahead of *Brooksfield*. But just barely. If the wind shifts, *Brooksfield* will have a better angle coming into the cape. As we approach Cape Reinga on January 22, I refuse to let up: grind *Brooksfield* down, keep pushing; the race is not over until we cross the finish line.

I am not so sure I want this leg to end. This has been our best passage so far, and the crew has come together. It showed in our performance, especially on January 18, when we logged the fastest day in the fleet.

We did 350 miles in twenty-four hours, and we worked for it: eight sail changes in the four-and-a-half hours before breakfast. Chute up, jib down, Code 5 up, peel to Code 6, change to jib top, chute down, Number 3 up, chute down: hauling sails in, hoisting halyards, packing and repacking gymnasium-sized pieces of sailcloth, dragging sails below deck, dragging new sails on deck. Our pumping-iron practice in Freo paid off. Only certain crew members regularly helm the boat, but on January 18 I made sure everyone took a turn at helming *Heineken:* I had a good feeling about our speed before the day was out and I wanted everyone to feel a part of our fastest day at sea.

Days after our record run, we had visitors: a pod of sperm whales charging in our direction. They were moving at about ten knots — their shiny muscular hides powering through the water. Flesh-and-blood torpedoes whose path was unknown to us. Were they playing, out for a walk, on a warpath? I didn't know. But at the last minute, the one closest to us — about fifty feet away — turned suddenly, then dove. Thank God. Collisions with whales have put holes in boats. But this time, the whale sensed us in time and turned on a dime. I have never seen a whale turn that fast; but, thank you, he-whale or she-whale, whichever you are; I am glad you have good brakes.

Barry and his *ENZA* crewmates, led by Peter Blake and Robin Knox-Johnston, had started their round-the-world time trial. We finally got our satellite-communications gear talking to each other, so I faxed Barry about the whales.

We had an active correspondence going by now — a romance via the satellites. On *ENZA,* with the crew squeezed into the small spaces onboard, it was not a totally private affair. Still, I faxed Barry personal notes and news — even if his crewmates did give him a hard time about the love letters beamed in from the Tasman Sea.

After Christmas, Barry and the *ENZA* crew sat through raw English-winter days, waiting for the right weather to move in. (*Dear Dawn, . . . It wouldn't surprise me if we are still bloody sitting here when you finish this leg: the weather here is crap. . . . Love, Barry.*)

By January 16 the right weather arrived, and the *ENZA* crew sailed away from the United Kingdom — passing the official start line between Ushant Light and the Lizard in a breeze of thirty-five knots. They flew from there. Barry kept me posted, telling me of 450-mile days, 508-mile days. *ENZA* is a catamaran, and on certain points of sail, the boat is expected to fly past monohulls like the Whitbread 60s. But they were logging amazing speeds to cover five hundred miles in a day! It was supersonic yachting, and I reported the highlights of the Kiwi boys on *ENZA* to Kerikeri Radio whenever I could.

Everyone's purpose in the crew has become better defined on this leg. Gloria is our in-house super-mechanic, fabricating generator belts out of the radar reflector and finding a loose wire connection in the desalinator just as we were beginning to brainstorm about ways to catch rainwater and boil it, already dreading pasty, freeze-dried chicken supreme made with two teaspoons of water. Jeni's nemesis continues to be our dinosaur-egg SatCom A, which she lovingly calls "the Beast." She now has an intimate knowledge of its miles of color-coded wiring, and she has wrestled with the Beast again and again, to get our pitching boat to lock on to the satellite long enough to get our transmissions out.

Kaori's helming is getting better and better; she steers to a compass number better than anyone. But, I am learning, that is the way Kaori works. If you ask her to helm for one hour at 089 degrees, she will do just that. Kaori's favorite English expression is, "It's OK." If we are driving through monster seas and pouring rain and she is on an hour-long stint on the wheel, and you ask her if she is tired at fifty-eight minutes: "No. It's OK." But at sixty minutes: "Kaori, do you want a break?" A big smile and a long "Yeeeeeeees" will emerge from her.

Kaori is a crusader. No Japanese woman has done what she has, venturing off to do this race. I do not think Kaori knows yet how unique she is in her country; her life will change forever when she goes home.

We have a new crew member: Marleen Cleyndert from Holland. Heineken stipulated that we add one Dutch woman to the crew with the sponsorship. I had met Marleen at a women's match-racing event in Portofino, Italy, and Howard and DG tracked her down through the yacht-racing authorities in the Netherlands. During my Christmas holiday I went up to the Heineken office in Amsterdam to interview the candidates for the Dutch crew position. I believed Marleen would be an asset to the boat. She is a nurse, a sailor without an enormous amount of offshore racing experience but an eagerness to learn, and a personality that I believed would fit in fine.

When I hired Marleen she had about twenty-four hours to pack up her life and join us. I already knew she was committed.

Sue Crafer, with a broken bone on the mend after fracturing her tibia in the Southern Ocean, sat this leg out. From here on, we would have to rotate one crew member off the boat for each leg to keep to a crew of twelve women.

We had one more new crewmate, a token male — a Ken doll we renamed HeineKen. Despite his too-good-to-be-true plastic perfection, he too is doing fine, hanging on in his perch in the galley.

At midnight, we round Cape Reinga in light winds. *Brooksfield* came in from the north, rounding ahead of us.

Now we are on a drag race to Auckland, jib-reaching in a breeze that I pray fills in from behind to push us closer to *Brooksfield*.

I go below to tune in to Kerikeri Radio on the VHF. The operator reads the weather report. Then she promises the Whitbread report. "But first, the Lotto . . . " First things first, I guess.

I switch off the radio and go on deck to find Gloria plugged blissfully into her Walkman in the cockpit. Either she has a very strange music-listening style, or she is not listening to funk, rock, or pop at all: her head motions and hand motions are too irregular. It looks like commentary, to a game of some sort. Just as I start to figure it out —

"Hey, Jeni, come listen to this! *Endeavour*'s coming into the finish," said Gloria. Jeni's boyfriend Spike is racing on the Maxi *New Zealand Endeavour*, and *Endeavour* and *Tokio* are the first boats approaching the finish line.

The *Endeavour* crew is all–New Zealand. They did promotional tours around the country months before the start of the Whitbread. They trained at home and built a replica *Endeavour* that was trucked from coast to coast for all to see. During the legs, their story is covered daily on New Zealand television, at the evening-news hour; by now, the *Endeavour* boys are local heroes. Chris Dickson, at the wheel of *Tokio*, is also a Kiwi; but many consider him more of a mercenary — extremely talented, a proved winner, but not the one who warms the hearts of the nation.

Jeni moved in quickly to share the Walkman with Gloria; now they both are tuned into the same pair of headphones, making synchronized reactions to what sounded to be a very close fight to the finish narrated by New Zealand sports announcer Peter Montgomery. Watching a sailboat race has

the reputation of being as exciting as watching grass grow —
but not when Peter Montgomery is calling the play-by-play
action. His voice speaks exclamation marks, and sailing turns
into a sport with edge-of-your-seat excitement.

I was at the wheel, but motioning with my hands, with
my feet: "Hey, guys, over here. Guys, over here. Over here."
I stamped my foot and barked: *"Over here!!!"* I got their
attention. "Keep me posted; let me know what's happening."

"Well, Dawn, we don't have a speaker for this thing. I
mean, so how do you . . . ?" Gloria kidded.

"All right, all right. Just drop a few hints every so often,
or do your own Peter Montgomery imitation. Just so I
know who's winning," I said — as I dropped the ham-it-up
bait right into Gloria's mouth.

"OK, they're coming in. They're coming in. They're
approaching Tiriititititti — whasisname? — Island. . . .
They're close. They're very close. *Tokio* is still in the lead
with Chris Dickson at the helm, and he's intense. He's
intense. The *Endeavour* crew can see the whites of his eyes,"
echoed Gloria.

Endeavour pulled out her whole sail locker, with two
spinnakers flying: one from her mainmast, one from her
mizzen. She passed *Tokio* in the Rangitoto Channel. It must
have caused pandemonium on shore; the radio estimated
that twenty thousand people were watching from the waterfront. The television carried live coverage in the middle of
the night. One taxicab was reported to have stopped, while
the passengers listened to the race to the background tune of
the meter running. There were hundreds of spectator boats
swarming around the big racing machines charging in from
the ocean like Thoroughbreds headed for the wire.

Endeavour beat *Tokio* to the line by 2 minutes, 12 seconds, and she only took that lead in the final three miles of the race. Jeni was happy for Spike. It must have been an amazing finish, and I wished we had been there. At least closer, in the thick of the front-runners. I knew the boys on *Winston* felt worse. Their early lead, which stretched to 146 miles at one point, evaporated in the middle of the leg. But if they keep their pace up, it looks like they will be the second Whitbread 60 to finish after *Tokio.*

At sunrise, New Zealand comes into view and we pass the famous hole-in-the-rock landmark of the Bay of Islands. We surge past, still reaching with jib and mainsail up, powering past the coastline — past blue skies and long, green hills. Small local boats have already started coming out from coastal towns, saying hello, waving us on. "Hello, girls! . . . Good work, ladies. . . . Welcome to New Zealand — How's the weather out there?" The occasional greetings continue throughout the day. The only inconvenience is that we have to scan the horizon before venturing to the aft deck for a shower and shampoo. But that was all right. We would have most of the day to make our preparations for landing on shore; Adrienne calculates our arrival in Auckland by sundown.

We do not succeed in catching *Brooksfield.* They got around Cape Reinga and got a head start down the coast. *Brooksfield* crossed the finish line at 16:04:57. Now, it is pedal-down, get the most out of our boat in these final hours.

As we sail toward Hauraki Gulf, we change course enough that we can put up our spinnaker. It goes up perfectly, and the crew is in phase now, spinnaker trimmers and winch grinders working in synchronized thought and action — our own kind of ballet.

We sail into Auckland at sunset and cross the finish line to a resounding roar of the crowd-monster sprawled out along the waterfront. We douse our spinnaker perfectly in a tight-turn maneuver before the dock, and head into the Viaduct Basin.

I knew what the crowds would be like, because I had done this race before. The first-timers in our crew were awed by the number of people. It would be an exciting land-fall for them — champagne all around, autographs to sign, television cameras and radio reporters stopping us all in our tracks. We would be celebrities for a day: we, the women Whitbread sailors, the ones who the world thought would sail off the edge of the world as soon as we got a taste of the Southern Ocean.

But we didn't. Our finish today — at 18:08:10, at sunset, in eighth place in the Whitbread 60 class — is about sixteen hours behind the lead boat. Our timing is getting better.

We sail toward the sea of spectators waiting in the Viaduct Basin. They cheer us home as if we were local heroes. We are not first to finish, but we feel every bit a winner. Who would have thought, in our most desperate days in the ice, we would have reached this moment?

We sail into the Viaduct Basin, through the skinny draw-bridge passage. Barry's mom has secured herself a place in the front lines and she is waving proudly. It feels good to have my soon-to-be family here to welcome me back to Auckland.

I know this homecoming means a lot to Leah. Auckland is home, and she ventured away a young sailor and came home a Whitbread racer. It has not all been a glory ride, and I am sure there were days when she asked herself, Is this worth it? Is this *crazy*? We all do, as we circumnavigate the globe and collect physical scars, mental scars — and strengths we never thought we had.

Leah traveled further than physical distance to come home from the other side of the world. The look on her face as we sail toward the crowd in the Viaduct Basin is proof enough: she feels twenty feet tall.

So do we all.

7

I'm not so sure we have changed the perspective of men, but I think that women are saying to themselves, "If they can do it, why can't I?"

— Dawn Riley, as quoted in the *Miami Herald*

January 24, 1994

I wanted the party to last all night long.

It began at the docks after our finish in Auckland and traveled up to Vine Street, to Barry's and my house — a small and tall house nestled on a hill overlooking the harbor, the ocean, and the great beyond. It is our domestic crow's nest, our perch over the sea that we return to after each adventure.

The crew and friends trailed up to the house. Little by little, our small house filled up. Howard had organized food and drink, which, when mixed with a bunch of ocean-weary sailors, made for an instant party.

By the early hours of the morning, I still did not want everyone to leave. Some of the crew stayed at the house (some by design; others because it was simply where they landed for the night). Everyone was either gone or asleep, and so I made myself one last gin and tonic and took my mail up to bed to read. I fell asleep — awash in junk mail, letters, and magazines. My gin and tonic sat untouched.

So much for all-night-party ambitions.

Crossing the Tasman Sea, I dreamed of eating a leisurely breakfast at home: fresh bread, New Zealand butter, avocados, espresso alfresco, out on the wooden deck that Barry and I built. It was already summer in Auckland, and I had visions of spending hours in the garden weeding, planting, collecting herbs, tending to my lemon trees, my orange tree. I wanted to spend hours in the 120-year-old house Barry and I had restored together, looking over our books and photos of racing campaigns and places visited — the house with the *Miami Vice* shade of purple-blue-gray walls that Barry painted one day, with the paint he mixed himself and covered nearly every wall with (until I stopped him on the stairs). Still, I liked the by-accident mix of colors that Barry spread all over the house in his usual get-the-job-done way. I wanted to be at home with the kitty, who, even if she is too tired, still follows me wherever I go.

But it was not to be. Within ten days, I would be gone.

On February 3, Jan Beijerinck of Heineken and I hopped on a plane bound for Washington, D.C., for a ten-day, six-city tour of U.S. airports, newspaper offices, radio studios, television studios — with a short stop for me to visit my family (and media contacts) in Detroit.

I should have been suspicious when I received Howard's fax one morning, in the middle of riding the monster waves of the Tasman Sea: *Message from the leader of the circus, Mr. Gibbons. Here is your schedule for your U.S. tour. I hope you like it.* But at the time, I had other things on my mind.

We flew away from summer in New Zealand, into Washington and winter storms that were paralyzing the East Coast. Roads were closed, highways were mirror-sheets of ice, airports were flooded with refugees from flights that never arrived or departed. But I did not mind much. For the first time in a long time, I was simply a passenger, asked to adhere to a detailed schedule of interviews, limousine rides, hotel check-ins and check-outs. I sat back and did my job, which was to tell the press the tale of *Heineken*.

Winter clothes were nonexistent in New Zealand, so I asked the limousine driver to make a quick pit stop at Banana Republic. I whooshed in, threw my credit card down, and said, "Hello, I need two turtlenecks, two pairs of socks, and a pair of trousers." The saleswoman — who was used to offering a leisurely, "Hello, can I help you?" and getting a leisurely response of, "No, just looking," or "Maybe," or "Can you show me what you have in chinos?" followed by a thorough tour of the store racks, was a little taken aback. Garments flew in and out of the dressing room as I tried everything on with lightning speed. "Yes, this is fine. Two more turtlenecks please, tan and cream. Another pair of trousers, just like these only in brown. And three more pairs of socks." A quick signing of the credit-card slip. Thank you. Good-bye. And in seconds I was gone, jumping into the limousine, which took off immediately, leaving the saleswoman dazed.

We had an entourage of people for the media tour, the core of which was me, Jan, and a man named Eric Handler, the publicist from New York City with whom we worked. Eric had everything planned with split-second precision: 7:30 AM hotel departure, 8:00 interview with the *Washington Post*, 9:00 interview with the *Baltimore Sun*, 9:45 limousine pickup, 11:00 taped in-studio interview at CBS affiliate . . . And so it went, for days.

We stopped in Annapolis and worked out of the office of Gary Jobson, a fellow sailor who has turned himself into a unique small company — racing boats, consulting, writing, doing television commentary on sailboat racing. We did interviews in Gary's office, toured Washington and Arlington for in-studio interviews, hooked up with *USA Today* by telephone. The next day we all flew to Atlantic City in a chartered six-seater to Sail Expo — a national winter rendezvous for sailors, with boats and gear on display and seminars and panel discussions for sailing enthusiasts and the marine industry.

It was a perfect place to be, and I saw many friends — America's Cup crews, racing friends who were planning solo races around the world, fellow sailors from my days sailing in the Caribbean and Florida who now had real jobs, kids, spouses, houses. I wanted just to stay and visit, but the schedule (and Eric) kept pulling me away.

Despite all the regimented activities, I was out of sync and still living in a different time zone after flying out so recently from the other side of the world. I couldn't sleep at night, and so I did a tour of the Atlantic City casinos, by myself. It was interesting: everyone said I am gambling doing the Whitbread and banking my future on a sport like sailing. But I am taking calculated risks. All those people in the casinos — in the bright lights of the slot machines, with cocktails going down and chips and wagers flying — *they* were gambling: opening themselves up to arbitrary pot luck, or ruin. In comparison, my life felt logical, well planned: I knew my percentages for success and survival.

After Atlantic City, we flew to Detroit. Jan got a hotel. Eric returned to New York. And I had an entire night at home with my family in our house on the canal — the A-frame made of pink brick down the street from where I learned to sail. I was impressed when I pulled up to the house in a limousine and my mom did not run out the front door with a video camera in hand and a spare still-camera strapped to her waist. I was impressed, until my sister Dana told me she had ripped the camera out of Mom's hands seconds before the limo rolled up to the door.

Mom and I fax back and forth about three times during each leg of the race. She already told me about all the snow-storms, about the snow shoveling that spooked the new kittens, about the nights they could only walk along the canal for transport because the roads were not yet plowed. Mom and her husband Charlie's boat, a thirty-two-foot Tartan called the *Mary Prudence,* was tucked away for the winter. The canal was quiet.

It was good to be home, in the 1950s house that Mom decorated in a style that she proudly calls "eclectic." All the things from our travels are here: batiks from the Caribbean, an old straw hat that I remember buying in a market by myself, lots of photos. I looked under my old bed, and it was chock-full of mementos. There wasn't enough time to exca-vate under the bed that night.

My friend Tish and her husband Dan were over. Tish is a midwife. She calls it "baby catching." Tish is a longtime friend; before she started in the baby business, she helped me deliver a lot of boats too. She is happy for Barry and me, and she gave me a useful gift: a guide to long-distance wedding planning.

When I did my first Whitbread in 1989/90, my family got to see the pressures that the race puts on people. So we didn't talk much about the Whitbread. I did give them a *Heineken* videotape to watch, with Southern Ocean scenes, wild speed rides through crashing waves, arrivals in port, sharp-toothed icebergs, interviews with half-asleep skippers just going through the motions of one more watch at sea.

During this Whitbread, my family has also followed the updates I file from sea on the CompuServe computer network, so they know what's been happening in the race. Our discussion of my life at sea was short: to my family's credit, they have never imposed on me their concerns about the kinds of sailing I am doing.

My parents were always like that. When I was growing up, they were strict about things like doing the dishes and saying please and thank you. But when it came to adventure, the idea of fear was never introduced. Do it, but do it right; take time to make the proper preparations and don't ever be afraid. It was a gift they gave to us all: me, Dana, and Todd, our younger brother.

The next morning, I said good-bye to my family after a too-brief visit and headed into Detroit to talk to local media contacts: women's writers, radio stations, the *Detroit Free Press*, the *Oakland Press*. At 8:35 that night, Jan and I flew away from winter and headed to Florida.

Fort Lauderdale was sunny and the breeze was warm. I had a beautiful tower room at Pier 66 overlooking the ocean. "Jan, do you think I could stay here for a week or so?" That was the question I was only brave enough to pose in my dreams. In reality, I knew what the answer would be: we had a schedule to keep.

Florida was a good stop. The Fort Lauderdale and Miami media were especially interested in the Whitbread, because the fleet would be returning here in the spring after racing a 5,475-mile leg from Uruguay to Fort Lauderdale.

In Florida we also had time to take reporters sailing on a fast, twenty-four-foot rocketship of a boat called a Melges 24. It was an afternoon of tacking, jibing, flying fast under the sun. I was a constant coach: "Sit here, please. Now move to this side. Quicker, please. . . . Watch your head — and could you get that line unwrapped from around your foot so we don't hoist you in the spinnaker set? . . . Please move over here now. No, right here. A little farther. Yes, that's fine, but watch out for that — spray. Sorry." I had a blast; I hoped they liked it.

The interviews in the States forced me to outline our goals on *Heineken*. By now, we knew what we were up against. There were five Whitbread 60s, all built later than *Heineken*, that I considered to have superior boat speed to ours: the New Zealand/Japan entry *Tokio*, with Chris Dickson at the helm; Lawrie Smith's *Intrum Justitia*; *Yamaha*, also owned by Ocean Ventures; the Spanish entry *Galicia 93 Pescanova*; and the other U.S. entry, *Winston*. Our boat is a first-generation Bruce Farr–designed Whitbread 60, the first one ever to be built. She was commissioned as the first boat to be sailed by the *Yamaha* crew, and they put her through the paces: racing her around Hawaii, taking her on sea trials on a trans-Pacific trip to Japan. *Heineken* was an old girl: she was the test bed for these newer-generation 60s that we were competing against.

I knew we did not have the same potential for boat speed as the top five 60s — but our goal was to beat one of them, on one leg, and to shoot for a midfleet standing in the ten-boat Whitbread 60 class by the time we reached England. I know some of the reporters were baiting me: they wanted me to say, *Yes, we will trounce all the men. We will win! We will be the golden girls of the sea.* I didn't bite. We had our goals, and they were realistic.

The Whitbread was the focus of my interviews, but there was one subject that kept coming up in nearly every interview I did: "Dawn, what are your America's Cup plans?" "Do you have any America's Cup plans?" "Can you confirm that Bill Koch will field the first-ever all-female America's Cup team in sport history, and will you be a part of it?" "Do you think a crew of women could be competitive in the America's Cup?" "Do you have plans to return to San Diego soon?"

They all posed the question in a different way, but they were all looking for the same answer.

Bill Koch, the man who led our *America³* team to a win in the 1992 America's Cup, was rumored in the press to be fielding the first women's team in the 142-year history of the Cup. A story had broken in the *New York Times* earlier that fall, and it sparked a rash of media interest.

I had sailed for Koch in the 1992 Cup as part of the *America³* team. Twelve syndicates from around the world entered to defend or challenge for the Cup. I was the only woman in the competition.

In the '92 Cup Koch concentrated on building a team effort, taking many disparate segments — technical experts, sailors, managers, business administrators, support crews — and pulling them all into the single focus of winning. The odds makers labeled *America³* a longshot for the Cup. We became the wildcard out in San Diego, and we won. I believed that Bill Koch could do it again.

I was not at liberty to offer any information to the press, even though I had intentions of becoming part of the all-women's team for which plans were brewing. All I could say was that I wanted to do another Cup campaign. That was the whole truth — for I left unfinished business in San Diego, and I had every intention of returning to complete something I had started in 1992.

In January 1991, the winter after I returned home after completing my first Whitbread, I got a tryout with Bill

Koch's *America³* Cup campaign in San Diego. I almost could not believe that there was a door open anywhere in the Cup for a female crew member: I flew myself to the tryout as fast as I could.

For the tryout, they put me in the "pit," a position in the center of the boat where you haul halyards and lines and coordinate with all the foredeck crew on hoisting, dousing, and trimming the headsails. You need to have a strong upper body. You need quick reactions.

After the tryout, I had no idea if I would make the team, so I prepared myself. To make the team would be awesome; if I did not make the team, I still had had the experience of sailing on the second IACC (International America's Cup Class) boat ever built.

I made the team, I stayed in the pit, and I spent many more hours on this boat. Six days a week, I was up at 5:15 AM to make phone calls to the East Coast. Then I made the twenty-minute commute to the compound for crew training at 6:15.

We alternated between aerobic and weight training. I had been abusing my knees since I was little, skiing moguls and running. By the time I moved to San Diego, my knees were already shot. But I refused to make excuses for myself, and I kept pace with the boys on the four- to six-mile runs. What really hurt my knees were the plyometric exercises: running up hills, running down, changing directions fast to develop quick reaction skills, carrying our crewmates up the hill to develop strength (some of the smaller crew members and I were popular on those days). The result was that I had to get laser surgery on my knee after the campaign was over.

Beyond the knee area, my legs were strong. I worked on upper-body strength in the weight room. I worked up to a bench press of 125 pounds, at three sets of ten to twelve reps. By the end of the campaign, I was stronger than some of the guys in my upper body. But I was only in the middle in terms of strength; the bigger guys beat me out.

After workouts, we had a crew breakfast, then a meeting at 8:45. After we had made all the preparations getting sails and equipment onto the boat, we sailed off the dock at 10:00 AM. The goal was to have the mainsail up by 10:30. We sailed until sundown; in the winter months, we were landing on the dock after it was completely dark.

Being the only woman, I got a lot of attention from the media. I did interviews outside of work: the East Coast ones were done on the phone at 5:15 AM; the West Coast interviews were done after work. I was also part of a trio of crew who traveled to fund-raisers and public relations events. We called ourselves the Mod Squad: me, the white girl with blond hair; Marty Stephan, our winch grinder, who is black; and handsome Billy Ruh.

The boat and the crew and the campaign became my life.

It was not always a smooth, six-day-a-week, clockwork effort. We hit our rough spots and we had our problems. But the team hung together, and Buddy Melges — one of the three helmsmen on the crew who a lot of us came to view as a cross between God and a surrogate father — was one of the forces who kept us all going.

All the sweat and hard work paid off, and we surprised many people when we beat Dennis Conner and won the right to defend the Cup in the winter of 1992. A fever pitch of power and possibility ran through our camp, and we moved into the finals.

Only some of us would make the final team to defend the Cup against *Il Moro di Venezia*, the Italian boat that had

won the right to challenge for the Cup. And when the list of
the final crew was published and posted in the gym, my
name was not on it. I knew I was the best person to be in the
pit. I was stunned, more disappointed than I have been about
anything before. I had worked for this, and I knew I had
earned it. No one said anything; no one explained why. I was
simply and silently left off the final team.

I did have a small moment of revenge. The day came
when I was walking into a gym in San Diego when the crew
member who had lobbied to replace me on the final team
was walking out. He was about twenty-five pounds heavier
than I was. I did not premeditate this moment, but the idea
came to me in flash. I punched him in the jaw and he fell to
the ground. Then I simply kept walking into the gym.

It felt good to do that, and I was proud of one thing: I did
not turn the defeat into a weakness and cry about my final
cut to the rest of the team. Barry — who was out in San
Diego, sailing for New Zealand — saw my tears. But I never
let the team see me cry.

On the final day of the 1992 America's Cup, *America³*
sailed to a victory. Mayhem broke out on the water: cheers
sounded, horns blasted, spectator boats buzzed through the
sidelines, champagne poured over the winning sailors, the
crew jumped into gargantuan high-fives and hugs. The team
I had been a part of had won the America's Cup, but I
played no part in that final victory on the water.

I will never forget that day.

We flew away from Fort Lauderdale on February 10 and
headed north to New York City to rendezvous with Eric
Handler, for more winter weather and another round of
interviews.

Our first day in New York was what I always think New York is like. We rushed out of the hotel. We rushed in to an interview. We rushed back out, rushed in, and out again, and in the face of delays Eric acted cool and collected on his pocket cellular phone, his tool of survival in the urban jungle. *"Hello, this is Eric Handler. . . . Yes, fine. Dawn Riley is with me now. . . . Yes . . . oh, that's nice. But we are running a little behind schedule. We'll be a few minutes late. . . . You say we air live in fifteen minutes? OK. We'll be there. Good-bye."*

It was at those moments that we were typically stuck in a limo parked in traffic. Eric looked at his watch a lot and made a lot of phone calls, and I think I heard his blood pressure rise. I really didn't mind the delays. I watched soap operas on TV. I had never had a TV in a car before.

The next day, New York changed completely — and I loved it. A huge snowstorm came during the night. In the morning the sounds on the street were quiet. There were fewer cars and fewer people. I took a walk in the morning, to look for a pharmacy to buy sunscreen for the next leg of the race.

"Leaving us so soon?" the cashier said, probably thinking I was going home to pack my bikini and fly to the Virgin Islands. I just smiled. He would never believe I was heading to an ocean of ice, where the weather is worse.

From New York, we flew to San Francisco to see my dad and to make an appearance at the Armchair Sailor Bookstore in Sausalito. There, I met some of the schoolchildren who were following our progress in their classroom. Two fourth-grade girls from Berkeley had written me a letter.

At school we are learning about the Whitbread race. We wrote this letter to you because you are are favroit team in the race and even though your not in first place we will be routing for you all the way. . . . We would love, Love, LOVE if Dawn could come and visit our class. We also want to know, is it very scary at sea? And we wondered how it feels to have the pride to be in the race.

The fourth-graders came to the bookstore with candy and a class picture, and the look in their eyes and the articles that were published in the daily papers during the days I was in the United States proved to me that I was very wrong about one thing. I had thought it would be difficult to tell the press about the positive aspects of what we were doing — twelve women racing through the world's oceans on *Heineken*. The last time I'd talked to many of the American reporters, I was in Uruguay. I had just arrived to take over a splintered crew and an underfunded boat. At the time, the press were all digging for the deep, dark side of what they saw as controversy. *Nance Frank is off the boat and now you are on. How did this happen? Why are you the new skipper? How do you think you can get this boat and this crew across the Southern Ocean? Do you think you can make it around the entire world?*

The stories written during my U.S. tour were positive. In three months' time, our crew on *Heineken* had proved that we could pull together, that we could make a bad situation into something good. The race was not over, not yet. But we had turned our story around.

As I flew away from California and headed back to Auckland — to the crew and our boat, to Barry's and my house on the hill and the Whitbread world I was anxious to return to — I knew one thing more.

Last November, when I got the crazy, unexpected phone call from Uruguay, I did the right thing.

8

The 5,914-mile leg from Auckland to Punta del Este, Uruguay, via the notorious Cape Horn, takes the 14-strong fleet back into the Roaring Forties and the iceberg-strewn Southern Ocean.

— "Whitbread Fax News"

February 19, 1994

Tomorrow we sail back into the Southern Ocean. No one on the crew is talking about the fact that we are going back. Everyone deals with the prospect of more cold, more ice, and more danger quietly — like something you don't verbalize, for fear of giving it more power than it deserves to have.

I know we are a stronger crew now, compared to the first time we sailed into the Southern Ocean on this boat. I also know that the Southern Ocean is still a deadly place. Today, we all go through the motions in a robotlike, mechanical way. We are going back to hell. Period. No further discussion.

Summer vanished from New Zealand when the rains and gray skies arrived. It has been raining a lot. That was obvious today, when I went down to the boat to stow my crew bag. Already, the boat smells down below after being closed up tightly for the wet weather.

It usually takes a few days at sea for the air below deck to develop its own stench — a mix of a crew in five-day-old clothes, wet sails, moldy sleeping bags, diesel fuel, seaboots, trapped aromas from Wednesday's lamb curry and Thursday's chicken supreme. We got used to the air quality down below, gradually, as we endured one more day without a shower and one more day of getting thrashed at sea.

Once I stowed my gear, I switched on the electronics and powered up the laptop computer to try to send a fax out to Barry. He had been at sea for a month now, and I knew what his life on the ocean was like: a strange, isolated, basic-survival existence of eating, sleeping, and sailing. Any contact from the outside world, even mundane news from home, can be a welcome and reassuring distraction.

Being in the States and not having access to the right communications software to fax *ENZA* directly, I did not communicate with Barry much during the Auckland stopover. I updated him now on the engagement presents we had received. I told him about meeting his mom for coffee and her plan, from now on, to buy lotto tickets in case we have the wedding in the United States. I relayed some information from his dad about making radio contact with home. I told him about the sponsor meetings I had scheduled for tomorrow morning before the start, and about the festive send-off dinner party I had hosted the night before I flew away to the States — sit-down for twelve, alfresco, on our wooden-deck veranda overlooking the harbor. I told him about my pending trip to the ice-cream shop, after I finished checking the gear stowed onboard and closed up the *Heineken* machine for one last night of rest before heading into the Southern Ocean.

It was only small talk — the kind my mom and friends send me when I am out at sea. I assumed Barry liked hearing much of the same.

There were footstops on deck, then footsteps coming down the companionway stairs.

"Hey, Dawn," said Renee, who stood dripping wet, looking as if she'd just fallen into a swimming pool fully clothed in her wet-weather gear. "It's pouring out."

"No kidding. What are you up to?" I asked her. We tried to make the day before a restart a relaxing one: a day for personal business with some time mixed in to make sure we have each taken care of all our responsibilities on the boat before going back out to sea. If we are organized, the days before a restart never have to be flat-out, crazy days of wiring, lubricating, installing, and troubleshooting systems after the deadline for ordering parts has passed — the way they were when we left Punta last November.

"I just came down to make sure the video camera and batteries were stowed onboard properly, double-check the supply of duct tape, batteries, spare light bulbs. You know, the usual."

Because Renee was experienced at running racing boats, she naturally began to slot into the position of captain — overseeing the general maintenance on the boat and purchasing parts and inventory. But she did not move into a leadership role with ease on *Heineken*. When she got onto the boat in Punta, some of the crew viewed her only as my friend. They doubted that her hundred-pound frame could be strong enough. I knew Renee would hold her own in the crew, and I wanted to tell the skeptics to piss off. At first I hoped to dictate that Renee would take a leadership role and make clear that she was to be respected by the crew. But I figured, no, I can't do that. Plus, that would not do Renee any favors. She had to sink or swim on her own.

I hoped Renee could learn to demonstrate her strengths

on the boat and diminish her weaknesses, and I left her to find her own way into the crew. Now, Renee was swimming just fine.

Renee had also become the campaign filmmaker. With the Heineken sponsorship came the onboard video equipment to tape our action at sea, edit it, and send it to land via the satellites for the television news. We had had a video camera on the leg from Punta, but we had not had the capability to send feeds to land.

Renee had proven her journalistic tendencies by recording, with religious regularity, her personal take on the tale of *Heineken* in her journal. Now she had electronic means to tell our story, and she quickly assumed the role of the roving reporter with the camcorder eyes. She would hunt us down at all hours to capture the documentary-style story of our life at sea: sleeping in our bunks; perched on the side of the galley and eating freeze-dried mush out of a plastic bowl; riding a Southern Ocean wave to the end of a tether; helming, winch grinding, trimming sails on deck. It was not Hollywood. Renee would wait until Marleen's hair looked just as stringy as the spaghetti bolognese she was eating; until our chef was sweating, sauce-stained, and looking like a marathon short-order cook; until I was my most sleep-deprived; until all of us donned our most elegant, all-the-rage, feminine ensembles of long johns, T-shirts, Synchilla everything, face masks, and shapely foul-weather gear. Sending the footage to land was not easy. Renee spent hours staring at the small video screen in the navigation station. Here, at a viewer the size of a television for a family of mice, she edited her footage.

Auckland was the stopover we needed. The crowds who cheered us over the finish line, the positive reception of our story in the press — these were the signals that we were turning our fate around. But I knew now — after returning from the States and getting back into the day-to-day management of our campaign — that we still had a long way to go. The crowds, the publicity — they were the halftime festivities. Now, we were back on the field.

By the time we arrived in Auckland, I had gone through a crash course in do-it-yourself management. I have never before been a campaign leader for this amount of time — and I am learning. Fast. It is not easy taking all these individuals and meshing them into a crew, an entity that becomes one monster personality with twelve heads.

By the time we were ready to leave New Zealand, I had already had individual, sit-down meetings with some members of the team. Our crew had its own ecology; if one part of the operation was not working, the whole system was out of whack. Some of the crew saw the criticisms given in the sit-down meetings as constructive, and they worked hard to change. Some saw it only as criticism.

Lisa Beecham, our cook and doctor, was one person I had to let off the crew in Auckland. I did not feel she was fitting into a professional campaign the way I needed her to. Letting a crew member go had its aftershocks. Those who felt insecure about their jobs and abilities felt even more vulnerable after seeing a crewmate depart. Personnel changes were not a good thing for the team, but I could not afford to take a crew member offshore — through the rugged conditions we faced in the race — if I felt I could not rely on her to do the job I needed her to do.

I also learned the hard way not to ask the crew how they thought things should be run. When I did that, I had twelve different opinions. When I chose one, I had eleven disgruntled crew members who took potshots at my path of action. I had never realized how detrimental this could be. So the laissez-faire mode of leadership that I adopted to ease my way into the campaign changed. I began to pull away from the crew, to tell them how things would be done. For our own survival, I let go of democratic ideals. Every crew member had her say in her own area of expertise, but I maintained the ultimate decision-making power. Some members of the crew deposed me in their own personal-fantasy schemes: . . . *If I were in charge, that never would have happened. . . . We never would have blown out that sail. . . . We would have won.*

I know. I play the same twenty-twenty hindsight, I-would-have-done-it-differently game when I am not in charge. It's innocuous enough — until you start politicking, building momentum, creating support for your fantasized strengths. Being the skipper is harder than I thought it would be.

"Hey, Renee, do you want to go get an ice cream?" I asked her.

"No, no thanks. I have some things here I want to finish up. What are you doing for dinner?" she asked.

"Home cooking. Maybe some pasta and vegetables. Something fresh and not freeze-dried. I also have an article to write and fax to London before we leave. Plus, I need a good night's rest," I said.

The Auckland stopover had been tiring. There was a lot of media activity. There were day sails in the harbor with sponsor guests and members of the press. And I was just getting over my jet lag from the U.S. tour.

The crew was onstage for the nearly one month we were in Auckland. Behind the scenes, we still had to make time to maintain the boat, ready the sail wardrobe for the Southern Ocean, check all the systems, survey the running and standing rigging, and fix our much-needed heater for the ice region. (We were unsuccessful; after one round of parts replacements, we did diagnose the problem — but not in time to get the additional parts we needed shipped to Auckland.)

There was one thing about the boat that haunted me. Renee dove under the hull to check the underbody, and she saw that there were still arteries of rust running around the area of the keel attachment. We hauled the boat to take a closer look, and I called Dave Powys — who had handled our refit in Freo while I was in England — in the middle of the night to check with him. They had ground out some of the rust in Freo and refilled those areas. I wanted to know what it looked like before the repairs, to know how far the rust had moved since then. I totally trusted Dave's expertise, and after comparing notes, I felt sure that the attachment was fine.

You can break a lot of things at sea and still keep sailing — but not the keel, the weighted underbody appendage that keeps the boat upright. It was not long ago that the American solo racer Mike Plant lost the weighted bulb on the end of his keel while crossing the Atlantic Ocean. The boat capsized; no one knew what happened and no one knew exactly where he was. Days later, a Liberian freighter sighted the boat — overturned, bobbing like a cork — several hundred miles north of the Azores. A team of French rescue divers went out to survey the vessel. When the divers got inside the boat, they found the life raft partially inflated. Plant must have acted fast when the boat flipped, but not fast enough. His body was never found.

I felt certain that our keel attachment was sound. Still, I

was haunted by what had happened to Mike Plant. As far as we all knew, he too set sail with every confidence that his boat would hold up fine.

Renee interrupted my daydream-nightmare. "Auckland's been a blast, and I'm sorry to leave. But yeah, a good night's rest is the best idea for tonight. I'm looking forward to my last night in my warm, dry bed. As of tomorrow it's back to a wet, cold bunk. . . . Hey, Dawn, are you nervous about going back into the Southern Ocean?" Renee tossed the question off casually, still looking over her stores of supplies and waiting eagerly for my answer.

"No. Not really. We're ready to go back," I said.

"Yeah. . . . See you tomorrow," said Renee.

It wasn't really ice-cream weather, with all the rain and all the gray skies. Still, I put on my wet-weather gear and went out to get some before heading home. It was a routine by now. Ice cream is one thing I crave once I get offshore. So I have to have my fill before I leave.

At home, I made dinner. I tried to finish the column I was writing on my experiences in the Whitbread race for *Seahorse,* the monthly journal of the Royal Ocean Racing Club published in London, but Ginger Kitty — the neighborhood cat with the loosest morals, who liked to crash at our house best — kept walking all over my notes. I straightened Barry's and my room up. Our housemate Martin, who was living in our place and taking care of Ginger Kitty while we were both away, would be staying on, so I did not have to worry about closing everything down. Still, I was sad to be leaving home.

Later that night, Barry got a phone call through to home via the SSB (single-sideband) radio. *ENZA* had been at sea about thirty-five days now. They had just come through a

Southern Ocean passage and were sailing south of New Zealand, well on schedule and nearing the halfway mark of their 27,000-mile time trial.

We just made small talk: "Yes, I am ready to go back into the ice. . . . The house is fine; it's good to be home. . . . The garden is a disaster area. . . . Ginger Kitty is up to her old tricks."

When I was in the States, I had spoken further with the organizers of the all-female America's Cup crew. Barry knew I had every hope of joining this historic women's quest for the Cup. I had worked hard to sail the big, powerful, grand-prix boats typically sailed by men. If there was to be a women's Cup crew, I would put a lot of my life on hold to be a part of the campaign.

"I talked to the organizers of the women's team while I was in the States. Barry, I think it's really going to happen," I told him, and I updated him on the plans with full-steam-ahead enthusiasm: a pending big announcement, crew trials, the prospect of moving to San Diego for a year, the excitement brewing in the United States about this effort. But Barry's reaction spelled out one thing, very clearly: running around the world and leading this Whitbread campaign, I had become the big-lady skipper, the one in the newspapers, on the TV; the one with the basketball-sized head that would get even bigger once I signed on with the first-ever all-female Cup crew. I could hear it in his voice: *Why did you even bother to get engaged if you had every intention of leaving home in Auckland, to move to the other side of the world and conquer the sailing world?*

We had talked before about my hope of joining the women's team in San Diego. But now that we were engaged, the Cup became the monster storm looming over our horizon. My doing the Whitbread, Barry racing around the world on *ENZA*, both of us spending weeks and months apart sailing on different oceans: they all fueled the fire. In trying to build a life together from two sailing careers that keep us a world apart, I wondered, would it always be like this? One racing campaign after the next with little time together? As we head out to conquer another ocean, or another racing circuit, will we lose each other along the way?

Our conversation did not last much longer. Soon, Barry signed off the radio, and the sound of his voice trailed away, far away, back to the ocean. I was left at home alone, with Ginger Kitty.

The next day, we sailed away from Auckland to head back into the Southern Ocean. The crowds along the Viaduct Basin were in full force by the time we powered away from the dock and out to the starting area. We estimated several hundred thousand people on shore and a few thousand spectator craft buzzing around the fleet — everything from one-man Windsurfers to catamarans that carried two hundred people. We counted over twenty helicopters overhead and an entire fleet of fixed-wing aircraft. This race is, after all, a Kiwi Super Bowl.

The crowd roared as we motored out of the skinny drawbridge passage and we waved goodbye. We were not winners yet, or losers: the hopes of some people in the crowd were riding with us into the Southern Ocean, and what we were about to do inspired some observers, especially the children following our progress in school programs.

It was a good feeling, to know we could fuel the ideals of the kids. But as we sailed away from the Auckland crowds, I did not feel like a happy heroine.

There is a downside to this fairy tale. We all pay a price to sail at this level, and mine could be a big one.

The ice arrived today, February 28, our ninth day out at sea. The water temperature is down to four degrees centigrade. Frostbite and chilblains have returned to our patches of exposed skin. A mix of snow and sleet fell today. Cape Horn is still twenty-two hundred miles away, which translates to about six days of sailing. Over two thousand miles to go until we turn the corner. Will we ever get there?

Life is slightly boring out here. At least it was until Leah went below to turn the deck lights off and looked at the radar: "Dawn, there is something out there — about two miles away on the radar."

I knew it had to be ice. I was on deck at 0300 hours earlier that morning. I thought I smelled ice, but when I looked on the horizon, I could see nothing but an endless black sky. I thought my mind was playing tricks on me. It does that sometimes. You see things that don't belong in the middle of the ocean — a Windsurfer speeding by, a person walking past the boat — but it is only a figment, a thought that is really inside your head and not out there floating past you on the sea.

With Leah's warning, the on-watch crew searched the horizon. The shadow of an iceberg took shape. Soon it was clear: a monster berg, its sharp-as-steel edges glittering in the diffused moonlight. The iceberg was about five degrees off our bow, and we were not on a collision course with it. But we needed to know it was there so we did not veer the wrong way and feel the wrath of its sharp teeth.

The nearby berg added a few moments of butterflies to my stomach. Soon, we were back to business as usual, another day at the office. This is, after all, our job.

The moon is out tonight for the first time in a week. There are stars, too. It is not a clear night, but at least we can see something of the heavens beyond the patches of cloud — as opposed to the wash of overcast sky we have been looking at ever since we left New Zealand. Star light, star bright: I made a wish. I cannot say what it was, but it has a lot to do with being someplace warm and dry.

We have been averaging some decent velocities: 12.4 knots, 12.5. Those are the averages. Our top boat speeds in the gusts are much faster, but they are wet and wild and through (not over) the waves.

Everything onboard is soaked, and having a bone-dry sleeping bag is just as farfetched a fantasy as winning the lottery. But we all try. I attempted to dry one of the bags by boiling the kettle, getting it steaming hot, and wrapping the sleeping bag around it. The theory of my spot-drying was the heat would drive the dampness out of the cloth. It worked, marginally. For a short time afterward my bunk passed as soggy rather than wet.

Without the heater, there is nothing to pull the moisture out of the cabin. We keep a hatch board over the companionway, the open passageway that runs from the cabin to the cockpit outside, to act as a makeshift door to keep as much cold and wet out as possible. Still, the air in the cabin has a wet, icy chill. We are living in an antarctic rainforest.

Our latitude/longitude is 58°17.92' S, 126°30.37' W. *Brooksfield* is nineteen miles ahead, according to the distance-to-the-finish calculations sent from the race office. But *Brooksfield* is sailing much farther north than we are. We won't know how our north-south positioning will pan out until we turn the corner at Cape Horn. The boys on *Dolphin & Youth* — our other nemesis in the fleet — are doing well on this leg; they are among the southerly pack of lead boats. Again, the answer will be at the Horn — where the fleet will turn the corner to head up the coast of South America, and where the winds and waves can be hell.

We all left Auckland on February 20 and sailed through the teacup-shaped Bay of Plenty. DG sent us a fax shortly after our start: "Good Morning Ladies. . . . How is the Bay of Plenty treating you?" Don't rub it in, DG. He obviously knew what it was like — rain, gray skies, with near–gale force northwesterlies that pushed us all fast through the bay, over the East Cape rim of New Zealand, and into a long, southeasterly dive down into the Southern Ocean. We took the fast-forward swan dive through the Bay of Plenty, toward the ice, and away from the last land we would see until Cape Horn. After that, the strong winds lasted for three days.

The vocabulary among the fleet was limited during those first days out: wet, wild, wet, cold, miserable, cold, wet, miserable, fast. Grant Dalton, skipper of the Maxi *New Zealand Endeavour,* reported in to race headquarters: "Waves are crashing over the deck and the boat is soaking wet below deck and our clothes are not drying out. I'm struggling to be enthusiastic when I say that I am enjoying this." For the fleet leaders and all the also-rans, the first days out from Auckland were equal-opportunity purgatory; we all got the same flogging from the weather.

By today, everyone has plateaued out into a general easterly course — but all of us are picking our route and our weather systems carefully as we head toward the Horn.

Diving off the edge of New Zealand and taking the big leap across the Southern Ocean puts us in a barren stretch of open water where weather information is not reliable. The navigator on *Intrum Justitia,* Marcel van Triest, informed race headquarters of this today, reporting that these days have been trying, that he was dealing with "tricky weather patterns" and relying on weather information from as far afield as New Zealand, Australia, Chile, and Russia. Still, *Intrum Justitia* must be doing something right; as of today's positions, she is walking away with an approximate thirty-five-mile lead in the Whitbread 60 class. On the first night at sea, *Intrum* also broke her own 425-mile record with a 428.7-mile run in a twenty-four-hour period. I think the boat has wings.

Intrum has several Whitbread veterans onboard, led by British skipper Lawrie Smith. A kind of Outward Bound version of James Bond with surfer-blond hair, Smith is ultra-cool and competent and, at this point in the race, he is a too-close-for-comfort threat to *Tokio*'s overall lead.

Our start from Auckland could have been perfect if we had held the boat back a few seconds longer from the starting line. The start was upwind, which meant we could drive fast with our sails close-hauled and not worry about the complications of hoisting up a balloonlike spinnaker.

Seconds before the start, the fleet started to charge for the line, surging forward like a train with nonstop momentum. We all sailed across the line, but eight out of fourteen boats crossed the line early. That is a very high number of boats to jump the gun.

Under the Whitbread rules, if you cross the line early, you either sail back and recross the line legally or you take a time penalty. We opted for a penalty of seventeen minutes. We figured that sailing back through the chaos of the spectator fleet could eat up more time than our penalty. Six boats, however, saw it differently, and they went back and re-crossed the line.

The first miles of the race were exciting racing. Because we have to shift the water in our water-ballast tanks every time we tack — which means turning through the eye of the wind and changing the angle of the boat's heel — Gloria stayed down below to operate the system of gravity-fed passages and clutch pumps.

New Zealand Endeavour crossed just in front of us with her majestic rig, a tree trunk flying with sails, while hundreds of spectator boats buzzed in our wakes like flies. A close encounter, perfectly executed. Within minutes, a close encounter of a different kind began to develop.

Winston's red-and-white cigarette-package hull was charging up, below our sail. One of our crew climbed down to the low, leeward side of the boat with a report: "*Winston* is coming, *fast*. They are on starboard tack [which meant they had the right-of-way]. We may not be able to get across their bow, and if we go for it, it is going to be very, very close."

Trying to cross a too-close starboard-tack boat on the water is like running a red light well after it's turned red and praying you make it. Well, it's more scientific than that, and you have to gauge your relative speeds — but it feels like a red-light run in your stomach. "*Winston*, cross or tack? Cross or tack?" I yelled. It was close, and I wanted to ask for a go-ahead to cross. That way, we would be clear about what was happening, and we would avoid the split-second, last-minute confusion that results in collisions. "Tack . . . Tack!" was *Winston*'s response. The crew was ready. I gave the command to tack and threw the helm over. Our sails slammed over. We sliced a perfect ninety-degree turn in the water alongside *Winston*.

"What the hell are you doing up there?" yelled Gloria from below deck.

"Tacking — sorry we didn't tell you," Renee informed her.

According to all except Gloria, the tack was a good one, but it was almost too close, the kind where you could see the whites of their eyes. Turning into *Winston*'s leeward bow threw some of our "dirty" used air into their sails and slowed them down. It felt pretty good. After we turned sharp inside *Winston*'s path, it was pedal down, don't let *Winston* with her full-throttle momentum roll right over us. At the second channel mark, the Spanish Whitbread 60 *Galicia 93 Pescanova, Merit Cup*, and we were only forty-five seconds apart. We all went for maximum speed, like a herd of buffalo thundering over the ground — only our noises were waves crashing, rigging groaning from the constant adjustment of sails, orders being shouted in the wind. *Brooksfield* was one minute behind us at the mark. Our crew was focused and we were in the hunt. This leg had every sign of being a good one for us.

Once we were past the mark, I knew we would be on this tack for a while, so I asked Renee and Leah to tie the leeward runner forward. The runners are a set of two wires of adjustable length that run from the mast to the back of the boat that we use to help control the bend of the mast, to help shape the sails, and to help hold the rig up. We need to use only one runner at a time, so the leeward runner is let off.

Leah took one runner forward to clip it in and get it out of the way. Just as she did, we got hit with a big wave. Leah got washed down the deck, and all she had to hold on to was the runner clip. She was still holding it when the wave passed and the water on deck washed back into the sea. But Leah did not get right back up.

Renee went to help her, and she quietly took something out of Leah's hand, which was bleeding fast. The runner clip, a hook made out of quarter-inch-thick stainless steel, had gone clear through Leah's hand, in the meaty part between the thumb and forefinger.

Renee helped Leah back to the cockpit and down below. Sue and Marleen gave her painkillers first, then seventeen stitches. Leah was stoic throughout the operation.

Leah was banished below deck to keep her hand dry. Her only complaint was that she would mess up the watch system, forcing me to keep her watches. And she was back to being a cook — something Leah is professionally trained for, but not the job she wanted to do on a Whitbread boat.

Since our cook Lisa Beecham was no longer on the crew, we had planned a rotating cook schedule among several crew members for this leg. But for now, as Leah said, "All I can do is play Mum," and she did, tirelessly. Even though her hand was strapped up, she cooked, kept the interior of the boat clean, and offered, "Another cup of tea?" to all who looked as if they could use a warm drink — which was just about everyone, most of the time. Within days, Leah was back on deck.

Nine days out and Barry and I are still slinging faxes at each other across the Southern Ocean. I think we really are having our first full-blown satellite fight, courtesy of the modern communications systems we carry onboard.

Dear Dawn, What's more important: careers & egos or each other?

Dear Barry, I am happy that we are finally talking.

Dear Dawn, I am wondering why we got enagaged if we can't be together.

Dear Barry, We could both move to San Diego. I could sail for *America*[3]; you could work in San Diego for a Cup syndicate, or work on making contacts for your own sailing sponsorship.

Dear Dawn, I am not moving to San Diego.

Dear Barry, I know that we can work this out.

Dear Dawn, I am not moving to San Diego.

If Barry and I were a caveman-cavewoman couple, would we return to each other after long journeys and long silences and still be blissfully in love? Hard to say. Communication is a good thing — at the right time and in the right place. Maybe in our case, old-fashioned absence and mystery would be better. At least for now.

We both have a bad case of Southern Ocean fever, and our discussion about our sailing careers and our life together that began the night before I sailed away from Auckland has spiraled into a blow-by-blow fax dialogue rehashing our past, present, and future. We are trying to establish a new understanding of our future together from faxes that are as good as hieroglyphics when it comes to discussing emotions.

I still believe in my heart that Barry and I have what it takes to make a life together. We just need time — face-to-face, in the same port — to work it out. Is it the Southern Ocean, the cold, the pressures and risks of pushing a boat constantly to beat a world-speed record? Or is Barry having a change of heart? I have not stopped thinking about him, as he sails farther and farther away on *ENZA*, since we left Auckland.

Beyond the cold, the wet, my futile attempts at satellite romance, and the continual push to the Horn, life onboard has its ups and downs.

Dehydrated macaroni and cheese tastes better in the Southern Ocean. The mystery of Adrienne's missing seaboot — which had been MIA since Australia — took on a new light when Susie Crafer stepped on deck wearing two left feet. All our bodies are bruised, sore, torn, and tired, and we are eating pink ibuprofen pills like candy. In addition to being one of our best heavy-air chutes, our Code 7 is also a good sea anchor: the shackle that fastens the sail to the top of the mast opened and the sail blew up into assorted pieces, one of which ended up as an underwater anchor until we got it onboard; the sail has now been proclaimed toast. Our rudder bearing is groaning, causing us mild concern about one of the rudder-attachment points. Merritt made a rare foray into the galley and filled the kettle from the salt-water pump (we have a salt-water pump that draws water directly from the ocean, in addition to the fresh-water pump, which we use for our drinking water). Now we know who the culprit is behind that strange-tasting coffee. Our port primary winch is not working, even after Mikki and Gloria meticulously pulled the entire thing apart — revealing its inner workings, like that of a large clock — with their frozen hands. Gloria rebeled when she discovered we did not pack enough Cocoa Puffs for breakfast; the day we ran out, she retaliated by chewing the purplest grape gum any of us had ever seen.

The barometer has taken a dive in the last two hours, from 1004 to 998. I am going to sleep in my full foul-weather gear, to be ready when the weather comes.

9

Half our rudder is gone. I am guessing, but it has been bad for a few days. The steering has been light and we have to oversteer. But we can still steer if we take it easy. . . . The only thing that I am worried about is that, if the rudder has started to delaminate, and it has not just broken off, how long is the stub going to last? We are assessing the situation.

— fax from Dawn Riley to
race headquarters

March 7, 1994

I could always count on Gloria, our engineer, our five-foot-two-inch ball of fire from Texas. She would dive headfirst into any engine or mechanical system, tear it apart, assess the problem, and fix it. From her days in the pits at NASCAR races, Gloria is used to working fast under pressure, and we dubbed her our drag-strip queen.

She was born in a hotel in El Paso. According to Gloria, this was a sign that she was destined to travel and use small pieces of soap. She was a beach bum in California before she was ten and has had a colorful life since then.

Gloria is Court-Jester-Miss-Fix-It rolled into one. She keeps this boat's systems together: the engine, desalinator, generator. She is good at improvisation (both mechanical and otherwise). And Gloria has an uncanny knack for knowing what is going on inside the hearts and heads of the crew. In short, she is an unappointed mascot and the glue of this boat: if Gloria is down, we are all in trouble.

A few days ago, she gave us a big scare when she came running out of the head, threw herself on her bunk, flipped over onto her back, and started wrapping toilet paper madly around her tongue. "Gloria, what's wrong?" asked Jeni.

"Poison. I've poisoned myself. I'm going to die!" she said, through a wad of toilet paper.

It took a long time to get the story out of Gloria and Jeni. Jeni was hysterical with laughter; Gloria's tongue was mummy-wrapped in toilet paper.

Gloria was told by Sue to gargle with antiseptic because she had a sore in her mouth. Gloria grabbed the red-liquid bottle in the head, took a huge gulp, swallowed part of it (she always, Gloria informed us later, swallows part of her mouthwash), only to find out that she had taken a swig of disinfectant household cleaner. Potpourri flavor.

It was a long time before Gloria got off her bunk and took the toilet paper off her tongue. The jokes continued for a few days, even from across the Southern Ocean, where Howard and Victoria remained to pack up our office in Auckland: *That is all for now. I am off to the bar for a Mount Gay rum with a Toilet Duck chaser. Cheers, Howard.*

Up until now, Gloria has had a way of keeping us all going. But last night, I thought I saw fear in her eyes. She would never want me to see, and I never let on.

I wanted to say, I know, I get scared too in these conditions. But how could I? By now, we had come to depend on Gloria as the one person who could ward off a wave of negative thinking. Gloria, please, don't let us down: do something to make us laugh.

Our eleventh day at sea was the calm before the storm. The wind had gone to sleep. We only had whispers of breeze, and our drifter and superlight headsails — named for their suitability in light air — got a workout. We did circles chasing what breeze we could find. It was not bad to have the wind machine turned off for a few hours, except the rest of the fleet was charging ahead and any mileage we had gained was quickly evaporating.

Some of the crew took advantage of a stable platform. Renee pulled the hacksaw out and shortened up the life-lines to make a better "fence" around the topsides of the boat; Leah caught up on sail repairs; the black-hole area under the galley stove was excavated, unearthing an odd assortment of dried and dehydrated foods and utensils that had gone AWOL a long time ago.

Then the wind woke up like a monster-genie bottled up for five hundred years and ready to rage — 35 knots, 38, 41, 43, 47, 50 knots. We pared the big light-air sails we were flying down to the size of a handkerchief: Number 3, triple-reefed main. We rode out the fronts that kept coming through over the next thirty-five hours.

With the wind came the waves. It was like the old days. We were getting slammed in the Southern Ocean, again. Gloria described it just right. The boat became an express elevator: we'd zoom up five floors on a wave, leaving most of our stomachs behind; we'd zoom back down on a wave. At the bottom the doors would open and we'd get a big bucket of seawater thrown in our faces. Then, up we go again: lingerie, fifth floor.

On March 3, *Dolphin & Youth* reported problems with her keel. According to the Whitbread office, three of her twenty-two keel bolts, which are part of the keel-to-hull attachment system, have sheared, and there is movement between the hull and the keel.

The boat's designer, based back in England, is reassuring: there are three keel-attachment systems that can each hold the seven-ton keel in place, independent of each other. But I trust *Dolphin*'s skipper Matt Humphries not to put 100 percent faith in what people on dry land are saying: *Dolphin* is still in the middle of the ocean, and she has about twelve hundred miles to go to reach the nearest point of land, which is the formidable rock-cliff of Cape Horn. The situation is not life-threatening — not yet — but if *Dolphin*'s keel falls off, or if the keel keeps moving and works a fracture into the hull, it will be.

Over the next days, we learn more. The *Dolphin* crew has rigged lines out of the companionway that extend out to the edge of the deck so if the boat flips, they can feel their way out by following the lines. The crew is sleeping near the hatch, ready for escape. Humphries went swimming to look at the keel. When he got out of the water, he vomited from the shock of the cold water.

The Whitbread office tells us the Chilean navy has a guard vessel at the Horn, and they are aware of the situation. Our boat and *Brooksfield* are not far behind *Dolphin*; we both must be ready in case a rescue is needed.

Hours after learning of *Dolphin*'s problems, we have problems of our own when our steering cable blows out. The steering wheel of the boat is attached to the steering cable; the cable is attached to the steering quadrant; and the quadrant is attached to the rudder. Every piece is linked into a mechanical system so the wheel can transfer direction to the rudder.

Leah was steering when the cable broke. It was no

different from driving seventy miles per hour down a highway and having the steering wheel come off in your hands. Luckily, our helm station has two wheels. Leah was strapped into her safety harness and she quickly grabbed the other, leeward wheel and regained control of the boat.

We have a system onboard during the rough weather: whoever drives the boat wears two safety harnesses. The harness is a nylon webbing strapped around the body, attached to a leash. The leash clips on to the boat to keep the driver connected in case something knocks her overboard — a rushing wave, a loss of footing, a boat that bucks like a bronco. This precaution is crucial in the cold, rough water. Once someone goes overboard, finding her in a big sea is like looking for a needle in a haystack. The problem is time: the cold can kill you before the boat finds you. The safety harness is a rule. And we have another crew on standby next to the wheel, just in case the driver gets washed off. It is vital to keep this beast of a boat under control at all times.

Gloria and Merritt fixed the cable. We had no spares onboard, since the cables were replaced when we were in Fremantle. Going offshore, we have to be ready to repair anything that breaks — but we have to hedge our bets and keep the boat light.

The cable is made of Vectran, a line made of Spectra and Kevlar, materials that are used to create a rope with the qualities of low stretch and high strength. Gloria and Merritt spliced a new section of Vectran into the cable. Once the repair was made, we checked to make sure the cable had the right amount of tension. Soon we were up and running again.

The Horn was not far away now. By March 6, we had about 450 miles to go. Around the Horn, the weather systems and the currents squeeze through the narrow passageway between the Horn and Antarctica — and conditions intensify. The hellish conditions at the Horn are legendary among sailors.

Yes, there is a science to sailing around the Horn, but in the realms of dreams and myths, it is as if something is alive down there. Maybe there is a huge ghost of Cabo de Hornos, with seaweed hair and crazed eyes the color of the sky during a storm. Maybe he sits on a perch on the legendary rock wall. Maybe he gets bored. Maybe he looks down at the tiny sailboats passing by and says, "OK, you little sailboat out there, I am going to have some fun with you now." He points a gnarly finger, takes a deep breath, and blows. The sea turns into a raging torrent of white water. And then he laughs.

According to the meteorological files we have access to, the wind should be about thirty knots from the west when we reach the Horn. The westerlies are expected to build to fifty knots. Not exactly a summer-afternoon breeze.

The Horn is our gate out of the Southern Ocean. Once we turn that corner, our navigational charts will take on an optimistic hue. Then we can follow the paper trail under the foot of Chile, up the long coast of Argentina, past the Falklands, and on to Uruguay. This is the home stretch to Punta del Este, the resort town that promises blue sky, sun, a dry bed, cheeseburgers, boys, movies, parties. But first, we have to get around the Horn.

After our steering cable broke, the rudder never felt right again. Every person who drove the boat complained that the helm felt soft. We checked and rechecked the steering cable, the quadrant; it seemed to be operating fine. There was a lot of play in the rudder bearing, which had been groaning for days. But those things could not account for the feel of the helm. Something was not right with the rudder section.

And then it all came clear in the fifty or so miles we had left before the Horn. The breeze calmed down to around twenty knots and we could put more sail up. Sue was on the wheel, and we had our full mainsail and a jib top flying. The waves grew into steady swells. These were not the kind of conditions that our boat would round up and broach in — but we did. The twenty-five-knot wind pushed our rig down, and the boat lost its footing in the water just long enough for the hull to skid out sideways. Pot lids flew out of the galley; sleeping bags rolled off their bunks. I think Marleen's teddy bear got its first offshore flying lesson and crashed in the bilge, and some of the off-watch crew were rudely awakened.

The boat was fine, but what bothered me was that we should not have broached in these conditions.

Sue got control of the boat quickly. But we rolled over again. I got on the helm, to see for myself if these broaches could be avoided. The same thing happened to me, so we shortened sail to reduce our power aloft.

"Dawn, this shouldn't be happening. We don't have enough sail up and we don't have enough wind to be rounding up like this," said Renee, out of breath from holding herself up on the high, weather side of the boat.

"I know, I know. You're right," I said. "It's been bothering me ever since the cable broke, but the only thing I can think of is that we don't have a whole rudder down there. That would explain the light steering; there isn't enough of a blade in the water to create any resistance."

"But Dawn, we didn't hit anything. Not that we know of. Why would the rudder be sheared off?" asked Gloria.

"That's what bothers me. If the rudder has a clean break, then it will stay broken at that point. But if the rudder is delaminating, then we have a potential problem," I answered. Delamination is like cancer; it can deteriorate and deteriorate a rudder section, until there is only a small stub left.

By this time, it was dusk and we were heading fast to Cape Horn. There was no use in lowering someone over the side to look at the rudder in this light.

"Anyway, look, we just have to keep a close watch on our steering until we can figure out what shape the rudder is in. We'll take it easy around the Horn," I said.

This sounded like a cool, calm, logical plan, the kind you would read in a manual. *If boat broaches with full mainsail and jib top in 25 knots of wind blowing over steady sea swells, you have lost part of your rudder. Reduce sail area. Watch your steering carefully. Take two aspirin.*

I have no idea how much of a rudder we do have. And with potential weather brewing at the Horn, the one thing I do know is that we need steerage to turn the corner.

I write a fax to race headquarters, to keep them apprised of the situation. Then all we can do is watch the steering closely. And wait.

And pray that we have enough of a rudder to sail around Cape Horn and out of the Southern Ocean forever.

We rounded Cape Horn around five AM, local time, on March 8. As we approached the Horn, the weather appeared as if it might be relatively calm. When the moon was only a sliver knifing through the clouds, and the silhouette of the landmark rock was a black shadow on the horizon, I went to sleep.

I hate seeing land in the middle of a passage. Part of it is that land is so near — near enough to sail to and almost touch. But we can't stop, not now. We have to keep sailing — one thousand, two thousand, three thousand more miles. It is a bad joke. Then I have the opposite reaction. When land looks dark and dismal, it is a letdown: you mean, the solid masses of earth are that forbidding? Then why are we killing ourselves to reach a land destination? Let's just stay on this boat and keep circling the globe forever. . . . They are opposing reactions, so I went to sleep to avoid confusion.

When we passed the great, dark Horn, the crew woke me up, but I elected to stay in my bunk. I'd seen the Horn before. The first-timers were not happy with me: How can she miss this? How can she miss the rite of turning the corner?

Renee compensated; she took photos of the crew holding a sign that pointed to the rock: "Cape Horn, that way." For posterity's sake. They would be the kind of pictures that, one day, a granddaughter will stumble upon in an old shoebox: "That was grandma? Wow, cool . . ." Or whatever it is, at that futuristic time, a granddaughter would say when experiencing disbelief, then awe.

I learned later that Mikaela had a fit that we had no champagne onboard to celebrate the ceremonious turn around the corner: "What, no champagne? Who. Forgot. The champagne?" Whoever it was (if it was any one person at all), Mikki's exclamation was a kind of off-with-her-head denouncement. I pity the absentminded crew.

I learned that Susie Crafer — our strawberry-blond version of the absentminded professor who is at one moment articulate and smart, then totally scattered — threw her knickers overboard. "It's a tradition for a woman to throw her knickers overboard when she passes the Horn," she was reported to say as she tossed her knickers out onto the sea.

I have never heard of the tradition, but there weren't that many women who sailed around the Horn, so maybe it was our job to start establishing some. I was glad I missed the ceremonious toss; I had only one pair of clean underwear left. I doubt King Neptune would want my dirty laundry.

On another ceremonious note, Kaori celebrated her thirtieth birthday as she rounded the Horn. Not a bad birthday present.

I was up at first light. Conditions had calmed, so Gloria held my feet while I hung headfirst over the transom to get a closer look at the underwater section of our rudder. Our theory was right: we had only part of a blade left. The break looked pretty clean, and it looked as if the rudder broke just beneath the stock — the structure that is the backbone of the blade. Only being able to peer at the rudder section underwater, I still did not know if this was a break or delamination. But at least we knew how much of a blade we still had under us.

We transferred any movable weight aft to push the stern of the boat down in the water, and in turn push our rudder blade down into the water as far as it would go. We would keep a vigil on the rudder all the way to Punta.

"Fuck you, Marie-Claude! Fuck you!" yelled Susie up on deck. Susie's voice is a sonic roar. She is yelling loudly to be heard so clearly above the racket of the wind and the crashing of the seas that are literally and figuratively pulling us apart in the South Atlantic.

Susie's voice is the first thing I hear when I wake up in the Le Maire Strait and think to myself, please, God. The tension on this boat is about to explode. We don't need this. Not now.

I storm on deck. The crew on watch is in the middle of taking a reef in the mainsail. "I don't know *what* the problem is, but deal with it," I yell. "You are waking up the off-watch crew — and we all need as much rest as we can get. Just. Deal. With. It!" By now, I am barking.

We thought we had already been to hell. But we had not yet sailed through the Le Maire Strait.

We are now 117 miles past Cape Horn, sailing in the sixty-mile-wide channel that wraps around the toe of Tierra del Fuego. We are traveling at a rate of eighteen knots over the bottom of the sea. The current — which squeezes faster through this channel, just as toothpaste oozes faster through the throat of a toothpaste tube — is with us, running at around three knots. The wind is on our beam, and it is raging somewhere around forty-five to fifty knots. We don't know for sure, because by now our wind instruments have been wiped out.

But it's the waves that are the worst thing about this strait. The moving water forced through the narrow channel creates walls of water that are steep and close together: twenty-five, thirty, thirty-five feet. It is hard to know exactly how big they are. They look like giant walls of water rolling toward us — a rank-and-file of skyscraper waves that don't stop coming.

Helming the boat in these seas is tricky, like driving seventy miles per hour on ice; you have to be good at recovering from potential disaster. I cannot always see the walls of water coming up because the waves are rolling into us from about ten degrees off the aft corner of our stern, and they are beyond my field of vision. But I can tell what's coming from behind by looking at the crew in front of me. If their grip on the boat tenses up, their knuckles turn white, their faces freeze into a "Holy shit, holy shit" mask, then I know it is a big one. I bend my knees, I brace myself, I get ready for the shock as the wave throws the boat up and drops her. Flat.

White water never stops rushing over the boat; it comes over the topsides, over the bow. Buckets of it come constantly at our faces. One wave knocked my feet out from under and washed me off the helm. The same happened to Jeni, and she crashed, hitting her leg. To these seas, we are featherlight, fluff — and we are getting thrashed.

Life is not bearable onboard. When I use the head, I levitate and hit my head as the boat torpedoes down, flying fast from a third-floor-window height into the level of a back alley. When I was trying to type at the computer and get a message out, I caught the laptop in midair when it flew up off the chart table as the table descended fast below. But it is not quality of life I am concerned about; survival is foremost on my mind.

There is one thing — and one thing only — I am thankful for: the wind is not against us. If we were facing a headwind and trying to sail upwind in these seas while crippled by having only a fraction of a rudder left, I have no doubt that we would end up on the rocks. We need to make as much headway as possible while the current and the wind are still with us.

After Susie and Marie-Claude's all-out shouting match on deck, I go below to get back into my bunk. It is not easy to move about on the boat; crawling is the best way to go. I stay low and hang on while the boat soars, flies, lurches, crashes — like the motion of a car having a thousand accidents. It takes several minutes to travel the few feet back to my bunk and get my wet jacket off. Just as I put my feet in my sleeping bag and zip up for warmth, the boat spins out of control. I fly out, into a jacket, crouching and crawling as fast as I can to get back on deck.

The waves have spun the boat head-to-wind. Our jib is flogging out of control. The jib sheets attached to one triangle point of the sail, to control the jib, have let loose. They have already tied themselves hopelessly in knots. Like a whip that is innocuous enough when it is not in motion, the sail and the sheets are dangerous now, flailing wildly in the wind.

Mayhem prevails. The flogging jib and the sheets sound like thunder and I can barely hear myself think. Everyone is so bundled up in wet-weather gear that if we had not written our initials in big red letters on the backs of our jackets, there would be no way of knowing who was who.

I find MC's initials, and I have to hit her — hard, again and again — to get her to turn and read my lips and understand what I am trying to tell her.

"Get that Number Three *down*. Before it pulls the rig down!" I tell her, mouthing the words slowly with my face contorted like a madwoman.

The Number 3 jib is shredding itself in the wind, pulling at the rigging like a wild animal as it whips around. But it's not coming down fast enough. Part of the sail has fallen into the water, and part of it is still wrapped tight in the rigging.

"Cut it! Cut it! *Cut it off!*" I mouth — again and again — to the crew, hoping they can understand my message in the confusion. Cutting a sail off and throwing it overboard is a last resort. But we have to get rid of the jib before the sail in the water turns into a huge sea anchor and pulls down the rig. We cut the jib off and deep-six it in the ocean. We finally get a smaller storm jib on, and we get some forward momentum and some steerage.

This takes a very long time.

By nightfall, the seas are still big, but they are not as steep and as sharp as before; the hell of the Le Maire Strait may be behind us. We hope.

Hours after spinning out of control and shredding our jib, there is a sense of aftershock on the boat. We are all bruised and beaten — by flogging sails and by the motions of our own bodies flying and colliding, again and again, with the hard surfaces of the boat. Everyone onboard is shattered.

Susie and MC's yelling match is long over. Kaori is always quiet onboard, but she is even quieter tonight. Gloria — our resident cheerleader — is silent.

10

We are parked. In the last four hours we did a total of six miles. Jeni has figured that, at this speed, it will take 60 days to get to Punta.

> — fax from Dawn Riley to
> Barry McKay

March 11, 1994

The skyscraper seas of the Le Maire Strait are gone now. Last night we had thunderstorms with a light show better than the Fourth of July. The barometer is rising and we are becalmed in fog. Jeni threatened to quit when she threw her cigarette butt in the water and it passed us.

Our supply of propane, which fuels our galley stove, is out, so we are eating interesting freeze-dried "salads" with cool drinks and cold coffee. Our supply of pink ibuprofen pills is nearly exhausted. We left Auckland with a store of six hundred of them. By today, our shore-support crew is in Punta organizing an office, crew accommodations, and stopover festivities. They have already watched sunsets from their apartment verandas overlooking the *rambla*, the cafés, the sea. Ben tells us we are missing a good party. And Howard has already faxed us an invite for Sunday dinner, which today, we have to decline: *Forget Sunday dinner. . . . Maybe next week.*

We are isolated out here, somewhere between the Southern Ocean ice and South America. When I fax DG to sort out our needs for parts, repairs, new sails, I slip in a request for news, any news. What is going on beyond the small world of this boat?

DG replies with updates on Hillary Clinton and Whitewater, news of the hailstorms back home on Hawke Bay that wiped out orchard exports, cricket scores of matches with South Africa and Pakistan, happy news of a healthy "wee girl" born to friends in New Zealand. He only transmits a few lines, but they are enough for now. It is nice to know there is still a world out there. We are ready to return to it. It may take us a while, though, for the weather maps are forecasting more light headwinds ahead.

Punta is close, 406 miles away as of our latest fix. But at this rate we may never get there. The leaders in the fleet should be finishing through the night. *Intrum Justitia* looks as if she can reach Punta before midnight; *Tokio* and *Yamaha* should arrive before the sun rises. And here we are. Drifting.

Barry and I fax each other often. Our plans, our future are not being discussed anymore. I still have a million questions and a million things to talk about, but the best we seem to be able to do in these conditions is support each other while we are both trying to survive.

ENZA turned the corner between South America and Antarctica on March 5. Just before reaching the Horn, they had bad weather: front after front peeling off the low-pressure systems, fifty-five-knot northerly winds, breaking seas close to eighteen meters high, snow squalls, and one watch where they took all their sails down and ran under bare poles. *ENZA* is flying, on schedule to break the Around-the-World-in-Eighty-Days record. I am curious about what it must be like to sail nonstop around the world: *Dear Barry, What is it like to sail that fast for that long?* Barry's answers come in bits and pieces, about the ups and downs of flying around the globe on a fast cat called *ENZA.*

I want to be in France when they finish their record run. But if they are delayed at all, there will not be enough time for me to fly to France, see *ENZA* cross the finish line, and get back to Uruguay in time for our restart to Fort Lauderdale.

By today, *Dolphin & Youth* has been nursing her keel with the missing keel bolts for ten days. We have already passed them, but this leg is not a fair gauge. Not only do they have a keel with missing bolts, but they shredded their mainsail and their Number 3 headsail as soon as they hit the Le Maire Strait. They have retrofitted a jib to act as a jury-rigged mainsail until they make it to port.

We have been concerned about *Dolphin* ever since her crew reported the problem with their keel in the Southern Ocean. But this is still a race; we want them to be safe, but we also want to beat them.

Our sail inventory, too, is limited. Since we left Auckland, we have blown up a series of headsails, including our heavy Number 1 genoa, our Code 7 spinnaker, our Number 3 jib. The Number 3 is buried somewhere off the coast of Argentina; the other sails are packed below deck, in assorted pieces.

Our upwind headsail choices now go from a medium-weight Number 1 genoa, which we would use in light winds under fifteen knots, to a small storm jib, which we use in the highest winds. There is a big gap in sailcloth area between these two headsails — as big as a winter coat compared to a bikini. In a certain wind range, we are crippled by the limits of our headsail choices.

After the seas of the Le Maire Strait settled down, we did a thorough check of the hull and rigging. Merritt went aloft to take a look for chafe, loose pins, or other potential problems on the mast, shrouds, and halyards. Gloria surveyed the mechanical systems. We checked our rudder. I checked the keel bolts to make sure our keel attachment was sound. The biggest surprise was in the forward section of the hull. It was flexing, up and down; it looked as if it were breathing.

In the old days, boats were built of wood. Then aluminum hulls began to appear. Then synthetics and plastics were developed. The modern plastics were considered magic; they did not rot, there was none of the electrolysis between metals that threatened to turn an aluminum hull into a structure resembling swiss cheese, and the plastic boats could be made lighter and just as strong as wood.

Our hull has a sandwich construction with inner and outer skins of fiberglass and Kevlar and an inner foam core. But the day after our thrashing in the strait, we discovered a three-foot-square section of the hull that was panting like a live creature. The area is located between ring frames seven and eight (the ring frames being the rib cage of the boat).

The flexing could be the result of a separation between the foam and the fiberglass skin. The foam inside could be water-damaged and breaking down. Several of the Whitbread 60s have already experienced hull delamination, so we are familiar with the phenomenon on this new design. So far every boat has been able to handle the problem by shoring up the area with the materials onboard — frying pans, floorboards, spinnaker poles, bunks — for additional interior support to the hull. The delaminated areas are then cut away, refilled, and relaminated in port.

The motion of our inner hull skin is minimal now, about two millimeters, so we will watch the strange, breathing motion of the hull — and hope it does not get any worse.

Our work list for the stopover is already growing: rebuild rudder, fix delamination in hull, recondition groaning rudder bearing, replace steering cables, not to mention an entire laundry list of repairs to be made to sails, rigging, and deck gear, and — I almost forgot — a reminder to launder the clothes of our token male, HeineKen.

With no proper boatyard facilities in Punta to haul out a boat of our size, we will have to sail to Montevideo and use the military facilities there to haul *Heineken* out of the water for repairs. I already know that our crew will be on the road between Punta and Montevideo a lot in the next month. Howard knows that too: *Dear Dawn, Montevideo is very nice this time of year,* he writes from sunny Punta del Este.

The rudder will have to be repaired. There are crews who have boat-building expertise, and they will have a look at the blade. Astillero del Estuario in Buenos Aires is a boat builder who has constructed several racing boats by Bruce Farr, the same naval architect who designed our boat. We may have to solicit their help in the repair.

But before we can think of repairs, we have a race to finish. Jeni is happy now. We are finally moving forward. The wind has come up and we are making 7.8 knots toward the finish line.

Dinner is a less-than-exciting salad of freeze-dried vegetables thawed in salad dressing and washed down with a cocktail of an electrolyte-powder drink mix we consume to keep from getting dehydrated. After the evening meal, the wind and the seas begin to build and we are pounding into waves again. Normally, this breeze would be a welcome change to the drifting we did today, but things are not normal onboard.

The rudder blade has not altered shape since the Horn; still, it is hard to steer in a straight line with only part of a blade. And the breathing section of the hull is growing; I outlined the original area with a marker so I could gauge any expansion. The hull is panting now outside my marked guidelines, and Gloria is concerned. She is having fantasies of our boat ripping open out here, several hundred miles from shore. My visions are not that dramatic, but I concur: we need to do something. I am also joining the effort because Gloria is brandishing a hacksaw and eyeing our jockey pole, which we use during our spinnaker runs to deflect a heavily loaded line away from potential chafe points. We need this pole, and it would be too difficult and too expensive to get a replacement pole shipped to Punta. I steer Gloria in another direction.

"These floorboards . . . Here. These would be perfect," I tell her. "Here, give me the hacksaw, Gloria . . . Gloria . . . *Gloria* . . . Can I have the hacksaw?" She finally relinquishes control of the hacksaw blade. The jockey pole is safe. For now.

The pounding is getting worse. It may be my imagination, but with each wave it seems as if the girth of the bulge is getting bigger and bigger. The only thing between us and disaster is two skins of fiberglass and some foam. I don't need to reiterate this to Gloria; I see in her eyes that she concurs.

We cut one long, fiberglass floorboard into shorter lengths and rebolt them together to shape the single board into a platform of inner support. Bolts and washers are something we still have a good supply of, so we use a lot of them. It is not easy to boat-build using the spare materials onboard. We go to sea as light as possible, even limiting the cassette tapes, books, and food we carry onboard. So it is no wonder that we do not have some spare two-by-fours lying around.

Gloria and I are up in the breathing section of the hull for two hours. Our repair looks like an atrocity, but I know it will get us through the night.

By daybreak, the wind has decreased. The sun is coming out. Soon it will be warm again.

We have rigged a cassette-player speaker up on deck. For the first time, we have piped-in music. Our selection is limited. Jimmy Buffet is singing about being a pirate two hundred years too late. We have Christmas carols. (Who brought Christmas carols?) Kaori has some Japanese tapes. And we have soul-sister dance music: *What you only dream about, wild women do . . .* We can all relate.

Our hull is still in one piece. If our weather predictions are right, we should be in Punta in thirty hours. For the first time since we left Auckland, the crew has stopped asking, Will we make it? Instead, we are all wondering: When should I wash my hair?

By lunchtime, on March 14, we are having the first non-freeze-dried food we have eaten in twenty-three days. We are only eating cheeseburgers in a sidewalk café with bubble-gum-pink walls, but this feels like gourmet heaven. Pitchers of sangria keep coming.

No one's mouth has stopped moving since we sat down, working to consume one more cheeseburger or talking, talking, talking. *Remember breaking that steering cable; Leah — even with a hole in your hand — you were a star.*

. . . God, I never thought we would make it through the Le Maire Strait; those seas were un-fucking believable. . . . No, my chilblains were worse. Did you see my face after we got around the Horn? . . . Gloria, sure you don't want a Toilet Duck cocktail instead of this plain old sangria?

Some of the boys from the other boats come by, grab a burger, a glass of sangria, and we trade stories: *The Horn wasn't bad; it was what came after. What kinds of conditions did you have in the Le Maire Strait? . . . You should see our rudder. . . . Yeah, we had some delam too, up forward.*

Our boat and our crew are bruised and beaten up — but we are not down. Not at all. If anything, we are beaming with pride. We have made it through the ice and returned to Punta in one piece. I can tell, today, when we compare notes and do our media interviews and remember the worst days onboard since Auckland, we are proud of our war wounds. We are pushing our boat as hard as the boys now.

We have already sailed a circle around Antarctica, sailing from Punta to Australia, to New Zealand, and back to Punta, but our 32,000-mile course is an England-to-England circumnavigation. In past races, the Whitbread course used to travel from England, then to South Africa, then on to Australia, New Zealand, and on to South America. But the fleet no longer goes to South Africa and two Punta stopovers were added instead. After this leg, we are in seventh place in the ten-boat Whitbread 60 class. Behind us are *Dolphin & Youth* from England and the Ukranian entries *Hetman Sahaidachny* and *Odessa*.

The winds on the next leg — past the coast of Brazil, across the equator, past the eastern edge of the Caribbean island chain, and on to Fort Lauderdale — are expected to be lighter. The next leg could be our strongest finish yet.

The day of our finish in Punta, I beat a path between our *Heineken*-green container and the bubblegum-pink café across the street. I sit down with friends in the café, then I think to myself that I should be checking faxes received, answering faxes, answering phone calls, mapping out a work schedule for the stopover. I go across to our container office with my Ziploc-bag pocketbook filled with documents, keys, telephone numbers, notes. In the container, Vicki and Howard have set up phones, computers, fax, refrigerator, supplies of press releases and photos. I waffle all day long between wanting to relax with friends and feeling obligated to work, and I make many round trips between the open-air veranda of the café and our office-container. By nightfall, I am back in the café with Gail and Andrew Cape. Gail is a good friend from Auckland and she is working for our race director, Ian Bailey-Willmot; her husband Andrew—"Capey"— navigates on *Tokio.* I know Gail and Capey will take care of me, so I have no problem falling asleep at the table.

Gail and Capey get me back to my land digs in the Bahia Palace. I am beyond tired. I am quite drunk. I insist they stay in the apartment. After living in close quarters on a boat, this apartment, with its unoccupied empty spaces, is unsettling.

Gail and Capey must have ignored my half-asleep orders, because in the morning, they are gone. My head hurts. Renee, one of my flatmates for the stopover, is not looking too special either. She too had a big night, and she collected stories on her way, which she tells me while I search for aspirin.

"Dawn, we missed the big party," calls Renee, a lifeless voice from the other room.

"Yeah, well, I had a party of my own yesterday," I said.

"No, the *really* big one, at the Moby Dick pub. . . . The night the first boats reached Punta," she said.

By early Sunday morning, two racers had already gone to the hospital after suffering self-inflicted injuries incurred from falling down. Some of the press is critical, but this happens when a crew of fatigued, ocean-weary, sleep-deprived sailors reach port and celebrate.

I want to invite the critics to try it for themselves: go sail through the ice, get cold and miserable and scared, and then see what you do when your feet touch solid land again.

The Whitbread is a macho race, and maybe some of us won't admit — to ourselves or to anyone — what it was like trying to get through the most hellish days in the Southern Ocean. The parties, the crazy celebrations, they are our collective sigh of relief. The worst of the race is behind us now.

Within a day, most of our crew is settled into flats in the Bahia Palace. This is not really a palace, but a high-rise stack of apartments that towers above the shops and cafés of Gorlero, the main street that cuts through the middle of Punta's seabound peninsula. The *Winston* crew has moved into a house on the coastal road. It is easy to tell where they reside, with the *Winston* banner flying out the window. The *Endeavour* crew is living in a house behind race headquarters with a spiral staircase and sea-green walls. The *Merit* crew quarters are easy to spot; their trademark white-and-yellow foul-weather gear is hanging off their veranda balustrade–turned–clothesline, drying in Punta's sunshine.

Within a day, we are all immersed full-time in our jobs: sorting through gear in our containers, working on our boats, repairing sails in a local sail loft, fabricating deck gear repairs wherever facilities can be found.

The last time I was in Punta to join this boat, I had no

time to explore. Now, I have a chance to update my knowledge on this place, and within a day, I know where to buy *café con leche* and croissants. I know the schedule at the movie theaters airing English-language films with Spanish subtitles, where the marquees change often: *Philadelphia, The Age of Innocence, Pelican Brief.* I know that the Moby Dick pub is the place to go at night for beers and conversation, and I know how much the laundry now costs.

The Whitbread community arrives in port and settles in quickly. We are a prefab society. We sail in, dock our boats, throw up our banners and offices, find homes and jobs and social lives. Presto — instant community. For our crew, being in port — making repairs from the last leg and getting ready to go back to sea — is the closest any of us come to a nine-to-five life. But the community never stays in one place for long. Within a few weeks, we will all be gone again.

The day after recuperating from our arrival celebrations, we sailed *Heineken* down the coast and into Montevideo, about 120 kilometers along the coast and two hours from Punta by car. The boat is sitting up on a metal-framed cradle, on a stretch of cobblestone yard next to the dock where the ferry to Buenos Aires lands. We are in a naval courtyard, not a proper boatyard, but this is the best we can do. The boatyard facilities at the Punta stopover leave a lot to be desired.

Every morning our crew meets at the *Heineken* container. We have one container that houses our office, and one next door for all our gear. If it's raining, we squeeze into the office container; if the sky is clear, we sit on the asphalt terrace Vicki and Howard have set up with plastic tables and chairs. The morning meetings are where we sort out the assignments for the day.

Leah, Marie-Claude, and Sue head to the sail loft every

day, sharing the mopeds we have rented to get back and forth to the loft located a few miles down the ocean road in Punta, to recondition, recut, and repair the inventory of sails we plan to take on the next leg. Leah takes charge of the food; she estimates our time at sea on the next leg, writes up a week-long menu, then runs through our stores of dehydrated cuisine and rations out a one-day supply of cereal, coffee, tea, dehydrated pasta dish for lunch, biscuits, chocolate, dehydrated entrée of beef or lamb or chicken for dinner, then packages the day-by-day supplies into waterproof grab bags that are stored in the back of the boat and pulled out easily at sea. Mikki tends to all the deck gear — pulling apart our winches, checking blocks and tracks. Merritt, with Kaori's help, tends to the rigging; she surveys the mast, the pins, the shrouds; she makes new halyards and fabricates rope-to-wire splices and Nico-press wire attachments, and checks the condition of all our jib sheets and spinnaker sheets. Renee is our purchasing agent, and she is always venturing off to scout out sources for supplies in Montevideo, Maldonado, Punta. When not working on the boat, Adrienne is in the office, working at the computer and tracking down the weather information we need for the next leg.

Crews of varying combinations drive into Montevideo to work on *Heineken.* Jeni and I are the steady travelers, and we go to the boat nearly every day.

On some days, Merritt joins us. Merritt is not fazed by the crazy Uruguayan drivers who pass slow trucks, carrying supplies or workers or food into the countryside, at highway speeds in the face of oncoming traffic. Jeni, who usually drives, is catching on to the Uruguayan customs. We *zoooooom* past a truck carrying livestock, and — like the locals — we just miss the oncoming traffic.

"All right, Jeni, good driving, eh?" says Merritt, nonchalantly from the backseat. Merritt, a tomboy at heart, enjoys the ride.

Some days we have Marleen, Renee, and Sue in the car. Sue is a good talker and she keeps the conversation going. Marleen and Renee are somehow similar — both calm, go-with-the-flow personalities. Sometimes Sue does a soliloquy. Sometimes Renee and Marleen chime in.

Some days Howard comes with us. Howard has a dry sense of humor, he keeps us on our toes, and he is also well practiced at the kind of camp-counselor tasks his job can require. One day, he collects me when I fall fast asleep on the couch in the car-rental agency in Montevideo (the only place we found that rents cellular phones) and the local staff does not know quite what to do with me at closing time.

Sunday is our one day off. On Sundays we do the kind of things normal people do on Sundays. We wear our crew uniforms from Monday to Saturday. It is not as military as it sounds; we have choices of *Heineken* tank tops, bathing suits, polo shirts, T-shirts, sweatshirts, and red and green shorts. But on Sundays, it is anything goes, except for Merritt, whose bag of land clothes did not make it into the container that was shipped from Auckland. Merritt wears a *Heineken* uniform every day of the week. In the evenings, she borrows clothes. I gave her a choice of my nicer clothes one night. She rummaged through them and moved quickly into my work-clothes pile, choosing jeans and a faded old green polo shirt.

Merritt has her own tomboy style. She is not bothered much by fashion. Merritt is the kind of person who, if it were her wedding day, and if she misplaced her white pumps that went with her white dress, the sneakers would come out in a matter of seconds. Merritt is practical when it comes to such matters.

On Sundays, we all head in our own directions. Jeni and Spike ship their golf clubs around the world, and they play at each stopover. Mikki is mad for horses, and, although her back is bad, she rides whenever she can. Renee and Kaori and Marleen and Sue will find diversions: go-carts or mountain hikes or river trips or zoos. Gloria went home to the States for a few days to see her mom.

One non-Sunday is declared a fun day by Heineken — who sponsored the overall race trophy before they came in as our title sponsor — and a golf tournament for the fleet is organized at the local golf club.

Jeni and I pair up for the tournament. At the top end, the competition is stiff, but there are other levels of competition, too. I spend a certain percentage of time foraging for golf balls in the woods. I catch one or two players who sheepishly pick their balls up off the green after a frustrating thirteen strokes. The golf-cart driving becomes extremely creative as the day wears on. When Spike's team from *New Zealand Endeavour* wins, the *Dolphin* crew captures the prize for golf-cart handling after driving up the stairs. Heineken also organized a party on the beach, in a cave that was turned into a disco. There was dancing, food, disco lights, and lots of people. The next morning everyone was late for the daily meeting, and DG's rental car was found fifteen feet in the air, parked on top of *Intrum*'s container. No one laid claim to the feat of getting a car to fly up to a container rooftop, but Ben and Howard were grinning. All day long.

By March 26, we have one more week until our restart for Florida, and the pressure is back on. The work list is still long, and it outlines every task we must complete in order to be ready for the restart. We have a tight work schedule ahead of us. I realized this last night, when I ran over the list and mapped out the hours we have left in port.

Today, I am riding shotgun with Jeni driving the van, heading for the boat in the naval yard in Montevideo. The weather is changeable. First it is raining as we drive away from Punta's beaches. Then the sun comes out. The rains return, followed by sun again, then rain.

Jeni drives fast. She is every bit the well-bred, well-traveled, well-educated Englishwoman from Surrey, but behind the wheel of our car she becomes a Briticized version of cigarette-blond, Ray Bans cool, barreling down the road to Montevideo in a crew van moving out with hot-rod speed. By now, the scenes of the Punta-Montevideo run are familiar: the turnoff for the Club de Golf, the long, green plains, the not-too-faraway hill of Pan du Azucar, and the rest stops that sell gas and food.

"There's one," I say, pointing to a roadside rest stop. "Let's get off. I really need some breakfast." Jeni turns — fast — off the road.

We only fuel ourselves: Pringles, Diet Coke, and wafer cookies with cream filling dyed the color of pink lipstick. They taste, well, like sugar. A breakfast of sugar and salt and chemicals. It reminds me how much I miss junk food at sea.

We reach Montevideo in the late morning in the pouring rain, enter the city, pass the row of worn, carved-stone houses that look like wedding cakes melting in the rain. Then we dive left, down into the web of backstreets that we know well by now, past the leather shop, the cafeteria that sells *chivitos*. Jeni is good at getting past the four-way intersections where it is not clear who has the right of way. She has a certain panache navigating near-misses with the local drivers.

Adrienne and Ross Field of *Yamaha* and one of the *Winston* crew are onboard *Heineken,* cleaning up after repairing the last of the delamination in the forward section of the hull. All our lines, sails, and crew gear have been stripped off the boat; our offshore home is now a workshop, filled with tools and fiberglass dust.

Jeni has some work to do on the SatCom A wiring. I need to get some of the rust around the keel ground out and reepoxied.

This is not an easy place to work. We are in the middle of a courtyard, and we have no facilities to speak of; we have to run extension cords across the yard to use our power tools. The nearest bathrooms are at the ferry terminal; they are the bring-your-own-toilet-paper kind. Forget chandlery supplies like many yards have; if you don't have them with you, you are out of luck. The one saving grace is that the *Dolphin* team has moved their container here, and inside they can boil water for coffee, which is welcome on these rainy days.

The day we lifted the boat out of the water we had our first indication of how crude the facilities were. The mast was lifted out of the boat by a huge industrial crane and put into a travel lift with two slings by fourteen Uruguayans who scurried to guide the tall unbalanced stick into the slings. Then the travel lift crawled no faster than four miles an hour around the yard, to the oil drums set up as our mast's temporary cradle. The trip took a full hour. Next came the boat, after the travel lift again took its hour-long trek (plus coffee breaks) back to the crane.

Next, *Heineken* was lifted out. After we survived the rugged pounding of the waves in the Le Maire Strait, I told DG our boat was so bulletproof we could drop it off a truck traveling sixty miles an hour and it would still survive. This was an image I was glad to have in my head as I watched *Heineken* being lifted out of the water by the crane, while the fourteen Uruguayan workers scurried — now with a heightened sense of urgency — to guide the boat into the slings of the travel lift. Operation successful. Then the long, tedious journey of the travel lift followed, taking — again — an hour.

By the time we managed to get the boat to its perch, the sun was starting to go down and it was raining. It was then that we discovered that we had yet another snag: our boat did not fit into its cradle.

We needed to redrill some new adjustment points into the cradle. A mad scramble followed to find a power drill. Then another mad scramble followed for the power cord, which was forgotten in the rush to find the drill. Then another (unsuccessful) mad scramble followed for an extension cord. All during the search, *Heineken* hung in its sling over the pavement — like Humpty Dumpty teetering in the balance.

When the search for a power cord failed, the Uruguayans made one of their own. They took two cords, stripped them to the core, and one little man held the two live wires together, in the rain.

It took thirteen long days to complete all our repairs in Montevideo, and we had a number of boats to thank for assistance: *Dolphin* for a warm container and use of some tools; *Yamaha, Intrum, Winston,* and *Endeavour* for the help of their crews with boat-building expertise.

We did not build much of a rapport with the Uruguayan workers in the yard, except for one man. None of us spoke Spanish well, but one worker used a limited English vocabulary that was very clear. It was one word, actually two words that he combined and used throughout our very short conversations amidst the shrieking of drills and the clouds of fiberglass dust: "Tool . . . fuck-shit." "Drill . . . fuck-shit." "Government . . . fuck-shit." We understood each other very well.

The rudder was dropped out of the boat and taken to Astillero del Estuario in Buenos Aires for repairs. There, the blade was stripped back to the stock and a new section was built.

Adrienne took the ferry over to Argentina to collect the rudder blade. Needless to say, the small woman with the Australian accent lugging the odd-shaped blade onto the ferry did not go unnoticed, and Adrienne met long delays at customs.

Barry and the *ENZA* crew finished their trip around the world on April 1. They logged a record-breaking time of 74 days, 22 hours, 17 minutes and broke the existing record by several days.

Barry and I did manage to keep in close touch through most of their circumnavigation, although, with *Heineken* sitting in a military area in Montevideo, I was not able to use our computer to communicate via the satellites with Barry in the final days of their trip.

After our long correspondences, with details of the weather and the seas and our own thoughts, Barry's last transmission from *ENZA* was an anticlimax: *01 April 1994 14:22. To: Dawn. Just Finished — 74 Days, 22 Hours, approximately. Love, Barry.* A few last words, and then, the transmissions from *ENZA* faded out.

Barry wanted me to get to France to see him come in, and I should have been there; there would not be a next time that he would return to land as one of the crew on the fastest round-the-world catamaran. But our restart to Fort Lauderdale is tomorrow, and there is no way I could have been in France today and traveled back to Uruguay in time for our departure to Lauderdale. Still, it is a big disappointment to Barry and to me.

The pressures of the Southern Ocean hit both of us hard. Getting through that bad patch of the ocean had meant one thing: we would see each other again. In every fax we speculated that maybe *ENZA* would finish in time, maybe I would be waiting at the finish line in France . . .

By today I know: it didn't happen. The wind just wasn't fast enough, I tell myself. So why do I feel as if Barry and I are falling apart?

Heineken is now back in Punta and docked at the cement pier — clean, repaired, and ready to hoist her battle flag tomorrow. By tomorrow morning, I have to be focused on the leg ahead of us to Florida. This next stage of the race could give our crew our kind of weather conditions. It is time we gave the boys in the front of the fleet a scare.

11

It was billed as a Caribbean cruise, but . . . the fifth stage of the Whitbread Round-the-World Race from Uruguay to Fort Lauderdale has been anything but a tropical cruise.

— *The Times* (London)

April 8, 1994

We changed our clocks to Florida time the day we sailed away from Punta. It was one way to exit South America quickly: motor off the dock, switch the hour onboard, and zoom into a time zone five thousand miles away.

But after seven days of sailing away from Uruguay and along the coast of Brazil, our clocks are still not making any sense. Lunchtime is after sundown and dinner is in the middle of the night. Florida time still eludes us.

This fifth leg of the race was supposed to be "the girlie leg," predicted Lawrie Smith, skipper of the Whitbread 60 *Intrum Justitia.* This Uruguay-to-Florida passage was supposed to be easy, belonging — if you believe Smith's lingo — to us: 5,475 miles past Brazil, over the equator, through the fickle winds of the doldrums, into gentle tradewinds, and up to Florida sunshine.

So much for predictions. This leg is slow, and frustrating, and Florida seems as though it will never materialize. If we own this leg, we have bought the equivalent of swamp land with no value, so thank you, but no thank you — title to this patch of ocean is not one we care to claim.

We sailed away from Punta on April 2, the day before Easter Sunday. Renee's face was an interesting shade of Easter-egg green when we left, and she swore it was from a six-foot Easter rabbit who had kicked her in the stomach. The nefarious rabbit who was lurking in South America must be riding with us by now; other members of the crew have suffered from the short-lived disease. I spent most of last night throwing up.

Maladies aside, we are pushing the boat, and ourselves.

The first days of this leg were quiet, with light winds and hazy skies. The whales, the sharks, the birds — they were all gone, leaving us to sail through an empty sea. The only noises were the water roiling behind us in our wake, the growling of the winches onboard, the calls from on-deck for more headsail trim, a sail change, more runner, more halyard tension: commands called out at unexpected intervals, at all hours of the day and night, and dropped into the air off the coast of South America. At night, the stars came out, and it was the exact same routine onboard: no whales, no sharks, no birds, and only hull noises, growling winches, and on-deck commands.

The progress of the entire fleet was slower than any of us had expected, with light winds coming off the South Atlantic high-pressure system. After the first forty-six hours out from Punta, the lead boats had only covered 330 miles. Compared to the record of sailing 428.7 miles in twenty-four hours, the pace of this leg has been a crawl. By the third day out from Punta, some boats had already started to ration their food.

This was slow sailing, but not easy sailing. The breeze was not gentle and predictable. It was fluky and unstable, giving none of us any assurance that it could carry us all the way to Florida. The conditions threw a minefield of traps in our path. Falling into a hole of no wind was commonplace; losing several miles to a competitor after hitting one unlucky wind shift was part of the game. It was almost impossible to get any speed out of these conditions. It was as if we were runners sprinting on a surface as slippery as glass.

Leads in the Maxi and the Whitbread 60 classes switched every day, and we awaited the position reports from race headquarters anxiously, with an artillery of questions: Who's leading? Where are they? How fast are they going? Where is *Brooksfield, Winston, Intrum?* Are we ahead now, or are we behind? If we did not like what we saw in one position report, there was always a different one coming in a few hours. In these unstable conditions, things changed quickly.

During the first days out, all the boats were close enough that, during some hours, we ghosted into each others' views and then ghosted away again — like a mirage that materialized quietly and then vanished when the haze slowly wrapped around the boat, making it fainter and fainter and fainter until, finally, there was nothing there. Some days the boats appeared to be mere apparitions. Was that *really Winston?* Was that *really* her hull, the one that looks like a cigarette-package billboard? Or am I imagining that she just sailed by?

It was a constant mental test: how many unanswered questions can you live with? Will we make it to Florida before our food runs out? Was it a wind shift or the current that caused us to lose those six miles in the last hour? Why is *Brooksfield* sailing so far east? What does her crew know that we don't? Should we tack now, or should we wait, and

where are the black holes — those still patches of sea with no
wind — that swallow up a lead? No matter what we did, we
would find the holes of no air, we would hit the unfavorable
wind shifts, we would gain miles only to lose them again. It
was enough to make us want to give up, but we had to keep
pushing. We were clawing our way to Florida and we had to
do everything we could to keep moving.

Our only consolation was that we were staying up with
the leaders. On the third day out, some of the boys' boats
ghosted into our view. We spied *Winston* and *Intrum* and
gauged them to be only three miles ahead of us. *Yamaha*, the
leader, was only thirteen miles ahead.

Then the wind came in, and the skyscraper seas returned.
Now, on our seventh day out, the steep seas are still with us.
The Brazil Current is running counter to the waves, kicking
them up even further. The sea around us is like the wild
waves of the Le Maire Strait — except the waves are not as
big, and the wind is calmer, at about twenty-five to thirty
knots. But these seas are lasting a long time. Too long. Our
boat has been slamming, shaking, shuddering. It is difficult
to sleep. Most of the crew are sleeping on the sails, because
it is hard to stay in your bunk. I have sores on my wrists and
hipbones from trying to stay in mine. Even if you can find a
secure place to lie down, sleep is another matter; none of us
is getting more than catnaps.

Our knees may be good shock absorbers by now. Still, it
is impossible to live in the crashing seas. Hours and hours of
these waves have taken their toll on us, and on our boat.

Our cabin reeks of diesel fuel, and it makes some of us
feel ill. We ruptured a fuel tank in the rough water, and our
bilge was soon awash in diesel. The slippery film of the fuel
turned the cabin into an ice-skating rink. We have all had our

share of flying fast below deck. Renee and Gloria tried to collect the diesel from the bilge, strain it, and put it back into our second tank. They salvaged some, but we will have to ration fuel until we get to Lauderdale.

We have also lost our wind instruments again. The wand at the top of the mast holding the equipment to monitor the wind direction and speed is broken. This is information we need, especially when it comes to making sail choices for the different strengths of breeze. Without the instruments, we can only guess if a given sail is strong enough to withstand the amount of wind blowing.

One of our water-ballast tanks needed to be reinforced. The wall of the tank located in our cabin was flexing, though it was not yet leaking. Sue and Merritt were especially sensitive to the bulge: their bunk was attached to the tank. I sanded and refiberglassed the area of the tank to keep it intact. It was not a difficult repair, except that I had to lie on my back and patch an area that was inches from my nose.

Everyone's boat and gear is tired from the battering of the ice regions, and we are all getting thrashed — yet again. Blown-up rigging, minor injuries, a constant watch for delaminating hull sections are the news among the fleet. Two boats have already turned west to sail to the coast of Brazil for repairs.

Dolphin & Youth discovered a six-foot crack in their inner hull skin, and by today they have already made it to Rio de Janeiro for repairs. We are disappointed to see them make a stopover: they were our closest competition in the overall standings.

After eighty-five days and twenty-two thousand miles at sea, *Tokio*, the Japan/New Zealand entry skippered by Chris Dickson, is out of the running. *Tokio* had about a fourteen-hour lead in our class when we sailed from Punta, and she was proving to be the hardest boat to catch — until three days ago, when the top of her mast crashed over the side.

It happened on the night of April 6, and several crew members took turns going into the water to secure lines to the top section of the fallen mast, to winch it back onboard. They had to collect the remains for two reasons. A section of mast hanging over the side could flail wildly in these waves and puncture the hull, and *Tokio*'s crew needed that mast section to make a jury rig to get to land. When the rig fell, they were some 260 miles from the Brazilian coast. Once a repair is made, *Tokio* can still continue in the race: but there is no way she can regain her edge in the standings: her chances for logging the fastest cumulative time around the world are shot now.

The *Tokio* crew took risks: they had pushed their boat to the edge to be the leading 60 after the Southern Ocean legs. All their risks mean nothing now, and *Tokio*'s hard-earned lead vanished the second her mast toppled over. The door to first place is wide open now.

We have a standard practice of surveying the boat every day before the sun goes down. One of the crew, usually Merritt, goes up the rig to check the fittings, pins, halyards, shrouds. We survey general wear and tear on deck and do a general cleanup: coil lines, clean out the cloth storage-pockets in the cockpit where we stow winch handles, coffee cups, sunscreen, and other small items of gear on deck, make sure flashlights and fresh batteries are within easy reach.

We are more diligent about housekeeping now, for *Tokio* is a reminder: keep a close eye on any weak points, any weakened fittings; back up stress points with a lashing of strong, low-stretch Spectra line — just in case.

In the end, this is an endurance test. But so far, we are making a passing grade.

Everyone is dealing with life on a sea that moves like washing-machine water. Everyone is enduring the diesel fumes, the stomach flus. Existence is no longer the Southern Ocean slide toward those moments of terror when your heart nearly stops, interspersed with long hours of cold misery. Back then, we were content just to get through another twenty-four hours in one piece. The waters are warmer now, the risks are more bland, and life is monotony — hour after hour of slamming on the Atlantic Ocean and looking for the next change-of-scene: the doldrums, the equator, the tradewinds, the Caribbean islands, landfall in Florida. None of them can come too soon.

So we keep reminding ourselves of our strongest-yet position: we are in fourth place, we are in fourth place. This is our silent war chant. Still, we need our diversions.

Very small things break up our existence. A little finchlike bird flew onto the boat and boldly moved in to eat all the moths onboard. We named him Boris.

Boris liked to be held and carried around the boat. He seemed content to stay with us until someone carried him above deck and he got caught on the way up in the crossfire of a flying, empty sail bag that was tossed below deck. Not long after that, Boris picked up his tail and flew away in a huff.

We have also revived an old game: *Name That Tune* (we have changed the rules, slightly, to make the game a Name-That-Artist challenge, because we like it better that way). One night, we had a showdown among the Americans: Renee, Merritt, Gloria, and me. The choices were not exactly current: Donny and Marie, the Captain and Tenille, Herb

Alpert and the Tijuana Brass, Lawrence Welk. We dated ourselves by our memories.

"Tie a yellow ribbon round the old oak tree . . . ," sang
Renee. I guessed it: Tony Orlando and Dawn.

"Who's Tony Orlando and Dawn?" asked Merritt.

"Who's Tony Orlando and Dawn? Don't you remember that yellow-ribbon song?" I asked her. But Tony
Orlando was before Merritt's time.

"OK, it's my turn," I said, cheerfully, because I thought I
had a hard-to-guess song in mind. The minute I sang a few
notes, Renee interrupted.

"Jimmy Buffet!"

"How did you know?" I asked her.

"Dawn, I know you. You only know the lyrics to Jimmy
Buffet songs." Renee, tragically, was right; my fate in the
game was sealed.

Renee hummed a few bars of Lawrence Welk, which
Gloria proudly guessed.

"Who's Lawrence Welk?" asked Young Merritt.

"Merritt, are you *really* an American?" Gloria asked.
"Are you sure you're not from somewhere else?"

We decided that Merritt was actually from Planet Merritt.
Our youngest crew member, our ace tomboy-style dresser,
our resident Pig Pen — she was our own alien. A crew
member from outer space. What a boon for press coverage
this will be.

We also have our dreams.

There are standard things that crop up in many of the
dreams: men, ice cream, beer, a hot shower, movie stars,
parties, a plush hotel room.

Batman and Robin have made an appearance. Renee has
gone one step further. She has dreamed up a new creature: a

"merman." He is a male version of a mermaid, and why not? If the male sailors of old had their lady fish, then we can have our equivalent. When the dolphins come and swim in our wake, we will all take a closer look.

Some of the crew's dream lives are more active than others. Gloria always comes back on watch with good dream stories. She has already taken a stretch limo to the ice-cream parlor with Sylvester Stallone. In the next dream, she became part of a band of superhero travelers: Batman, Robin, Catwoman, Tinkerbell, and Heineken Girl. I was Tinkerbell, which was a first; no one had ever called me small and dainty before. Gloria, of course, was Heineken Girl. She wore green (lycra and patent leather) and wherever she went, she left her mark: an empty can of Heineken. The music playing in her dream was the same music that played when Batman rode away in the Batmobile on TV. We know because Gloria sang it for us.

During Gloria's last off-watch sleep, the superheroes had a wild chase and solved the mystery, and Heineken Girl left her trademark can. Now, Heineken Girl is back on the boat in her everyday-humdrum persona of a round-the-world sailor.

The rest of us have more mundane dreams: bits and pieces of memory and imagination that make no sense — or make perfect sense, in light of what we are doing on this boat. Mostly, our dreams are not about boats. Maybe they are our collective unconscious wishing us all somewhere else.

Dreams are our necessary escape from the constant push to Lauderdale. When we wake up, it is back on deck, to helm the boat, trim sails, study weather faxes, to think, think, think: how can we pick our way faster through these unstable conditions?

Recife, the easternmost city of Brazil, is the next way-point we are focusing on. The city is still six hundred miles away, and from there, we have thirty-five hundred miles left to Lauderdale. We have yet to travel through the doldrums — the area of light wind, or no wind, located somewhere between seven degrees south and the equator. We still have a long way to go.

But for now — sailing in skyscraper seas and unpredictable weather — we are in fourth place. This is our incentive to push on.

On April 15, we crossed the equator. Very slowly.

The seas and wind had subsided, and it was too hot. With limited stores of diesel after rupturing our tank, we were still on rationed fuel and we were conserving power wherever we could. We could not run the small fans we had hooked up below deck to circulate air, and we had no cabin lights at night — only flashlights. A few weeks ago this boat was an icebox; now it is an oven, being baked by the equatorial sun.

We crept over the equatorial waters in light wind, and sometimes in no wind, so slowly and quietly that our passage into the Northern Hemisphere was an anticlimax. There were no neon signs or tollgates or fireworks, so the crew staged their own celebration.

King Neptune (Adrienne), who carried a scepter of hacksaw blades banded together by cello tape, and Queen Codfish (Leah) decided to initiate first-time equator crossers — a tradition on many boats. Renee and Marleen were called on deck and asked a list of ridiculous questions.

KING NEPTUNE: How many fish are under the boat?
MARLEEN: Fifty-two.

QUEEN CODFISH: Who won the match between the
   Wallabies and the All Blacks in 1959?
RENEE: Who cares?

For a wrong answer, Renee and Marleen got leftover lamb chaussure poured over their heads. Then they both went swimming in the sea to wash off, holding on to a line in case a breeze lifted the boat away. There were others among the crew who had never been through the equator-crossing ritual (me included), but I did not offer this information at the time. Every time I crossed the equator, the crew I was sailing with assumed I was such a seasoned ocean veteran that I must have already gone through the embarrassing rite. I never bothered to set the record straight.

Before we crossed the equator, it rained for twenty-four hours. It was not as bad as it sounds: rainwater felt good after being sweaty and salty for thirteen days; and with little diesel left to run our generator, we captured fresh water for our emergency containers in case we ran out of the fuel we needed to run the desalinator.

After the constant rain stopped, moving clouds carrying squalls still marched overhead, unleashing occasional showers. We learned to stay on the edges of the clouds and not sail into the middle, where the wind is sucked out of the air. The squalls come, their rain cools us off. Then the wind picks up, then shifts, then drops back down to nothing. This happens over and over again.

The rains were respite from the heat. When they stopped falling, it was sweltering on deck, in the sun. We kept pouring buckets of salt water over our heads to cool down, and bikini bottoms and sunscreen were as much clothing as most of us could manage in the heat. Adrienne was critical of our attire. She called the boat the "Continental Stir Fry," with Yankee, Asian, and European skin all burning up quickly. Except for Adrienne; she was sensible and covered up.

Our speeds had fallen way down: 1.5 knots, 2 knots, 3 knots over the bottom. We might as well be walking around the world. At this rate, we are not getting to Lauderdale quickly enough. The only good news is that neither is *Brooksfield,* the 60 just ahead of us in the overall standings. On April 14, we sailed up to *Brooksfield* and passed her. The crew sent us a fax: *Please slow down, because we want to invite you for lunch. . . . Our tortellini is ready in ten minutes.*

We declined the lunch date, and we made macaroni and cheese instead. Then, more rain came, a school of tuna surrounded our boat, and a bird the size of a New York City pigeon swooped down and landed right on Susie's head. It was an eventful day.

By the time we reached the equator, we had moved back to sixth place. *Yamaha* was leading. Ross Field and his crew were the first Whitbread 60 to escape the doldrums and catch a ride on the tradewinds. On April 15, *Yamaha* had a 140-mile lead over the second-place 60, *Galicia 93 Pescanova.* For those of us still stuck in the unstable weather around the equator, *Yamaha* was on a train ride out of this region. The rest of us were still in the train station, waiting for a ride.

We were surviving the long, hot, slow days around the equator. Barely. Even Marleen, our Dutch crew member who is the picture of poise and an even temper, was stomping up to the foredeck, swearing under her breath during our sail changes. Marleen vowed never to let a bad mood last longer than the four-hour term of one watch. This was a serious challenge in these conditions, because the lack of wind, the incessant slatting sails, the swaying hull and rigging was our real-life version of Chinese water torture.

Everyone was getting on one anothers' nerves. Eating habits, talking patterns, otherwise normal modes of behavior were fair targets, and everyone got her share of potshots at the most unexpected times: *Why* do you always have to eat first? . . . Why are you talking about *that?* . . . Why don't you put your shit away? . . . This galley is *disgusting.* Whose turn is it to do the dishes, anyway?

Lack of wind. Our snail-pace progress. Too much hot sun. It was starting to drive me mad, so I kept searching for signs of hope. Sailing at night under the stars was the most peaceful time. The sunlight was gone — and even though the on-watch crew was wide awake and working through those dark, nighttime hours — everyone was respectful of the silence of the night.

I found a sign one night, a configuration of stars that raised my spirits — the Big Dipper. The constellation was sitting on the horizon, balanced perfectly on the faraway plain where the sky drops into the sea. The Big Dipper was a welcome sight, and I knew its pattern of stars well: they are the ones I watched on those nights when my family and I flew away from everyday life in Detroit, to head south on an Atlantic Ocean highway. The Big Dipper was a sign: we are slowly getting deeper into the Northern Hemisphere, even though on some days it seems as if we are stuck at the equator. Forever.

The Big Dipper made me remember the nights that my sister Dana and I kept watch on our family's thirty-six-foot wooden boat, *Firefly,* as we sailed south to the Caribbean islands. Mom and Dad and Todd were down below, asleep. Dana and I sat in the cockpit, kept a watch out for ships, trimmed the sails, read *National Geographic* magazines by moonlight, and talked about anything and everything. On some nights dolphins came to visit. They swam alongside us during the hours when the moon was up as our escorts through the nighttime. Somehow they knew it was us: Dana and Dawn, back on deck again each night. During those moonlight sails especially, *Firefly* was a magic place.

The Big Dipper, the remembrances of the nights on *Firefly* — they soothed my about-to-jump-out-of-my-skin fits of frustration when the wind died and killed what little boat speed we had, when the heat of the sun became unbearable, when crew tempers flared. They were the signs that pulled me ahead, to remind me that the time would come when the equator would be far behind us.

On April 17, we reached the tradewinds. Twenty-knot winds swept under blue sky and puffy Caribbean clouds. We had a full mainsail and a jib top flying; they filled up with wind and took on a solid shape after hours and hours of hanging like deflated balloons in the hot sun of the equator.

Heineken lifted her tail and sailed — nine knots, eleven, thirteen knots of boat speed. We left the water behind us roiling in our wake. Our motion was enough to bring smiles to the crew's faces — and to melt the frustrations of the doldrums.

We had moved into a sixth-place standing in the fluky winds of the equator. Florida was still two thousand miles away, but the tradewind belt had a steady, dependable breeze; finally, we had caught our train ride into the Northern Hemisphere. Next stop: Fort Lauderdale.

The fact that we were moving again jump-started everyone's thoughts toward Florida.

"Dawn, can you ask Howard where my bike is?" asked

Leah, who had arranged to have her wheels container-shipped to Lauderdale.

"Dawn, what about my clothes?" asked Merritt. Merritt's missing clothes were still a mystery. They never made it to Punta and they are likely riding around the world inside some container. The question is, which one?

We had a long list of friends, family, and boyfriends coming to Lauderdale to visit with us: my mom, my sister, Barry, Barry's sister, Merritt's mom, Renee's Mike and her parents, and many more. Rooming arrangements were made. Party invitations were sent.

It would not be long before I would see Barry, who was coming to Lauderdale to stay with me during the stopover. Barry had stayed in France to take care of *ENZA* after their finish, living in Brest and touring the countryside on his days off. The last time I talked to him, he had gone walkabout in Paris, using his Kiwi survival instincts to navigate the big, romantic city without me. But that was OK; we were back on track again. Barry was on solid land; I was sailing in the tradewind region with stable weather and warm breeze. Life was good again. Still, I was desperate to see him.

The list of radio show call-ins we needed to do as we approached the finish in Lauderdale started to stack up. There were stations in Florida, Detroit, Toronto. DG informed me that one station wanted to do a piece using "extracts from your diary, how you fixed the teapot, etc." We had suffered through the same ice and storms and seas as the boys, and they want to know how we fixed the teapot. Interesting.

I did all the administrative duties during my off-watch hours. On deck, everyone was working hard, helming, trimming sails. In the nav station, we monitored the rest of the fleet and continually calculated our ETA in Florida. *Yamaha* was still walking away with this leg: her lead over second-place *Intrum Justitia* was approaching two hundred miles. The fleet was racing in a general northwesterly direction, up toward the Caribbean islands. We were holding on to our midfleet position, and we were gearing back up to hold our position in the tradewinds. Until dusk fell.

As the vibrant blue sky began to lose its color, we were taking puffs of wind and loading up our sails and rigging. Some puffs were strong enough that we would have to drop our mainsail traveler down and spill the wind from the mainsail to ease the pressure on the boat. After a series of puffs, Leah — who was on the helm — said the steering did not feel right. "Renee, you'd better check the cables and the steering quadrant," I told her.

Renee crawled into the aft section of the boat to check the steering system; she returned to report that it was fine. I did not think much more about it, until, a half-hour later I heard the rudder cavitating while I was lying in my bunk. It was a sound that made me flash back immediately to the sound of cavitation we had heard when we broke our rudder on our approach to Cape Horn. Not again, I thought. We could not have broken our rudder again.

Adrienne leaned over the transom and saw a crack in the rudder blade. We dropped the sails, and Merritt and I went in the water with diving masks to take a look.

The bottom third of the rudder was broken in about the same place where it had broken on the last leg. It was hanging at a ninety-degree angle to the blade, the port side of the laminate holding the broken bit like a thread. We had to take the hanging section off in order to keep sailing. I dove down to try again to yank it off, but I could not get enough force, floating underwater with nothing to brace myself against. Merritt and I tried together to muscle it off, but we couldn't. A hacksaw could work, but Merritt and I decided against it. With the boat lurching side-to-side in the waves, we were likely to saw into something else or into ourselves. Blood in the water at dusk would be an engraved invitation to any sharks in the area. Merritt and I agreed: we did not feel like being shark bait tonight.

Our next plan was to get out of the water and back onboard, start sailing again, and turn the boat in a tight circle. Ideally, the force of the water pushing against the hanging blade would snap it off.

Merritt and I got back onboard, and we turned the engine on to spin the boat in a fast, tight circle. We would have to file a report with the race committee, documenting the engine time we logged. But the fast engine-powered circle worked, and the broken blade came floating up to the surface.

After we were up and sailing again, I went below to fax Howard and DG. I told them everything: the sounds we heard, the inspections we made, the condition of the blade, the feel of the helm. I wanted them to have every bit of information, so they could start arranging immediately for a new rudder to be built.

Our elation at finding the tradewinds had not lasted very long, but there was no point in getting philosophical about it. We knew how to handle this boat with only two-thirds of a rudder by now, and the conditions of the tradewinds would not be as extreme as the weather we encountered going around Cape Horn. We would make it to Florida. But — damn it — just as we were starting to fly, it feels as if our wings have been clipped. Again.

12

More than 1,000 boisterous spectators witnessed teary reunions, a greeting from the White House and even an arrest Tuesday amid the excitement that followed the arrival of *Heineken,* the all-women's crew in the Whitbread Round-the-World Race. . . . Skipper Dawn Riley's homecoming began when her mother climbed on board and presented each sailor with a long-stemmed coral rose.

But it wasn't all rosy.

— *Miami Herald*

April 25, 1994

Our ETA in Lauderdale was set for April 26.

The midnight hour of April 25 came and went, and as we sailed toward the morning of the twenty-sixth, I couldn't sleep. The moon was unbelievable: full and bright, white-hot in the sky. This was a night for a magical romance cruise — not a race. The big moon was yet another reminder.

Adrienne was frustrated, as was I. We turned the question over and over: How can we get the crew motivated in these conditions? The end of this leg was more a cruise than a race. With only two-thirds of a rudder, we could not push hard. We sailed past Caribbean islands, toward the Bahama Bank, nursing *Heineken* toward her next landfall. Flying spinnakers in the northeast tradewinds, we could not put too much power aloft. When we did, we broached over onto our side, because our rudder did not have enough mass and area to bite into the sea and hold us there.

Broaching, which should only happen in extreme blasts of wind, was an everyday occurrence for us as we sailed through the tradewinds. We were operating under the laws of physics that prove if you travel too fast on a frictionless surface in one direction, you will simply keep flying. So we moved cautiously with our abbreviated blade. I estimated that our rudder fracture knocked our average speed off by 1 to 1.5 knots. That does not sound like much, but factor that over the two thousand miles we still had to go when the blade snapped, and it translates to precious hours.

By the twenty-sixth, we had exhausted many of our supplies. We managed to save a small amount of fuel to run our engine, for our motor into port after the finish. We were out of coffee, ketchup, batteries, soy sauce. One of our two alternators was down, so we were not able to get a good charge on our bank of batteries. When the moon melted into the horizon and the first rays of April 26 sun appeared, the light burned the haze away to reveal a flat sea; on our pass by the Bahamas and on to the coast of Florida, we were nearly out of wind, too.

Yamaha finished this leg first, pulling into Lauderdale on the night of April 24. On April 25, four more Whitbread 60s crossed the finish line, including *Brooksfield,* which finished in fifth place at 20:31:58. Our chances of catching *Brooksfield* in the overall standings were getting slimmer and slimmer with each leg.

When would we get there? We had been asking ourselves this question several times a day. By late morning on the twenty-sixth, we were within sight of land and monitoring our radio.

"Heineken, Heineken, Heineken," the race committee called, to raise us on the VHF.

"This is *Heineken.* Over," I answered.

"Please state your position and your ETA," they asked. I told them that we were approximately twenty-four miles from the finish and traveling at an approximate rate of two knots. They could figure out the rest. At this pace, we were looking at a nighttime arrival.

At twenty-four miles from the finish, there was no lack of activity. A helicopter carrying Japanese press was the first messenger from land. *Since you are taking so long to finish, we are getting tired of waiting, so we have come out to find you,* was what they were probably thinking in their impatience for us to arrive. The big mechanical bird hovering overhead put a halt to our aft-deck showers. Most of the crew moved their grooming maneuvers below deck, using the galley and the salad-bowl-sized sink in the head.

Some of us looked more frightful than others. I noticed that my skin looked awful days before we approached the Bahamas. I mixed up a homemade remedy of oatmeal, soap, and honey and pasted it on my face daily. No one else tried it, which made me think that the mask was not a miracle cure for too much sun, wind, cold, frostbite, and too little sleep. But it did feel good to pamper myself.

"Dawn . . . Dawn . . . *Dawn!*" Jeni said, catching my attention after a few tries, because my mind was someplace else. "Will you do something and stop pacing? You are driving us all crazy."

Jeni was one person from whom I could take criticism. Maybe it was an issue of mutual respect — and also the fact that Jeni was never catty or mean: only true-blue honest, logical, and fair.

"Yeah, OK. I just can't wait to finish and see Barry. I just want to get there. This is so *frustrating*," I told her.

"Well then, take the helm. Do something to stay busy," Jeni suggested.

I took the wheel and tried to direct my brain toward something constructive. I sent Merritt up the rig to look for breeze. Wind may be invisible, but we can see how it affects the water's surface. At the right angle, you can see the difference between flat water and water disturbed by a breeze. Merritt scouted for a while.

"Dawn, about thirty degrees off our bow, underneath that cloud," Merritt instructed.

I saw the cloud that marked the mini-weather system of breeze. We needed to jibe our spinnaker to hit the edge of the cloud system. We jibed over and crept toward the patch of breeze. The system had enough air to pick up our pace.

We stayed with the cloud system as long as we could. By late afternoon, we had a few miles left. By then, many more powerboats had come out to greet us: press, locals, race officials. One boat powered up with a crazy lady in short white shorts blowing an airhorn like mad. I did not have to look closely to know it was my mom; she did the same thing when I arrived in Florida onboard *Maiden*. Mom was forever supportive of my adventures. She stood on the boat, airhorn in one hand, roses for us in the other. And then I saw Barry on the small inflatable tender with "Heineken" branded all over it. I turned and waved, driving the boat off the wind without realizing it. Jeni called me back before we did a crash jibe by steering off course too far, potentially causing the wind to throw our sails to the opposite side of the boat. Jeni called the position of Barry and the breeze so I would not have to look.

"OK, Dawn, don't look. Barry is still over there. Come

up a little, up a little. There's not much pressure on the chute. OK, Barry's still over there. Puff coming in two seconds: one, two. Here it is. Another puff coming in four, three, two, one. Here it is. . . . Yes, Barry is still over there. Don't turn around."

We crossed the finish line at 16:23:15, Florida time, on April 26. As soon as we doused our spinnaker, Barry came over with the tender to tow us in. Barry and I had been in close touch via the fax machine, and he knew our fuel supply was nearly gone. We needed to save the last drops of diesel so we could dock the boat in port.

While we were being towed to shore, I forewarned the crew of several things. First:

"There is a local guy named Whale. He's a good friend and a lot of fun. I know he will surface in Lauderdale," I explained.

"*Whale?* Right, a guy named Whale," commented Gloria. "What kind of name is that?"

No one believed there was a Whale. I also warned the crew that our arrival in Florida would not be like our landing in Auckland; I explained that Americans do not treat sailors like national heroes.

On our way to the dock, Whale buzzed up in a power-boat with a big cooler of beer for us and a big "Hello, Ladies!" smile. We dropped our towline and powered on our own, and when we turned the corner as we entered Port Everglades, a huge crowd of people stood shoulder-to-shoulder along the docks.

The crew stood on deck, waving with both arms raised as we motored into the basin. As soon as we docked *Heineken* and secured all the lines, my mom zoomed over to us in a powerboat to deliver a dozen long-stemmed coral roses: one for each of the crew. Soon we were off the boat and headed into the crowd to shake hands and sign the kids' autograph books. Ben Pincus, with the *Heineken* shore-based team, was by our sides, surrounding us with a circle of people to travel through the crowds.

Broken rudder and all, we still finished in sixth place in the Whitbread 60 class, and we had a message waiting for us from the White House. Hillary Rodham Clinton wrote, "You and your crew are great role models for the young women of America. Bill joins me in saluting you on this challenging leg of your journey."

I was overwhelmed by our welcome and by the words of the First Lady. It was far more than the reception we received when we sailed into Florida four years ago, on *Maiden.* My family was around me — Mom and her husband, Charlie. My sister Dana, cousins, aunts, and uncles were expected later that week. Barry was finally close by after four months of our being thousands of miles apart and trying to keep our relationship alive via fax machines and satellites. He would stay with me in the United States during our entire stopover.

Minutes later, a woman in the crowd began to shout. It was embarrassing. She was yelling "Shame on you!" and she claimed that we had taken her boat away. She was escorted away by the police, and once she was gone, I did not think much more about the incident. Until I read the newspaper the next day.

The *Miami Herald* posted the headline in the sports section: "*Heineken* Sails Into Confrontation." There was a picture of our crew sailing to the finish, flying our spinnaker, with smiles all around, in gray bathing suits and green shorts: the collective persona of Miss Congeniality afloat, sailing toward Florida sunshine. Underneath was a picture of Susan Chiu, a member of Nance Frank's original crew of the

U.S. Women's Challenge, being arrested by Broward County sheriff's officers.

I was not surprised to see signs of Nance Frank's crew. The homeport of the *U.S. Women's Challenge* was listed as Key West, and Florida is Frank's backyard.

The *Herald* story reported one thing more. Nance Frank had already filed a $15-million lawsuit against Whitbread race officials, the Yamaha Motor Company, our sponsor Heineken, and Ocean Ventures Management.

Race organizers in Fort Lauderdale had set up a Whitbread "village" around the docks, which served as a base of operation for the crews as well as a lure to draw spectators to come and see the Whitbread fleet.

The boats' shipping containers were camouflaged by food concessions, booths selling marine apparel, big white tents for sponsor parties, and a small city of trailers that doubled as offices. The *Heineken* shore-based team had already set up a three-room air-conditioned office in a trailer by the time we arrived, complete with computers, faxes, Xerox, and telephones.

Air-conditioning was not a luxury; it was a necessity in Lauderdale's heat. The pavement around the docks had been baked frying-pan hot, and our already-browned skin was growing browner in the Florida sun as we cleaned the boat out and organized the work list for our month-long stopover.

On our Punta-to-Lauderdale leg, we did not blow out one sail, so Marie-Claude and Leah had a light workload of general maintenance on the sail wardrobe: checking for chafe, loose stitching, making some changes to our Code 7 spinnaker and our mainsail-batten system.

Jeni's beloved beasts, the SatComs A and C, needed

work. She also needed to repair our wind instruments and do a general maintenance check on all electronics.

Merritt had to make up some new sheets, and check halyards and sail controls for chafe. We planned to haul the rig out, and Merritt would do an overall check of the mast and rigging.

My priority was to get the rudder repaired. A half-repair would not be good enough on this rudder, which was made of carbon with a foam core. To make my point, Barry and I borrowed a circular skill saw and cut the blade off, so a builder could not simply slap a new lower section onto the existing blade. Then the rudder was shipped back to the boat's original builders in New Zealand, who I trusted would make a rudder that would last for our final leg.

During each stopover, one person gets hit with a work list that seems endless. After our voyage across the Southern Ocean, where we tore up sails like paper napkins, the sailmakers had a heavy workload in Fremantle. Lauderdale was Gloria's turn. For starters, she needed to fix the fuel tank, check and possibly replace the fuel lines, adjust the clutch and install a new impeller in the system of pumps that shifted our movable water ballast throughout the boat, fix the alternator, put new filters and oil in the generator, replace the motor mount, and rewire the VHF.

Yacht supplies and services were good in Lauderdale, so I had no doubt we could finish the work in time for the restart of our final trek to England. We used the last days of April to map out what we needed to do before the May 21 restart to England, then the crew had the first week in May off.

Sue had a false-alarm send-off to the Bahamas. She returned to collect her passport, not having realized that the nearby island group was another country.

Gloria led a band of travelers — including Marleen, Kaori, Leah, and friends who had come to the States to visit them — to Key West, where Gloria used to live. I imagined going home with Gloria to be an Alice-in-Wonderland descent south to the funky island where U.S. 1 drops into the ocean, where the taxicabs are pink, and where circus performers — fire-eaters, and people who jump through hoops, and trained monkeys — line the quay at sunset. I hoped Gloria and her band of travelers would all decide to return to *Heineken* once the fun was over.

On March 9, at a press conference at the Plaza Hotel in New York City, Bill Koch — who led the *America³* syndicate to a win in the 1992 America's Cup — had announced his plans to field the first all-female Cup crew in the 142-year history of the America's Cup. Many of us were waiting for the plan to be made public. I had agreed to be named as a potential member of the crew, as part of a nine-woman nucleus of experienced yacht racers and Olympic rowers. The core crew, in yacht-club blue blazers and white trousers, attended the conference. I, unfortunately, did not make the show. On the ninth, we were sailing up the coast of South America on *Heineken,* still 960 miles out from Punta.

No one, however, was officially on the team until she had a tryout in San Diego, along with the other women who would apply for crew positions. I sent Merritt and Renee out to San Diego the first week of May to try for a spot on the crew. So while Gloria and her band of travelers drank piña coladas at sundown, Merritt and Renee would be up at 6 AM, preparing for a day of pumping iron and intense sailing. But if they made the team, it would be a giant step for their sailing careers.

The campaign organizers wanted me in San Diego for

my tryout. But I risked my chances and told them I needed to postpone a tryout until after the Whitbread was over. By this time, I had also gotten an offer from the PACT '95 syndicate, another American group that was vying to defend the Cup.

The pressure was mounting for me to make a decision about the next America's Cup while the doors were still open. Barry and I had long talks about the possibilities. I doubted I had the energy to move right into another full-on racing campaign. I was exhausted from the rigors and the stress of being a Whitbread skipper. I was not in top shape either. I had dropped seventeen pounds since I joined the Whitbread, and I was not working with weights on any kind of regular basis.

My doing the Cup was still an issue between Barry and me. It meant that I would move to San Diego; Barry would stay in New Zealand to look for sponsorship for his future offshore-sailing endeavors. We are both strong-minded, and we were not making it easy on ourselves with our career choices. Could we stay together? Or did my doing the Cup mean good-bye for at least a year, with the risk of losing each other for good? It was a question I asked myself again and again. I never came up with an answer.

I was getting pushed and pushed for answers, and my public career and my private life were spiraling into dead-on opposites. Why did it have to be an either-or choice? I loved Barry and I wanted a life with him, especially after racing the Whitbread. But if I did not race the America's Cup when I had the opportunity, would it someday come back to haunt me?

Being back in Lauderdale, the place I'd called home in the late 1980s, brought some things into perspective. Barry and I drove by my old haunts: Chuck's, the steak house where all the yachties used to gather after a day's work; Pier 66 Marina; Derecktor-Gunnell boatyard. We cruised past backwater canals filled with every kind of boat, from small, shoestring-budget cruisers to a fleet of 100-foot-plus mega-yachts with so many lush details they might as well have been made of dollar bills: helicopter pads, Picasso line drawings on cabin walls, interiors that ranged in taste from good to bad — from elegant art deco to bordello-style with too much black, gold, and mirrors. We ran into friends who are still chasing the racing scene that travels through the backyards of the rich and famous in the Caribbean and the Mediterranean. Yes, the yachtie subculture of Fort Lauderdale that I remembered was alive and well.

Lauderdale made me remember how I had lived my life back then, when south Florida was "home": like a nomad running boats and racing on them out of Florida and everywhere else. I was free. Always free to hop a plane to Saint-Tropez one month, sail to Bermuda the next, take a job on a boat delivery through the Erie Canal with five days' notice, then take nine months to sail around the world. I was good at that kind of no-roots life then. My family was always home base, but I went off on my own — and I did not make the kind of attachments that would tie me down. The past, the present: they were just an odd assortment of the places I stopped in.

I wish the America's Cup offers had come back then.

Vacations were over on May 9. Merritt and Renee returned from San Diego looking the worse for wear. Merritt had an infected leg, and Renee had a bad cold. Gloria, Kaori, Leah, Marleen, and friends returned from Key West looking, well, relaxed.

Barry and I first spent time in Florida. Days after the finish, our family contingent in Lauderdale multiplied. My sister Dana arrived with my cousins Molly and Shannon and Shannon's husband Karl. My mom's sister, Aunt Pris, and Uncle Ron arrived. Barry's sister Vanessa came from New Zealand. It was the kind of group that would arrive for Thanksgiving or Christmas, except the festivities went on for days in southern steambath weather.

Barry and I then took a few days to visit my dad in California. We stopped in San Francisco to have a look at the boat in which Isabelle Autissier, a Frenchwoman who is a leading solo offshore racer, had just broken a New York–San Francisco record; we spent hours and hours looking over the deck-gear arrangement, the rig, the cockpit and cabin layout. We also made a short escape to Big Sur, to a cabin that was not connected to the outside world by telephone, fax, satellite, or carrier pigeon. It was my idea of heaven.

Heineken was waiting for us at the dock when we all returned to Florida. On the morning of May 9, the crew gathered onboard at 9:00 AM to run over the schedule for the remainder of the stopover.

Howard and Vicki had given us all an itinerary, including dates for the haul-out of the boat and the rig, required appearances at sponsor events and charity receptions, media appointments, photo shoots, parties, and a curious entry on Sunday, May 15, at 1900 hours: "Howard's End — A Birthday Drama." Howard was not forthcoming about what birthday this would be, but we knew we would find out — eventually.

Heineken was taken over to Derecktor's boatyard to be hauled out on the tenth. Once the boat was in the yard, our morning meetings moved over to the Crown Sterling Suites,

where we all stayed. We gathered in the big atrium dining
room filled with plants. Most of the other tables were occu-
pied with the ranks of the local business community: coiffed
executives, wearing elegant suits and carrying stylish brief-
cases, armed with spreadsheets and Filofaxes and laptop
computers. We were weather-beaten, in *Heineken* T-shirts
and shorts, armed with bits of rigging and line, our paperwork mainly in our heads. But I soon learned that there was
a parallel between our crew and the people who looked the
picture of corporate success.

Mary Wood, a Fort Lauderdale certified public accoun-
tant and partner with the firm KMPG Peat Marwick, was a
big reason why our crew had a warm welcome in Florida.
Wood and a group of Broward County businesswomen and
professionals pooled their efforts to generate local support
for our crew. Wood and her volunteers made about fifteen
hundred phone calls on our day of arrival to pull a crowd to
the docks. They arranged spa visits, salon visits, dentist visits,
dinners in the homes of local residents, and speaking engage-
ments for me and the crew.

I enjoyed speaking to the businesswomen's community.
They asked questions relevant to their own lives: How do
you deal with husbands and relationships while pursuing a
career in sailing? How do you handle finances being away
from home? How did you get your training?

They were also curious about a sport most of them knew
little about: Do you sail all night? What do you eat? What is
the procedure when you hit a storm? Do you have electric-
ity onboard?

I could relate to these women and their jobs, because
what was occupying all my time and energy was not so
much the sailing of a boat around the world; it was the man-

aging of people. I imagine skippering *Heineken* would be considered an unusual job. Written in a different setting, the job could be science fiction.

> Last November I walked into a room with a staff of eleven women, few of whom I had any say in selecting, and shut the door for thirty days. We had six bunks, so we slept in shifts. We ate freeze-dried food and had enough water to last the term. We were on an intense, round-the-clock problem-solving session that could potentially be life-threatening to us. Many of the staff did not have direct experience with this problem. They were getting on-the-job training under pressure. We had no control over the thermostat: sometimes it would be icebox cold, sometimes it would be sweltering hot. We had absolutely no privacy. We had no downtime, no hours away from the environment of work.
>
> After thirty days, the door opened. We took a break, but had to prepare to go back into the room again.
>
> We entered the room five times. And then, one day, I opened the door and said: "You can go now. There are few jobs in the world where you, as women, can reapply the technology you learned. But go now. Good luck. Take whatever you can from this experience and make a life for yourself."

Everyone on the crew was aware of the odd, no-safety-net situation we would be in once we reached England: our temporary home would be gone, our jobs would be over, and — after training together on *Heineken* for many months — job offers where we could use our offshore training were non-existent. That was why, in Lauderdale, the crew was preoccupied with the prospect of the afterlife of Whitbread sailors.

Each of the crew had only a vague idea of what was next. Merritt was waiting to hear if she would be part of the first all-female America's Cup team. With her engineering background, Gloria could move back to Florida and return to a job managing a charter fleet or maintaining the systems of a megayacht. Armed with her graduate degree in engineering, Jeni would look for jobs in England and New Zealand, where Spike lived. Marleen was among the minority: she had been trained to be a nurse and she had kept her flat in Amsterdam, but she wanted to stay around boats and prepare for the next Whitbread, which would start in 1997. Adrienne, who is a lawyer, had lined up work for herself in London for the summer. Renee was waiting for the America's Cup to call, and she had Mike and "Sparkin' Blue Vinyl," the blue-sided house near the power plant, to return to. Mikki is married, and she has a home in Helsinki. Kaori was planning to return to Japan and maybe write a book. Leah planned to see Europe before heading home to New Zealand. Marie-Claude wanted to move to shoreside operations on sailing campaigns, and she was planning to marry Richard and stay in England. Sue Crafer had been traveling around the world before she joined the Whitbread as our physio; for her, the next step was "the million-dollar question." In a few weeks I could be training hard for the America's Cup, or making curtains for Barry's and my house in New Zealand.

The lawsuit added a certain amount of stress. I was served papers to appear on May 19 at the Merit Reporting Center in Fort Lauderdale to give a deposition in the *U.S. Women's Challenge*/Nance Frank suit. Other members of the crew would also be called to appear. Our testimony would flesh out the story of a boat that sailed away from England last September with one crew and one name, and returned to Florida with a different crew and a different name eight months later. For most of us — except Adrienne — the only knowledge we had of a lawyer's line of questioning came from watching TV. The prospect of giving a deposition made me nervous.

The lawsuit was not the only source of stress. We had one more leg to prove we could finish this race and log a decent finishing time as an all-female team. We were in seventh place overall, out of ten Whitbread 60s. *Brooksfield,* ahead of us in the standings at sixth place, had an overall time that bettered ours by about two-and-a-half days. This was our last chance to improve our standing.

But beyond the pressure of the race and the lawsuit, we all knew that in about four weeks' time, the race would be over. The door to that imaginary room would be opened and we would be free to leave.

Few of us knew exactly where we were going once we made it to England.

13

I am the closest to having dreadlocks as I will ever be.
A week without shampoo, three days without brushing
my hair, and saltwater is all it takes. Leah and I have
decided not to bathe until the end of the race. After all,
when will I get the chance to wear the same clothes
and not have to worry about washing for two whole
weeks ever again?

— from the journal of
Renee Mehl

May 20, 1994

On the eve of our final restart for England, the this-will-be-
the-last-time notions began to kick in. That afternoon we
had the last skippers' meeting and the last navigators' briefing
of the race, where race officials and weather experts issue
information pertinent to the upcoming leg. That day, our
container was ready to ship to England for the last time. It
looked far more neat and orderly than it had previously,
when we were all traipsing in and out to rifle through the
stores in search of wire, vise grips, line, a hot knife, a shackle.
That night Barry and I packed my bags in the hotel while the
Miss Universe pageant flickered on the TV in the background. It would be the last time I would divide my possessions into piles to be sent across different oceans: one pile for
the boat, including everything from a bathing suit to warm

thermals for the cold weather of the North Atlantic; one pile for Barry to take home to New Zealand; one pile to ship to England for the few days I would spend there after the finish.

Before I even sailed out to the starting line, I knew the scene; farewells would be said at the docks, the sailors would crawl back into their boats, and the Whitbread fleet would charge out to the starting line, with battle flags and crews in T-shirts-and-shorts uniforms, while a mass of spectator boats followed the fleet in unruly rush-hour-traffic style. The scenario ran through my head like a movie I had seen one too many times. Still, it did not feel as if this would be the last time we would restart a leg, and I had a nightmarish notion that the race would keep going and going and going: more starts, more ice, more broken boats, more laps around the globe. It was only — I hoped — a delusion.

By the next morning, we were all more than ready to leave as we sat onboard the boat, berthed at dockside. *Heineken* was clean, repaired, and gleaming in the sun. Our rebuilt rudder arrived from New Zealand in time, and the long list of repairs was complete; there were no last-minute projects to do before we threw the dock lines, no frantic scrambles to tighten a final screw or stow the last bits of gear. The lawsuit filed by Nance Frank would continue, but a number of us had given our depositions. Now, everyone was in fast-forward mode once again, and we did not linger long at the dock.

There was a round of short and sweet farewells: waves to onlookers perched on the pier, hugs for families and friends. Our shoreside team came down from the trailer to handle our dock lines. The crew lined up along the starboard rail of *Heineken* to say our good-byes to Howard, Ben, Vicki, and Jan; they would be waiting for us when we arrived in

England. I said good-bye to Barry, thinking that this would be the last time that I would have to sail away from him to cross yet another ocean.

Crossing the Atlantic seemed like a short trip in comparison to the other passages we had made in this race. "A hop across the pond" is what offshore sailors with British affectations call the transatlantic run. Only a pond; I'll be in England soon, then home to New Zealand, I thought as I put our engine into forward gear, goosed the throttle up, and spun the wheel to port, then to starboard — the bearings gliding as smoothly as a giant roulette wheel. *Heineken* responded with a sway to the left, then to the right, and we snaked past a big motor-yacht filled with corporate-sponsor guests dressed in picnic clothes who had come out to party and watch the start. We waved. *Hello, good-bye, nice to meet you, but we have someplace important to get to.* England was 3,818 miles away.

The most recent weather report called for stiff northerly winds. The northerlies running counter to the Gulf Stream — a ribbon of current that runs fast in a south-to-north direction alongside the eastern seaboard — had the potential to produce nasty seas. The first part of this leg could be Punta redux, a repeat of the "Caribbean cruise" from Punta to Lauderdale that turned, in the first part of the leg, into a demolition derby of skyscraper seas. All the boats and their gear are that much more tired now, so if the Gulf Stream turned into a washing machine, we would have to watch the stress on the boat and the rig very carefully.

On this leg, we had to be prepared to encounter a range of conditions. We were sailing from Florida's hot weather, but we could reach regions populated by icebergs as we sailed north and across the North Atlantic.

There were hundreds of boats at the start — from Windsurfers, Wavejumpers, and runabouts with outboard engines to the *Sea Escape* cruise ship and the Navy frigate *USS Stark*, which was ready to fire a blank from a massive gun to signal our start to England.

Time flew when we got to the starting area. We raised our mainsail and our headsail and did some sailing to see what the wind was like. It was fairly light — ten knots or so, plus lots of wash from the spectator fleet. It would be hard to power in this wind through all the chop.

Adrienne did the ten-minute countdown. We were into the five-minute period, and a situation was developing that I should have avoided.

We ran the starting line with *Intrum Justitia* and *Brooksfield.* "Thirty seconds . . . twenty seconds . . . ten, nine, eight . . . ," Adrienne reeled. We were positioned between *Intrum Justitia* and the buoy end of the line: a between-a-rock-and-a-hard-place position that I did not want to be in. Merritt — who was eyeing the starting line from the bow — was signaling like mad: *slow down, Slow down!* It was too late.

One way out of the situation was to cross the starting line before the gun went off, so we sailed on, crossing the line three seconds early. Rather than weave our way back through the spectator-boat traffic and recross the line to remedy our early start, we kept sailing to the turning mark a few miles ahead. We would have to take a thirteen-minute penalty at the finish line: ten minutes for starting prematurely, then one minute for each second we were over the line.

We powered through the flood of spectator craft and on to the turning mark. *Intrum* was powering fast ahead, taking a front-line position in the fleet. Mikki took the wheel and I did a television interview with ESPN on the cellular phone.

(The leading questions were about our start.) Half of me was talking; the other half was eyeing our sail trim, boat speed, the other boats. I was mad at myself for that start, but all we could do now was put the pedal down and sail. We dropped the reporter from the *Washington Post* and the photographer shooting for Heineken, who were riding with us for the start, onto an inflatable boat. We sailed away from the spectators, and the waters churned up by their wakes, to find the Gulf Stream current.

We devoured our lunch, which was made fresh onshore that morning; it was the last fresh food we would eat until we reached England. By nightfall, we had found the Gulf Stream, complete with lumpy seas to remind us that, yes, we are back to living on washing-machine water.

By Sunday morning, the wind had gotten stronger and the pounding of the waves was worse. I tried to get some faxes out over the satellite-communications gear, but the system was not working. Our SSB radio, which allows us to make voice transmissions to anywhere after first linking up to the nearest land station, was not working either. Having no way to talk to land — having only the VHF radio that enabled us to make transmissions to boats and ships within a line-of-sight range — was a problem. Jeni's watch was over at noon. She would have a look at the system before getting into her bunk for her off-watch sleep.

"Who is *driving* this beast?" I overheard Renee say, from her bunk, under her breath. Renee — the lightest in weight of all of us — was the first to fly when the weather got rough. She flew up off her berth when the boat was launched in the waves, and she grabbed on to the metal frame of her bunk to curtail her flight and her eventual crash landing. It was not a motion conducive to sleep.

"Renee, how are you doing over there?" I asked her from the nav station, where I was having a wrestling match with the satellite-communications gear.

"Oh, just great. I won the free trip to the Gulf Stream Amusement Park. Roller coasters, water rides — " she said, nearly finishing the thought as she flew off her bunk again. "Only good thing," she said, pausing while she landed back down in her bunk, "is that this is the last time I'll ride this bunk!"

The this-is-the-last-time observations continued on through the leg. Some were noted with sadness, and some were relished with glee.

I would not trade the nights we flew over smooth, flat water under a million stars, or the wild rides in high winds when the boat picked up her tail and launched into boat speeds of over twenty knots. Harnessing the power of this big and powerful creature was something I would miss. But I would not miss the rough weather that threw us all around with a pinball-machine motion to collide with winches, the galley, bunk frames, each other. Speed on the water does have its price; we all have the bumps and bruises to show for it.

I would not miss going without a shower for thirty days. Renee, on the other hand, had a point. "When else can we wear the same clothes for two weeks and not worry about how we look?" she reminded us after a few days out, her hair more closely resembling a bird's nest than the long, straight hair she wears on land. The limited clothing supply we each packed allowed for about one change of under-clothes each week. No one did laundry en route; it was usually too cold or damp down below for anything to dry, and we did not have the water supply or the clothesline space for everyone to be doing hand-wash loads each day. I will admit to getting lazy about my wardrobe; there were times when I did not bother changing my clothes after a week. There was, after all, a certain freedom in being far from civilization and not having to worry about standards of appearance. We all took advantage of this.

This would be the last time we would all have regular access to Gloria's wild dreamworld. Dreams are more vivid at sea than they are on land. Ours are not hallucinations, not like the marooned sailor in a life raft I heard about, whose consumption of seawater led to madness: thinking he saw the 7-Eleven across the water, he stepped off the life raft and into a feeding frenzy of sharks. He was on his way to buy a package of cigarettes.

A few days out from Lauderdale, Gloria was already coming back on watch with more fantastic dream stories. Her last dream was about four little pigs and a kidnapping. In the end, the missing baby pig was found and the family was reunited. The whole *Heineken* crew was there with all their boyfriends, except all the couples were mixed up into new pairs. No one minded. Everyone had someone and everyone was happy.

What did it all mean? No one really knew. But I liked one part: the happy ending. Maybe it was a good omen for the end of our race.

Our speeds reported in the "scheds," the reports sent from race headquarters every six hours that tally the fleet's progress and position, were on a par with the leaders'. But we all questioned if we were going the right way.

Most of the boats opted to ride the Gulf Stream and travel the current's push up the coast toward Nova Scotia, then take the jump across the Atlantic to England. If you hit the Stream in the right spot, it is like being on a conveyor belt while everyone else is walking. It can get tricky, however. If you hit the edge of the Stream, you can get caught in back-eddies of current that slow you down.

Some boats opted not to catch the Stream. One was our nemesis just ahead of us in the overall standings, *Brooksfield.* The Italian crew sailed farther east than the rest of the fleet, and they took an early lead in the Whitbread 60 class — a lead that was growing successively with each sched. *Merit Cup*, the Swiss Maxi skippered by Whitbread veteran Pierre Fehlman, did the same; he was also walking away with the Maxi class lead.

Everyone knew that not taking the Stream could be a viable option. *Brooksfield* and *Merit* were obviously committed to the easterly route from the start. The question was, would their leads last all the way to England?

By our fourth night at sea, the Gulf Stream began to flatten out. Calmer seas would have been a welcome change, but with the waves went the breeze. We switched from our heavier Code 7 reaching spinnaker down to the lighter-air Code 5, then to the Code 3. Our speed-made-good for the latest sched was 9.8; *Brooksfield* was still logging an SMG of 16.4 knots.

By dawn, the sea around us was quiet: calm, and covered with a pink-sunrise sky. First light revealed a sea turtle swimming by. Then a whale erupted out of the ocean, pushing its mass out of the water and sending a spout up before diving down again. The dolphins were by now frequent visitors. They swam in the water streaming around our hull and dove — over and over again — alongside our boat.

The sea life made a good show, but it was not enough to lift our spirits. We were in eighth place, with about twenty-nine hundred miles to go. *Brooksfield* was in first place. Marie-Claude was quiet, clearly frustrated with our western Gulf Stream route. We did, however, have good company: *Winston, Intrum Justitia* — who was in second place overall, fighting to gain a few hours on the overall leader, *Yamaha* — and *Reebok* (*Dolphin & Youth* with a new title sponsor) were still close by. Adrienne was a voice of hope, informing us that a southwest breeze at twenty to twenty-five knots was expected in twenty-four hours.

The southwesterly came in, we changed our headsail to the Code 5, and we were off again. On the May 27 sched, we posted the highest speed in the fleet, and nightfall saw us blasting down waves, taking long, twenty-knot surfs toward England. We were just below Nova Scotia, and the temperature was warmed by the Gulf Stream. When Mikki came off her watch, the sweat rolled down her face from the athletic driving down the waves. When Renee got on the wheel, she named the patch of ocean "the Southern Ocean without ice" — exhilarating sailing without the temperature plunge.

The breeze stayed on, and we kept flying toward England at double-digit speeds with our spinnaker up and pulling hard, with spray flying and smiles all around. By now the crew was well practiced in this fast downwind sailing, and they handled *Heineken* with finesse.

The mood of the crew was directly linked to our wind speed and our knotmeter (the instrument that tells us how fast we are going); the wind and our speed were cranking up, and so were the spirits onboard.

The joking among the crew started again. Marleen played God and decided all our fates for us so we would not have to worry about it once we reached England. We had a wide array of careers: from Gloria the mud wrestler to Mikki, the Santa Claus helper from Helsinki; from me, the New Zealand lemon-tree farmer with a million kids to Jeni, the AT&T high-seas operator; from Kaori, the future prime minister of Japan to Renee, the astronaut.

A few days after the start, Merritt found out that she had made the all-women America's Cup team (Renee, unfortunately, had not been chosen). We could get a lot of mileage out of Merritt's new status as a member of this historic effort and her full-out enthusiasm to get out to San Diego to live and breathe the intense inshore racing of the Cup.

When it came time to pack the spinnaker, we all thought benevolently of Merritt. "You'll appreciate this early opportunity to train," I suggested. Whenever a chute came down, a chorus of, "Where's Merritt?" rang out. Merritt's fate was sealed: it was impossible to hide on a Whitbread 60.

Packing the chute is not a fun job. When the chute is doused, the tennis-court-sized piece of cloth is fed into the boat. Stuffed below deck, the sail becomes a confused mass of material that you need to sort out: find the points of the sail, organize the cloth, and then carefully pack the material into a bag so it can be hoisted properly the next time. Merritt was dressed for outdoor weather, with layers and layers of clothing on, when she went below to start the job. She would *zoom* below, quickly throw off an outer layer of clothing, then get down to business: pull the spinnaker cloth into the boat, wrestle with its mass, then pack it away. We all enjoyed the coaching role of watching, complete with stop-watches. Eleven minutes. Ten minutes, thirty seconds. Ten minutes. Merritt's timing was getting better, even though when she came back on deck — overheated from her spin-naker-packing workout — steam poured out of her jacket.

The boats in our area taking the Gulf Stream track all

reaped the benefits of the southwest breeze, and some of the boats inside us made bigger gains when the wind filled in. But the good news was that the eastern boats, including *Brooksfield,* were too far south to get the benefits of the low-presssure systems moving across the Atlantic, and the Azores High was moving dangerously close to their path. If they fell into the high, it would be like sailing into glue: lighter winds, smaller waves, slower speeds. The Gulf Stream boats were winding around outside of the eastern fleet. *Brooksfield*'s lead was vanishing.

Now we had to commit to a northerly or southerly route across to England. The fleet was traveling in a general east to east-northeast direction. *Intrum* made the first big move, taking a sharp turn north. She logged a course-made-good of twenty degrees on one afternoon sched.

Intrum, who was in second place in the overall standings, had to make up approximately 10.5 hours on *Yamaha* to win the entire race in the Whitbread 60 class. As of May 27, *Yamaha* was sailing ahead on this leg and *Intrum* was only lying in seventh position. *Intrum* skipper Lawrie Smith took his crew north — into the region where icebergs travel — to find the 10.5 hours they needed to win. *Intrum*'s navigator, Marcel van Triest, reported that they expected the temperature to plunge rapidly as they sailed north, from about nineteen degrees centigrade to one degree centigrade in the space of approximately half an hour.

Intrum was gambling, but if she followed *Yamaha*'s route, she would have no chance of making any gains. She needed to make a clean break.

We committed ourselves to a southerly route, deciding far north was not the way for us to go to make gains. By May

30, we had gained back about 130 miles from the leaders. We were still in eighth place, but we were closing the gap.

The crew was working better together than ever before. Gloria was watchdogging the mechanical systems, keeping an eye on potential trouble spots. Merritt kept a continual check on the rig. Mikki's back had been out earlier on this leg, and Marleen had to administer some shots of morphine; Mikki was back at the helm now, working the boat through the seas. Adrienne lived in the nav station. She studied the weather situation, charting the movements of the highs and lows and constantly updating her theories about what would happen next. This way we could stay one step ahead of the weather systems coming our way and be in the right place when the systems arrived.

This final approach to England was our last chance to reach our potential — and everyone on the crew knew it. Adrienne and I figured out the mental aspect of the miles ahead — the which-way-do-we-move part of the game. We studied the fleet as it fanned out across the Atlantic. Every boat was trying to make up time on their closest competition or protect an established lead. Adrienne made her recommendations on the weather situation, I drew up my own theories, and we made decisions about our strategy. The entire crew had to shoulder the mechanical burden of the boat: the job of moving as fast as possible without breaking anything.

By the morning of May 31, we had twelve hundred miles to go, and we factored our ETA in England for the afternoon of June 5. We would adjust this time again and again, based on our distance to the finish and our predicted speed, but we had a target to shoot for: we could be in England in five days.

Five days, five days, I thought to myself. Could we shorten that block of time?

More low-pressure systems, bringing stronger winds, were developing in the Atlantic. The lows could start rolling over us in thirty-six hours' time. If we wanted to cut our five-day prediction down, we needed to position ourselves to be in the path of the low-pressure weather when it hit.

By the night of June 1, we had caught the tail of one system. *Heineken* became a downwind sleigh. With spinnaker flying, the boat soared and hummed with speed at a steady pace of twenty to twenty-five knots — turning seawater into white-water spray that flew up into the air, then fell back down again into the black ocean around us.

As we approached the hour of midnight, it looked as if we were on our way to breaking our own speed barrier and logging our first over-one-hundred-mile sched. As soon as midnight hit, Adrienne could clock the miles and tell us for sure.

But as we flew down the waves, I already knew. I didn't need the final count. I knew we had clocked our fastest sched yet.

14

We have had a really bad break. Last night we were sailing with our smallest running spinnaker and a reef in the main. I was in my bunk when I heard a huge bang and felt the boat broach violently. . . . We are now wallowing along in 35-foot seas and 40 knots of wind with only the storm jib up and trailing warps off of the transom, trying to control our drift in the general direction of England.

— report from Dawn
Riley, filed on
CompuServe

June 1, 1994

The North Atlantic nights were cold. Renee woke up to get ready for her watch, and she turned the kettle on for hot drinks. The crew getting ready to go on deck did the usual cold-weather dressing routine: pile the layers on, throw back a hot coffee or a soup or a cocoa, finish off the costume with boots, outer layers of waterproof gear, and hats and gloves.

The midnight watch change went like clockwork, just as it had many times before. About twenty minutes after the switchover, peace and quiet settled back into the cabin. The new watch took over on deck, and the old watch peeled their wet, outer layers of clothing off and got inside their sleeping bags to warm up and sleep. I had finished my stint on deck, and I crawled into my bunk. The kettle flame went out, and the cabin went dark.

On deck, the boat was alive. I heard a round of cheers float below deck for our last sched: 102 miles in six hours. Our fastest run yet. The wind was up, and the challenge had already begun: can we do it again?

Mikki was leading the watch, while I lay below in my bunk, feeling the motion of the boat. *Heineken* kicked into high speed down a wave, then she crashed-stopped in the trough. The next wave came and picked her up. *Heineken* rose up again with the sea, to the top of the wave, then she started her descent into the next trough — at first slowly, then fast, with a burst of acceleration into pure speed that lasted all the way to the end of the wild surf.

This was nerve-racking sailing, but the fly-crash, fly-crash motion of the boat was situation-normal in these conditions. The winds were already in the forty-knot range, but that was only an estimate, because our wind instruments were broken again. I tried to relax once the new watch settled in; the motion of the boat felt all right for these sea conditions. I hugged Gizmo and curled up to try to get some sleep.

It was later that night that it all happened. I'm not sure when. I just remember being flipped out of my bunk when the boat rolled over forty-five degrees. Then I heard a huge bang. The wind slammed the rig down toward the sea, and *Heineken* rolled over onto her side in a violent broach. I grabbed the nearest bunk frame to get up. I got on deck as quickly as I could. With the boat pitched over on its side, no one could move easily. I trusted the crew on deck was already grabbing for the nearest stationary structure, to keep from flying across the cockpit to the low side of the boat that was by now dipping into the pitch-black sea. Everyone held on, and held on, and held on, until — finally — *Heineken* rolled back to an upright position.

I made it on deck. I did a quick check to make sure all the on-watch crew were still safely onboard. The sails were flogging wildly in the wind. Down below, when I heard that bang, I assumed it was the sound of our spinnaker pole exploding. But the pole was intact. What was that sound?

"Get the jib top on deck!" I called over the deafening sound of the spinnaker flailing in the forty-knot wind.

"Dawn, it's the rudder. I heard a big snap. It's the rudder again," Marie-Claude said, yelling over the mayhem.

"Let's get that *jib top up!*" I yelled. We had to get this boat under control. That was my only focus. I was not convinced that we had a rudder problem. Not yet.

The spinnaker was shredding, and we had to cut it away to get it down. The cockpit became a mass of spaghetti-like line, from long strings of abandoned spinnaker sheets and spinnaker guys no longer in use. It was nearly impossible to work on the boat: the waves were about thirty feet high and we were bobbing like a cork with no sails pulling. We finally managed to get the jib top on deck and set it up for a hoist. We raised the sail, and I waited for the boat to start moving again.

Thank God, I thought. We can finally get this boat back under control. The wind caught the jib and just pushed the boat down, away from the wind, then over onto her side again. We spun the wheel, but there was no response. Then we were thrown into a crash tack that spun us into a turn. Maybe the wind is stronger than I thought? Maybe the waves are throwing us over? I wondered, to myself, Why is the boat reacting like this?

"Get the jib top down. Get the storm jib up! *The storm jib!*" I yelled and yelled for our smallest jib. Maybe we could handle that sail in these conditions. We had to try.

We reran all the sheets, which control the trim of the jib, for the smaller storm jib. The spaghetti in the cockpit grew thicker. Finally, the jib was up and pulling. But it was the same reaction: the sail filled, started to pull, but we had no way to steer to keep moving forward in one direction. The storm jib was as useless as the jib top. MC was right: it must be the rudder.

I directed the crew to get all the sails down and straighten up the boat. We needed time to rethink this situation and diagnose the steering problem.

The steering cables were fine. The rudderpost that runs through the boat was sound. The problem was that we could not see the rudder blade underneath the boat. It was a pitch-black night — no moon, no phosphorescence in the water — and it was too cold to send anyone swimming to investigate. The blade must have broken off again — but there was no way of knowing how much of a blade we had left.

"Renee, organize some drogues and warps," I called up from the aft cabin compartment, after we had surveyed the rudderpost and the steering quadrant. The drogues and warps would be lines, anchor chain, whatever we could trail off the back of the boat to create some drag off our stern and, I hoped, keep us turned in one direction, rather than flying free and getting tossed all over by the waves.

Renee got to work, cutting apart a spinnaker net and some spare battens, which are rigid, corsetlike stays we use to shape the sails, to create an H-shaped grid we could trail off the stern. While Renee built the system, the crew worked on getting lines and anchor chain streaming in the meantime.

Once the spaghetti of lines was cleared out of the cockpit and we had warps streaming, we could try a sail again. We started small, with the storm jib. The sail would pull, we would spin our wheel, but from the way the boat behaved, it was clear we did not have much of a rudder blade — if we had one at all.

Daylight was breaking over the ocean. But rather than bringing a warm glow to the horizon, the dawn was a deep, ominous gray. The winds were already in the forty-knot range. Adrienne's weather projections showed that more lows were expected to roll through with stronger winds. We were in for a long stint of this kind of weather, and the nearest point of land was over five hundred miles away. There was no way we could make that distance in these conditions with a storm jib and a stub of a rudder.

We needed to fabricate some kind of structure to use as a rudder. The only piece of equipment halfway suitable was our spinnaker pole. But there were two problems with using this pole, a piece of carbon tubing with a diameter about double that of a coffee can. The pole could only work as a rudder in flatter seas and light to moderate winds, not the kind of rough weather we were expecting. And we had no way to butt the end of the pole up to the back of the boat. Without a proper attachment system, the pole could punch a hole into the back of the boat as soon as a following wave approached. A hole in our hull would make our situation even more serious than it was already.

The spinnaker pole was not a perfect substitute for a rudder blade. But it was all we had. We all put our minds to engineering the spinnaker-pole system. If the weather subsided, we would be ready to try the jury-rigged pole.

We sent faxes to keep everyone apprised of the situation.

I sent word to race headquarters, to the *Heineken* shore crew, and to DG. I also filed a report on the CompuServe computer network. Friends and family of our crew plugged into CompuServe to follow the race. This way, when they noticed how much our speed plummeted in the position reports filed on the network, they would understand why.

Once the effort to engineer the spinnaker-pole system was under way, there was no need for everyone to stay awake. One team was working on perfecting our drogue system, one team was working on the spinnaker pole. The rest of the crew could get some sleep. We had a certain amount of time; we would have to float a long way before we would hit land or rocks.

What would happen if we got too close to land and this violent weather was still with us? I knew there were private towing companies that could tow us away from danger. And with any emergency problem on a boat, there is always the possibility that the crew will have to abandon ship. But in my mind, this situation was not going to escalate to that level of seriousness. We could find a way to make a new rudder, and we all agreed: we wanted to finish the race under our own power. So we racked our brains for solutions.

Renee and Gloria have a talent for masterminding mechanical systems. I had been in enough tight situations on a boat that I trusted myself to be able to make use of the materials we had onboard to fabricate some kind of work-able solution. The crew was ready, able, and willing to carry out a plan. Jeni worked with Gloria well: their minds both worked in a logical, engineer kind of way. Jeni did not need to have explanations to carry out a plan. Merritt was always ready for action: "OK, OK. We have a plan. Let's go."

No one on the crew was hopeless or hysterical. But what

a depressing way to end this race. I wasn't quiet about how I felt. In my CompuServe report, which would be accessible to millions of subscribers, I ended my entry with this thought:

> It is extremely frustrating that we did not get a new rudder the first time it broke. Now we are in some danger. Extreme seas and conditions, and we still have 573 miles until we can get to land. I will keep you updated on how we manage to jury-rig a steering system. Unfortunately it will be very slow going in these conditions. That is all for now.

The only bright spot in the situation was the arrival of George and Mildred, two pigeons who landed in our rigging, on our first spreader, hours before we broke our rudder. In the broach, they fell off the rig and into the cockpit. Kaori and Mikki rescued them and put them safely below deck.

On June 2, the weather worsened. The winds were stronger; we estimated them closer to fifty knots. The seas were still running around thirty to thirty-five feet. The latest sched reported our course-made-good at 102 degrees, which was in the neighborhood of the direction we needed to head in, but our speed-made-good was only 3.2 knots.

The spinnaker-pole system was still under construction. We adapted the jockey pole, a smaller aluminum tubular strut normally used to deflect tensioned lines away from the rigging, as a crossbar. The end of the spinnaker pole would attach to the jockey pole, and that strut would absorb the load if the spinnkaker pole were to be pushed back toward the hull.

By nightfall, it was still too rough to attempt the spinnaker-pole system. We sat the night out with our storm jib up and warps streaming.

Friday, June 3, brought a break in the weather. By that time, the spinnaker pole had been enhanced with a skeg — an underwater fin added to increase the surface area of our new "pole-blade" — which we fashioned from some scrap aluminum we were carrying. We kept the scrap onboard in case we needed to make a sleeve of aluminum to mend the boom if it broke. We attached the spinnaker-pole system to a spare halyard. The halyard allowed us to lower the contraption into the water and fit it on the boat. The spaghetti-like proliferation of ropes and lines returned to the aft cockpit as we attached the system onto the back of the boat. We also had two lines attached to the pole, which ran to either side of our stern, to control the steering angle of the spinnaker pole once we had the system up and running.

By the afternoon of June 3, we had the pole-rudder operating. It took more than three people to operate the system. One person guided the boat, and two manned the lines that pulled the pole from side to side. The helmsman would watch the compass and the wind, and then call "Jeni!" — which meant that Jeni had to pull her line and drive the boat to starboard. When we needed to turn to port, "Kaori!" was called. The turns were slow and lumbering. And this system would eat up more crew energy than the normal wheel-steering system. The jury-rigged pole was far from a perfect solution. But for now, it was all we had.

I filed a report on the CompuServe network: "We are still struggling out here without a rudder. We have jury-rigged a spinnaker pole out of the back of the boat, but in 35-foot seas it is as much as we can do to keep the boat in the Eastern half of the compass."

No one in the crew wanted to say it, but this system would not work all the way to England. We needed to fabricate a new one, but with no large, flat, bladelike structures on the boat to use, we had little to work with. We knew it. Our shore crew knew it. Race headquarters knew it.

On June 3, *Uruguay Natural* — the Maxi boat from Uruguay — was approximately forty miles away from us. She was carrying an emergency rudder onboard. Most boats carried an emergency tiller, which they could link directly to the rudder stock in case the internal steering system failed. Few boats in the race carried spare, emergency rudders. That meant more weight, more parts onboard; it was not considered worth it on these stripped-out racing machines.

Uruguay, luckily for us, deemed a spare rudder worth its weight, so we planned a rendezvous. Even though the boat was nearly twenty feet longer than ours, we might be able to retrofit the system to fit *Heineken.* We waited for the rendezvous. It would be very difficult to pass anything between two boats in these pitching seas. There was no way our two craft could get close to each other in these waves without causing major damage to both hulls. We started to think of ways to make the transfer with *Uruguay* using a system of messenger lines, winches, pulleys. We would be ready when they arrived.

We expected to see *Uruguay Natural* sometime that evening. In the meantime, we could only wait and struggle on with the systems we had already fabricated, imperfect as they were. We started rationing food; we had only packed enough for about sixteen days at the outside. We had already been at sea for about thirteen days. Even though it was cold, and everyone was wearing thermals, foul-weather gear, and hats on deck, we also needed to ration hot drinks. If we didn't start a rationing system on soups and coffees, we were likely to run out of cooking gas for our galley stove before we actually ran out of food. If we ran dry on gas, we would be without hot water and have no way to prepare freeze-dried food.

George and Mildred were the fittest members of our crew. After a day or so aboard, they became very bold and started hopping around the galley during lunchtime. Jeni had a failed sense of humor about our new crew, so George and Mildred were moved and banished to new quarters in a milk crate stored in the aft section of the cabin. They were kept warm and dry, however, and were fed regularly with water and rolled oats (of which we had plenty onboard).

Uruguay Natural arrived in the early evening. They could not come too close, but in the light of dusk, we could see the crew onboard. It felt so good to see other human beings out there; everyone in our crew commented on how rough and rugged the men of *Uruguay Natural* all looked, standing on deck in foul-weather gear, their boat pounding in the distant surf.

Our boat was traveling stern-first down the waves, so we trailed a line off our bow with four life jackets attached at evenly spaced intervals to keep the line afloat. It took about half an hour for *Uruguay* to circle around and get a sense of how maneuverable the boats were in close quarters in these seas.

Once they were ready, we payed our line out so it would float downwind toward *Uruguay*. At 1715 hours GMT, *Uruguay*'s crew made a pass for the line and used a boat hook, a long, broomstick-like pole with a hook on the end, to pick the line out of the water and get it onboard their boat. They had packaged their steel emergency rudder like a raft. Attached to the rudder were wooden floorboards and rubber fenders (inflated cylinders used to cushion the hull of a boat when it sits at a dock) for flotation. *Uruguay* tied the raft onto our line. It was secured and they lowered it into the water and made a high sign to us. We winched the rudder back to our boat.

When we got the "raft" back, it was heavy, probably about 150 pounds, and it had an awkward shape for lifting onboard. We attached a halyard to the line they used to package up the raft, and we rigged up a system of ropes and snatch blocks to try to maneuver the rudder-raft onto the boat.

After a long wrestling match with the raft, coupled with a do-it-yourself course in the creative use of pulleys and line-purchase systems, we muscled the monstrosity on deck. Carrying the 150-pound structure to the back of the boat was an operation unto itself.

We waved good-bye and thank you to *Uruguay*. Then we needed to dismantle the 150-pound raft and start creating a way to attach it to our boat.

The rudder had a T-shaped bracket, with each section of the T about two feet long. We needed to attach the bracket to our boat, and then attach the rudder blade to the bracket, slap in the emergency tiller (the stick used to steer with), then sail away to England.

It was easier said than done.

The bracket had to be retrofitted to the shape of the transom area of our boat. So we thought it through. Everyone contributed ideas on how to adapt our transom area to fit the bracket and how to bolt the bracket on. We made a plan, then everyone went to work.

We needed to cut up the wooden floorboards so we could pad the back area of the boat and bolt the bracket on tight. We did not have woodworking tools onboard, but we did have a hacksaw. We also had a drill, and Jeni drilled a series of holes first; then her team followed the dots with saw and knives.

We needed to beef up the transom area more, so Adrienne went down below with fiberglass and epoxy (taking care to avoid George and Mildred along the way) to build up the transom by applying more glass to the inside aft section of the hull.

We had no long bolts to secure the bracket to the boat, so Gloria went scavaging to find some long, half-inch bolts. The generator became the victim of her search, and Gloria removed several long bolts from the generator shaft mount.

The worst part of the operation was drilling holes through the back of the boat so we could bolt the bracket on. It was not a comfortable feeling, drilling a hole right through the hull. We needed to drill from the water side of the boat, so I wrapped our cordless drill in a Ziploc bag and sealed the enclosure around the drill-bit section with electrical tape. We made four holes at the top of the T, then two holes in the bottom section. The boat was pitching in the waves, so our Ziploc waterproof system was a necessary new feature to our drill. After the holes were made, we had to file the openings out since the drill bit was too small for the bolts.

The entire operation absorbed most of June 4. George and Mildred were no doubt confused by the construction site outside their crate.

Once the bracket was on, we needed to attach the rudder blade onto it. Sue and Leah suited up in waterproof drysuits, which are one-piece jumpsuits with rubber seals at the neck, hands, and feet that keep the water out if you go swimming.

Sue — who was the most talkative member of the crew — was dressed in her suit, with a harness and some lines around her body so she could be lowered into the water. She slipped over the side of the boat and we eased her down with a halyard. We went too far, lowering her all the way underwater.

"Pull Sue up! Pull her up!" Marleen yelled to Adrienne, who was handling the line.

"How much?" asked Adrienne.

"Just so we can hear her talk again," Marleen said, totally unaware of the joke.

Leah went into the water with less fanfare.

Together they muscled the blade into place so it could be attached to the bracket. The operation took a while, because each time Sue and Leah got the blade into position and ready for attachment, a wave came and shifted the rudder, undoing all their work.

Finally, the rudder was attached. It took all hands on deck, four halyards, and six guidelines. But we did it. We went through several rounds of cheers, smiles, high-fives, and we got under way. I faxed the crew on *Uruguay Natural* to give them a progress report, but mostly to say thank you.

The tiller to the new rudder was low, right above the floor of the cockpit, so whoever helmed the boat had to sit on the floor and push and pull the heavy rudder while braced in the cockpit. All our arms would be strong by the time we reached England.

By the time we retrofitted the rudder, the first ten boats had already crossed the finish line in Southampton. The boys on *Tokio* and *Yamaha*, the two first boats in our class who finished on June 3, had by now had many champagne showers and hours and hours of celebration.

But we had victories of our own to celebrate — and a race to finish.

Everyone had her turn at having a wrestling match with the tiller. Jeni made the best faces. Merritt worked the boat hard, reaching speeds of ten to twelve knots; she said helming would be much easier if she had longer arms. We could jury-rig many things — but not Merritt's limbs.

We had a break in the weather. The sun struggled to get through the clouds, and we all started to warm up after our days of living in the cold, damp fog that hung over the Atlantic.

We still had several hundred miles left until we reached the finish. We were getting to England. Slowly. I checked the rudder regularly — taking mental notes on its condition. The system was clearly under stress. The rudder was not built for this type of boat, and I only hoped it could last, because the closer we got to England, the more risky it would be to lose our steerage. Once we were in closer range to land, we would not have the luxury of floating for hours and hours to brainstorm about new jury-rigs and repairs.

Our shore crew was in regular contact with us, monitoring our slow and steady pace to Southampton. I called them on the SSB radio via the Poitershead land station several times a day. It was important that they be kept up to date; if the situation worsened and we lost communication, they would have our last-known position and be current on our condition.

The crew was fatigued, but positive that we were going to make it to the finish line under our own power. One area of the cabin was transformed into an arts-and-crafts workshop, and the off-watch crew was busy cutting out letters from green sticky-back material so we could plaster HEINEKEN on our jib for the finish. It seemed a constructive enough activity until Renee threw the scissors and the sticky-back down in a fit of frustration. It was only a short tantrum. Renee was soon back to work, and everyone seemed to be holding together: contained, functioning, sane on the outside. No one had lost her sense of humor. Not yet.

But our supply of food and cooking gas was running out. By the morning of June 6, we had only enough propane to cook one meal. And our supply of non-freeze-dried food was two packets of cookies and three packets of crackers. We had other food left: soup, oatmeal, pasta — all of which required hot water for cooking. We rationed what little food we had left. If we could hold our speed all the way to England, we would be all right — hungry, but all right.

Later on June 6, I did a live press conference with the media center in Southampton. The news was all good now: *Yes, we are going to be able to sail across the finish line; yes, we are getting closer; yes, our speeds are still around eight to ten knots; yes, the crew is holding together fine.* I fielded the questions and, as the conference neared a close, the boat slammed over on its side again. I said nothing during the conference, hoping the audience would not detect in my voice that I was straining to stay put in the nav station. I answered the rest of the questions with short-and-sweet, yes-and-no answers. I quickly pushed for a conclusion, to cut the electronic cord to the journalists waiting for us in Southampton.

"What's happened?" I said, running on deck as soon as I could get away from the nav station.

One of the welds on the rudder shaft had broken, and the blade was working itself lose. The steel guillotine rudder blade was starting to fly free. The rudder system was deteriorating, fast. But we still had 367 miles to go to Southampton.

"What are we going to do now? Dawn, what next?" one of the crew asked me. It could have been said in chorus, everyone looking to me. Everyone asking me, What next? *What next?* All my ideas had been exhausted, and I was tired of the pressure.

"I don't know," I snapped back. "Can you give me *five minutes?*" For the first time, I had no clue what to do. I usually have a plan when something on the boat breaks or explodes. I have usually thought through the scenario in my mind: what are the steps, the priorities, the plan of action. But the rudder blade working loose from the shaft was not something I envisioned happening.

All I could think of was to get into the water, take a closer look at the rudder, and create a new solution. I went down below to put on more layers of warm clothing and I topped them off with my waterproof drysuit.

The crew lowered me into the water. We rewrapped our cordless drill in Ziploc bags, and I tried to drill back into the shaft to resecure the blade. But we could not get a strong enough connection. Next, I took extra line and tied the blade up like a Christmas present. My thinking was that we might be able to tie lines directly to the rudder blade and steer by manipulating the outboard end of the blade. If anything, this would buy us time.

I came out of the water after an hour and a half — cold, tired, still with no long-term solutions. The HEINEKEN letter-making stopped. The senses of humor turned off. The we-can-cope facades began to crumble. It was written on all their faces: *How will we get to the finish line now?*

The problem was, I had no clue.

The Christmas-wrapping-style lines tied around the rudder were working for now. But the system was deteriorating, and I kept checking it and checking it, feeling in my gut that it was about to explode.

We wanted to sail to the finish line on our own; but was our desire to push on becoming plain stubbornness? We needed welding equipment. We needed food. We needed propane to fuel our galley stove. Falmouth, one of the westernmost ports on England's south coast, with a well-protected harbor with good marine services, was still ahead. We would have to make the call whether we would stop or not as we got closer to Falmouth.

The crew was coping, contributing in the ways they best could. Gloria, our resident inventor, never tired of trying to fabricate a system of cooking burners to cook our last bits of freeze-dried food on. One morning I dreamt about toast. I actually smelled it. When I woke up and went on deck, Gloria was camping out: with a butter tin filled with alcohol and flaming wildly in the breeze, burning under a small pot of freeze-dried soup. The entire two-tiered system hung from our large coffee-grinder winch in the cockpit. It didn't work. But I couldn't fault her for trying.

The *Uruguay* rudder lasted for another two hundred miles, but the system required constant nursing. I could not risk going farther into the English Channel, with its strong tidal streams and heavy commercial shipping traffic, with such a fragile steering system. If we lost steerage then — close to land and shoals and rocks — we would really be in trouble.

At 0500 hours GMT on the morning of June 8, we waited off the coast of Falmouth. We had arranged a rendezvous with the *Heineken* shore crew. We could not risk going too close to shore with the rudder, so we waited for the shore team to come out and meet us by boat.

Howard called on the VHF radio as they motored out to the rendezvous point. One minute he was a voice inside a small, hand-held radio, and the next minute, the shore team appeared out of the fog — like a mirage, but real.

They drove toward *Heineken* in a small, inflatable tender: Howard, Dave Powys, who had been in charge of the refit of *Heineken* in Fremantle, one of our campaign photographers, and a welder.

Howard brought us newspapers and magazines, oranges and bananas, and some cooking gas. We now had a new committee of minds — our weary crew and the new arrivals, who were rested, fed, warm, and thinking much clearer than we were. We devoured the fruit and surveyed our options. It was futile to reweld the *Uruguay Natural* rudder; it would not last the 150 miles we now had to go to the finish.

Our rivals on the Whitbread 60 *Brooksfield,* who had finished on June 4, had already passed their emergency rudder off to Howard in case we could make use of it. The entire fleet knew exactly what we were going through, and *Brooksfield's* generosity was a godsend.

The decision was made to retrofit the *Brooksfield* rudder to the T-bracket already fitted on our transom. The modifications took about two hours, and it then took fifteen minutes to affix the *Brooksfield* system to our boat. *Brooksfield,* which had lost her entire rudder in the Southern Ocean, had a system that worked like a charm. There was a sleeve, which was affixed to our T-bracket. The long, dagger-shaped rudder dropped into the sleeve as easily as a saber fits into its sheath. There was no need to send anyone into the water to guide the rudder in. And the system had been fabricated especially for a Whitbread 60, so the engineering was perfectly suited to our boat.

We owed many thanks to *Uruguay Natural* and *Brooksfield,* who considered the extra emergency rudders worth their weight and bulk. We would be given a time penalty for stopping for supplies, but we were willing to take the hit if we could sail to the finish line ourselves.

Once the rudder was fitted, we had 150 miles to go. We waved good-bye to Howard and his crew. Soon our boat speed started to click back up to double-digit numbers: 10.5 knots, 11, 11.5. The wind came up and the sun came out revealing blue skies, puffy white clouds, and a perfect summer day. For the first time, the weather was on our side.

The crew had an instant about-face mood swing from the depression of watching the *Uruguay* rudder slowly self-destruct. For the moment, they were ecstatic, jubilant, and at last certain that we would reach the finish line and the end of this race. Sue, Adrienne, and MC all got on the radio to give the news to the shore-based team. "We have just taken another ride on the emotional roller coaster — but this time it's on the way up! We are on our way," said Adrienne. Sue and MC echoed her sentiments.

I was happy to be moving again. But we had miles to go before we could celebrate, and I was reserved. This was our third jury-rig; what a frustrating way to finish a race. My mood did not soar along with the crew's because I had isolated myself from the crew a long time ago. The ultimate decisions and responsibility for this boat fell on my head, and I needed my distance — my own territory to make decisions. We were all underfed. I was operating on little to no sleep. Those final miles were, to me, more like a cloud of delirium. The crew started to come out of the cloud the minute *Brooksfield*'s rudder was fitted and operating. But I held back.

The sun stayed with us through the day as we sailed along the south coast of England — past Eddystone Rocks, Plymouth, Lyme Bay, Portland, Saint Alban's Head, and finally into the Solent, the channel of water that squeezes between England and the Isle of Wight.

After the sun went down, the lights of land slowly broke through the dusk. We relied on the navigational lights and their patterns to show us the way, like road signs, to Southampton in the dark. Adrienne was directing me through the navigational markers as we sailed toward the finish. But as we made the turn at Calshot Spit, to go up the ribbon of water that snakes into Southampton, something was very wrong: MC was yelling, almost crying, telling me to turn. The numbers on our depth sounder, which tells us how much water we have under our keel, began to descend fast to shallow depths. I swung the boat about fifty degrees from course. Had we gone farther, we could have run aground.

My nerves were shot. Adrienne went down below to disappear into the nav station.

At 22:18:07 hours GMT, on the night of June 8, we crossed the finish line of the 1993/94 Whitbread Round-the-World Race in Southampton. The race committee sounded a finishing gun, to signal that we had sailed across the line. All the way around the world to cross that imaginary line.

There were a few pats on the back among the crew. A few high-fives. Halfhearted attempts to celebrate what should have been jubilation. We were all just relieved to be finished.

We were the very last boat in the race to cross the finish line.

Epilogue

The last time I saw *Heineken*, the boat was empty: a big eggshell with nothing left inside. The hooks we hung our wet-weather gear on were bare. The metal frames of our bunks no longer held sleeping bags, stuffed bears, and gremlins. Coffee, freeze-dried food packets, and pots and bowls were gone from the galley. The mounds of headsails, tools, spare lines, and rigging had been removed. The red potpourri-flavored disinfectant, which Gloria once used as mouthwash, was gone from its honorary perch in the head. Even our houseguest pigeons George and Mildred, who rode with us through the worst times, had moved on.

There was no sign of the twelve women who once lived on this boat. They were gone, and *Heineken* sat abandoned where we left her on the south coast of England. At rest after a long journey.

I have returned to New Zealand, to Barry, and to our house overlooking the sea. It is winter here. The flowers in our garden are asleep and the lemons on our tree are green. It is time for hibernation and a long-awaited rest.

The final miles of the Whitbread were a blur when I lived them. During those days in the Atlantic, I was all nerves and synapses; the chain of action and reaction came fast, without time to consider the turn of events. Now — far away from England, at home in New Zealand — it is all coming back to me.

For six days, ever since the rudder broke on that cold

night in the North Atlantic, the crew had been on a trek of emotional extremes. Depression and elation. Frustration and hope. Full of creative ideas for jury-rigs and then lost for any solutions. But no one wanted to quit. I was proud of everyone for that, and it wasn't something I asked of them. Everyone just kept pushing until we finished.

We reached the finish line late on a summer night in June. The final gun of the race sounded, and the overriding emotion onboard was not jubilation. It was relief.

We pulled our sails quietly down and slowly made our way to land. The crew lit hand-held flares in the dark, and they stood tall, one arm raised into the sky in commemoration: silent statues burning torches on the last Whitbread boat to sail into port.

Slowly, boats began to appear out of the dark as we motored to land: runabout powerboats, rubber-duck inflatables. They came out quietly, like a small navy, to escort us in. Their numbers grew, and more and more we could see faces onboard. Some of the boats were filled with close friends: Renee's and my friend Andy Ogilvy from the States; Jeni's sister, who surprised her by coming home from Nairobi; a few members of the *Maiden* crew. Some of the boats were filled with total strangers who wanted to come out late that night and greet us. There were so many boats, we had to wave them aside when we needed to change course.

We turned the corner, and a crowd waited at the dock. And as we motored closer, there was a sound. A cheer that kept sounding again and again. Once we got closer to the dock lights, we could see faces. The crowd was full of our competitors, waiting on the dock in their Wednesday-night best, waiting to grab our dock lines and welcome us back to reality. Crew members from *Tokio, Endeavour, Yamaha, Brooksfield,* and other boats. They knew, they all knew better than anyone, what we had gone through.

My legs wobbled when they touched solid ground for the first time in twenty days, but it felt good. Terra firma. I planted my feet and promised myself not to leave solid earth again for a long, long time.

I was numb then, slowly coming back down to earth. And I now remember it all: the hugs and the happy tears, the media questions asked and the TV spotlights, the prizes passed out, the champagne that flowed all night long. I got home at daybreak.

The morning after we finished, press interviews were held. Some of the reporters hunted down the negatives, the down-and-dirty details they could spin into "news" about a boat that sailed away from England last September and returned nine months later with a different crew, a new name, a new paint job, one mutiny, and a still-unresolved lawsuit filed on the other side of the Atlantic. Some of the reporters treated us fairly, as twelve sailors trying to overcome obstacles to get to the finish line in whatever way we could.

Now, the *Heineken* crew has scattered to many places: California, New Zealand, Holland, and points beyond. They are all gone, ready to start a life again someplace else.

Some of us will stay friends for life; some of us may never have reason to talk again. It is like that when you go offshore in such an intense endurance test. When you return, it is either all or nothing.

Why did we do it? Why is it that anyone does this race? Probably for a million good reasons and a thousand bad ones. Maybe to become a better sailor. Maybe to prove — to the world, but mostly to yourself — that you can survive the grueling endurance test. Maybe to escape the life you left behind, or to go beyond the limits of an existence you had on land. Maybe to break an old record or set a new one. Some of the reasons for going are deep and profound. Some are mundane.

When I left Detroit last November, I wanted to prove that women could compete in this race. We may have limped into the finish line, but in the end, we finished. Our time was docked by the International Jury for stopping to get assistance in Falmouth. After the six legs of the race, our overall time put us in ninth place in the ten-boat Whitbread 60 class. But this position does not reflect the ultimate test the crew passed in those final days. We all know we could have done better, but how well we could have finished if the rudder had held together is impossible to know now.

Every boat had its triumphs and its hardships.

New Zealand Endeavour, with Grant Dalton at the helm, won the Maxi class and clocked the fastest time around the world for this race: 120 days, 5 hours, 9 minutes, 23 seconds. Dalton and his crew shaved the 1989/90 Whitbread winner's record by some eight days. *Yamaha,* the Japan/New Zealand entry skippered by Ross Field, won the Whitbread 60 class overall. *Brooksfield* faced a near-disaster in the Southern Ocean, dropping out of the electronic tracking system on leg two for nearly twenty-four hours while three tons of ice-cold seawater poured into her hull. How hard was it for that crew to sail on after feeling cold ocean water lap at their feet? *Tokio* had an untouchable fourteen-hour lead in the race until her rig fell down off the coast of Brazil.

Now that I am back in New Zealand, I keep telling myself

that it is time to start again. Part of me wants to stay here, on the fringe of the Pacific Ocean, to relax and drop out of sailing for a while. The stress of getting *Heineken* around the world, the scrutiny of the press — they are not things I am looking forward to dealing with again. But sailing is my life, and I know I will return to it. When I do, Barry and I will still need to find a way to make a life out of two whirlwind sailing careers. And I should be making decisions about the next America's Cup now — whether I do it or not.

Not now, not yet, is what I tell people pushing me for answers. I need a little more time here at home because I am slowly coming back to a state where I can make those decisions. I certainly could not think straight to plot my next moves during those final days of the Whitbread. Getting *Heineken* around the world absorbed all my thought and energy, and existence spiraled down to one simple goal: cross the finish line. Once we did, I was lost for a few moments. I did not feel like a conqueror making a conquest. I felt very small.

But there was one thing that began to pull me out of the cloud of our final days at sea.

That night, as we motored from the finish line toward the docks in Southampton — our hull glowing with torch flames held high by the crew — there was one noise I remember. It was the crowd, with our Whitbread competitors among them. The crowd was cheering, and it kept cheering. We turned the corner to motor to Ocean Village and more cheers began to float out to us. They pulled us toward land, and the crew came alive — with smiles, with life to their movements, with pride.

Maybe more people came out to see us sail into Auckland harbor. The crowds may have been bigger as we reached the docks of Fort Lauderdale. And thousands came to wave good-bye to us as we sailed from New Zealand. But it was those cheers from the crowd on the dock in Southampton that outweighed every departure and every homecoming. The crowd roared again and again, and I will never forget the sound of their cheers.

They were the loudest cheers I had ever heard.

Afterword

In July 1994, Dawn Riley moved to San Diego, California, to join the *America³* syndicate — the first women's team in history to vie for the America's Cup. Barry McKay remained in Auckland, New Zealand, where he continues to organize future offshore sailing projects. The couple plans to marry in 1996.

The Crew

Gloria Borrego (b. 1961, Engineer, United States) returned to Key West to make the Florida island her base of operation from which she will pursue work as an engineer on boats. She is working with the *America³* syndicate during the 1995 America's Cup.

A lawyer by profession, *Adrienne Cahalan* (b. 1964, Navigator, Australia) returned home to Sydney to resume her career in law and to organize future sailing endeavors.

Maine native *Merritt Carey* (b. 1969, Foredeck/Rigger, United States) joined the *America³* women's team. After the completion of the 1995 America's Cup, Carey will be the second American woman (behind Dawn Riley) to have competed in both the Whitbread and the America's Cup.

Marie-Claude "MC" Kieffer (b. 1960, Sailmaker, France) and Richard Faulkner were married in October

1994. They reside in southern England. She is working at jobs in sales and language translation until the 1997 Whitbread; she hopes next time to travel the racecourse by plane, as part of a shoreside team.

A registered nurse by profession, *Marleen Cleyndert* (b. 1967, Medic, Holland) returned to her home in Amsterdam to pursue her sailing career. She is actively racing twenty-four-foot keelboats and exploring future sailing projects, including an Olympic campaign in the 470 dinghy class and another Whitbread.

Susan Crafer (b. 1967, Medic/Sail Trimmer, United Kingdom) relocated to Sydney, Australia, where she works as a sports physiotherapist at the New South Wales Academy of Sport, in addition to serving as a physiotherapist for the Australian Olympic sailing team.

Mikaela "Mikki" von Koskull (b. 1958, Watch Leader, Finland) returned to her home in Helsinki. A former radio operator for the Finnish Steamship Company, she took a job working on Baltic Sea ferries. A former member of the *Maiden* crew, she is the only Finnish woman to have raced two Whitbread campaigns.

Japan's only woman to compete in the Whitbread, *Kaori Matsunaga* (b. 1964, Helm, Japan) returned to Japan after the finish of the race. Within six months, she was back at sea as crew member of a research vessel working in the Southern Ocean.

Looking to start a new career after working as a professional boat captain and crew for five years, *Renee Mehl* (b. 1964, Purchaser/Cockpit, United States) is working her way into the sports marketing field. Her first job was acting as a media advisor at the Louis Vuitton Media Center for the 1995 America's Cup.

"After six years of galavanting around the world," *Jeni Mundy* (b. 1965, Helm/Electronics, United Kingdom) reports she has found a "real job" in New Zealand, as a radio frequency engineer for the Digital Mobile Company. She bought her first house, and a lawn mower. Mundy has completed two Whitbreads, the first as a crew member onboard *Maiden.*

Leah Newbold (b. 1967, Sailmaker/Sail Trimmer, New Zealand) returned to Auckland where she is actively racing sailboats in New Zealand and Australian waters, including a stint as watch captain in the 640-mile Sydney-Hobart race held in December 1994.

The next Whitbread Round-the-World Race starts from Southampton, England, in September 1997.

With special thanks . . .

To our *Heineken* shore crew, Jan and Iljia Beijerinck, Helen Campbell-Smith, Howard Gibbons, David Glen, Ben Pincus, and Victoria Stacey, for their unflagging support.

To our sponsor, Heineken, for making our voyage possible.

To Renee Mehl, for keeping a detailed record of the voyage of *Heineken* in the 1993/94 Whitbread Round-the-World Race and allowing us access to her journals for this book.

To *Brooksfield* and *Uruguay Natural,* for spare parts and a helping hand in a time of need.

And to Charlie Barthold, Peggy Barthold, Stephen E. Bates, Hugh Bosey, Jim Briscoe, Joe Clement, John Clotu-arthy, Vivian and F. Stephen Gauss, Nathan Gorenstein, Gary Jobson, Chris Johnson, Norman D. Lane, Linda Lindquist, Laura Lopez Shannon, Bill Lynch, Geoffery Mason, John H. Mitchell, Laura Monino, Dick and Barbara S. Neville, Briggs Palmer, Janet Ragon, John and Helen of Fremantle, Dr. Kerry K. Steward, G. D. Swensen, Keith Taylor, Sandra Welsh, Mary Wood, and Henry Young.